Directive Play Therapy

Elsa Soto Leggett, PhD, LPC-S, RPT-S, CSC, is an associate professor at the CACREP-accredited program in Counselor Education, University of Houston-Victoria, where she serves as the program coordinator of the Counselor Education Program. The current past president of the Association of Child and Adolescent Counseling, Dr. Leggett has also served as the president of the Texas Association for Counselor Education and Supervision. She has contributed original research and book reviews to such peer-reviewed journals as *The Journal of LGBT Issues in Counseling, Psychology in the Schools, The Family Journal, Journal of Creativity in Mental Health,* and *ACA Vistas,* and serves on the editorial review board of the *Journal of Child and Adolescent Counseling*. She has contributed chapters to a wide range of books, including *Human Growth and Development Across the Lifespan; Encyclopedia of Theory in Counseling and Psychotherapy; Innovative Career Counseling Interventions; Art and Creative Development for Young Children,* 8th edition; *Integrating the Expressive Arts Into Counseling Practice: Theory Based Interventions, ACA Encyclopedia of Counseling;* and *Critical Incidents in Counseling Children.* Dr. Leggett has presented numerous workshops and talks to national and regional audiences on topics such as school counseling, directive play therapy, solution-focused counseling, and counseling children and youth.

Jennifer N. Boswell, PhD, LPC-S, NCC, RPT, is an assistant professor at the CACREP-accredited program in Counselor Education, University of Houston-Victoria (UHV). A licensed professional counselor supervisor in Texas, she is also a registered play therapist. Dr. Boswell teaches a wide range of courses at UHV, including Counseling Techniques, Counseling Couples and Families, Introduction to Play Therapy, Child and Adolescent Counseling, and Program Evaluation. Her research focuses on play therapy, religious issues in counseling, counseling supervision, and engaging clients' families in counseling. She is the assistant editor of *Mentoring and Tutoring* and serves on the editorial review board of the *Journal of Child and Adolescent Counseling*. Dr. Boswell has published numerous peer-reviewed articles in *International Journal of Play Therapy, Journal of Counseling and Development, Professional Issues in Counseling, The Family Journal, Counseling and Values, Mental Health, Religion and Culture, The Journal of Creativity in Mental Health,* and *Journal of Individual Psychology.* She has made numerous presentations at national, regional, and state associations related to counseling, play therapy, education, and Adlerian psychology.

Directive Play Therapy

Theories and Techniques

Elsa Soto Leggett, PhD, LPC-S, RPT-S, CSC
Jennifer N. Boswell, PhD, LPC-S, NCC, RPT
Editors

SPRINGER PUBLISHING COMPANY
NEW YORK

Springer Publishing Company, LLC
11 West 42nd Street
New York, NY 10036
www.springerpub.com

Acquisitions Editor: Nancy Hale
Compositor: Newgen KnowledgeWorks

ISBN: 978-0-8261-3065-5
e-book ISBN: 978-0-8261-3066-2

16 17 18 19 20 / 5 4 3 2 1

Library of Congress Cataloging-in-Publication Data
Names: Leggett, Elsa Soto, editor. | Boswell, Jennifer N., editor.
Title: Directive play therapy: theories and techniques / Elsa Soto Leggett, Jennifer N. Boswell, editors.
Description: New York, NY: Springer Publishing Company, LLC, [2017] | Includes bibliographic references and index.
Identifiers: LCCN 2016025672 | ISBN 9780826130655 | ISBN 9780826130662 (e-book)
Subjects: | MESH: Play Therapy—methods | Child | Play and Playthings—psychology | Psychoanalytic Therapy—methods
Classification: LCC RJ505.P6 | NLM WS 350.4 | DDC 618.92/891653–dc23
LC record available at https://lccn.loc.gov/2016025672

Printed in the United States of America by McNaughton & Gunn.

To the young who play and the young in heart who still play
To our own young ones: Elliott, Annamarie, and Daniel

Contents

Contributors

Stephen A. Armstrong, PhD, LPC-S, RPT-S
Associate Professor
Texas A&M University–Commerce
Commerce, Texas

Linda L. Autry, PhD, LPC-S, CSC
Assistant Professor and School Counseling Coordinator
University of Houston–Victoria
Victoria, Texas

Jennifer N. Boswell, PhD, LPC-S, NCC, RPT
Assistant Professor and CACREP Liaison
University of Houston-Victoria
Katy, Texas

Tim Brown, MS, LPC
Texas A&M University–Commerce
Commerce, Texas

Joan Davis, PhD, LPC-S, LMFT
Associate Professor
Dallas Baptist University
Dallas, Texas

Jodie Elder, PhD, LPC-S, LMFT
Private Counseling Practice and Adjunct Faculty
University of Houston–Victoria
Dallas, Texas

Ryan D. Foster, PhD, LPC-S, CHST
Assistant Professor and Clinic Coordinator
Tarleton State University
Waco, Texas

Evette Horton, PhD, NCC, LPCS, RPT-S
Clinical Instructor
University of North Carolina–Chapel Hill
Chapel Hill, North Carolina

Elsa Soto Leggett, PhD, LPC-S, RPT-S, CSC
Association Professor and Counselor Education Program Coordinator
University of Houston–Victoria
Houston, Texas

Donna Potter, LCSW
Clinical Faculty
Department of Psychiatry and Behavioral Sciences
Duke University Medical Center; and
North Carolina Child Treatment Program
Center for Child and Family Health
Durham, North Carolina

Karen Sullivan, LCSW
Registered Play Therapist and Supervisor
Certified EMDR Therapist
NMT Trained—Phase I
Sugar Land, Texas

Kelly Sullivan, PhD
Assistant Professor
Department of Psychiatry and Behavioral Sciences
Duke University Medical Center
Durham, North Carolina

Gael Thompson, LPC
Certified EMDR Therapist
Self-Employed, Private Practice
Wimberley, Texas

Elaine Wittmann, MAEd, NCLPC
Supervisor
Registered Play Therapist and Supervisor, National Certified Counselor, Approved Clinical Supervisor
Pathways Counseling and Wellness, Banner Elk, North Carolina; and
Owner and Counselor
Rainbows End Retreat and Training Center, Beech Mountain, North Carolina; and
Owner, Supervisor and Trainer
Beech Mountain and Banner Elk, North Carolina

Preface

Play therapy has been recognized in the counseling profession as a developmentally appropriate model for working with children and adolescents. *Directive Play Therapy: Theories and Techniques* provides a comprehensive introduction to structured, prescriptive approaches to play therapy to those desiring to gain more information and knowledge about the use of different directive play therapy modalities. Through the years of teaching and presenting on this approach, it became clear that there was a gap in understanding directive play therapy and its potential for addressing specific needs and diversity of children and adolescents. Therefore, the primary intended audience for this book is those becoming trained as play therapists. This includes students enrolled in play therapy courses seeking to explore and understand a directive approach to play therapy. It is also written for clinicians and practitioners who would like to learn more about play therapy and gain a greater understanding of these directive approaches.

A notable strength of *Directive Play Therapy: Theories and Techniques* is the diversity of the theoretical approaches presented. Chapter 1 delivers the rich history of this approach, introducing the unique integration of play therapy and different theoretical models. It also encompasses the essential concepts and practices of directive play therapy. Most importantly, it shares some guidelines for planning and selecting toys and materials for a directive approach. The chapter also incorporates settings and skills necessary for effective implementation and addresses common questions asked about the use of these.

The following chapters provide the exploration and detailed description of various theoretical approaches to directive play therapy: "Post-Jungian

Directive Sandtray in Play Therapy," "Solution-Focused Play Therapy," "Eye Movement Desensitization and Reprocessing and Play Therapy," "Directive Play Therapy Techniques in Trauma-Focused Cognitive Behavioral Therapy," "Child Parent Relationship Therapy," "Creativity in Play Therapy Using Technology," "Directive Filial Therapy Models With Very Young Children," "Humanistic Sandtray Therapy With Children and Adults," and "Directive Approaches to Working With Parents." Each of these chapters includes a strong overview and introduction to each theory as well as empirical evidence and research. The distinctive techniques and processes of each of these approaches are explained. Finally, case examples are given to demonstrate their application and implementation.

Directive Play Therapy: Theories and Techniques is written by leading experts on each specific theoretical model. We believe that this book will help play therapists learn how to integrate various theoretical approaches with play therapy. Counselors, family therapists, social workers, psychologists, and psychiatrists will find *Directive Play Therapy: Theories and Techniques* informative and enlightening as well as clinically useful.

Elsa Soto Leggett, PhD, LPC-S, RPT-S, CSC
Jennifer N. Boswell, PhD, LPC-S, NCC, RPT

CHAPTER 1

Directive Play Therapy

ELSA SOTO LEGGETT AND
JENNIFER N. BOSWELL

In September 2000, the U.S. Surgeon General's Office held the *Surgeon General's Conference on Children's Mental Health: Developing a National Action Agenda*. At this conference the Surgeon General explained to children and families, practitioners, educational institutions, educators, physicians, and members of the mental health, scientific, and health care professions of the need to develop specific treatment recommendations for the well-being of children (Department of Health and Human Services, 2000). At this conference, several researchers noted that the prevalence of mental health disorders in children ranged from 16% to 22% (Costello et al., 1996; Roberts, Attkisson, & Rosenblatt, 1998). Later in life, Costello et al. (1996) and Roberts et al. (1998) noted that 74% of children who experience mental health disorders go on to have ongoing mental health needs into adulthood. At the Conference on Children's Mental Health, the Surgeon General's Office decided on four guiding principles to address the mental health needs of children in the United States. These were:

> (a) promoting the recognition of mental health as an essential part of child health, (b) integrating the family, child, and youth-centered mental health services into all systems that serve children and youth, (c) engaging families and incorporating the perspectives of children and youth in the development of all mental health care planning, and (d) developing and enhancing public-private health infrastructure to support these efforts to the fullest extent possible. (Department of Health and Human Services, 2000, p. 3)

The counseling profession has long recognized play therapy as a developmentally appropriate model for working with children presenting in counseling with a variety of mental health concerns. The beginnings of play therapy can be traced back to Sigmund Freud. Freud worked with the father of a young child, Little Hans. Through their interactions with the father, Freud made recommendations to the father about ways he could help his son improve. This is considered the first documented case of filial therapy. Freud was followed in his work by Hermine Hug-Hellmuth, Melanie Klein, and Anna Freud. Each of these practitioners used play with children in various ways as a means to either build a relationship with the child or assist in analyzing the strength of the child's ego. Later, relationship play therapy emerged with a focus on the child's present environment and emotional state. Developers of relationship play therapy (e.g., Jessie Taft, Frederick Allen, and Clark Moustakas) allowed the child permission to engage in any type of play the child was interested in and would play with the child, if invited.

From relationship play, the field moved to nondirective play. This model was created by Virginia Axline (1947) as she adapted the work of Carl Rogers to her work with children. Axline's focus was on building a relationship with the child as a means to create a safe environment in which change could be explored at his or her own pace. Axline, like Rogers, believed that individuals (including children) have an innate ability for self-growth and healing and that all play is a reflection of this ability for or drive toward growth. Due to this belief, Axline allowed children the freedom to play with all of the items and toys in the playroom as she focused on reflecting the child's feelings, thoughts, and behaviors. By doing so, the child would then be able to recognize and deal with those feelings. In 2002, Garry Landreth defined this approach as child-centered play therapy. Since the early 1900s, practitioners and researchers from a wide variety of theoretical orientations (psychoanalysis, cognitive behavior therapy [CBT], gestalt, Adlerian, family therapy, etc.) have begun to explore the use of play therapy. Many of these more directive approaches, including common techniques and case applications, are discussed later in this book.

OVERVIEW OF DIRECTIVE PLAY THERAPY

Directive play therapy is an integrative approach that combines different theoretical models in a manner that responds to and addresses the needs of children (Kenney-Noziska, Schaefer, & Homeyer, 2012). Other names for this integrative approach include: structured, prescriptive, focused, and non-humanistic. Counselors use directive play therapy to focus attention, stimulate further activity, gain information, interpret, or set limits (Jones, Casado, & Robinson, 2003). Purposeful activities, such as games or make-believe, are structured by the counselor to elicit imaginative responses from the client. The counselor assumes the responsibility for the guidance and interpretation of the play interactions (Rasmussen & Cunningham, 1995). Therefore, the work of Anna Freud and Melanie Klein continued within the form of structured play therapy. David Levy (1939) developed release therapy in the 1930s using toys to help children relive traumatic events and thereby release negative emotions. Levy would review the child's case history to understand the struggle and then control the play by providing selected toys to allow the child to work out the problem (Frost, Wortham, & Reifel, 2001; Jones et al., 2003). Gove Hambidge (1955) disapproved of the idea of flooding or pushing the child to release strong negative feelings. As a result, he developed a *structured play therapy* which was implemented only after a relationship had already been established through nondirective play therapy. His method promoted a slow start, using less threatening toys and materials to recreate events, and then using the play to recover from the events (Hambidge, 1955). Consequently, much thought and deliberation was required in the selection of an activity with the client's need and goal in mind. Activities used in directive play therapy cannot be randomly selected but must have a rationale for being chosen (Hambidge, 1955; Jones et al., 2003).

Jones et al. (2003) provide some guidelines for planning and selecting toys and materials that are based on the model of structured play therapy. This group of authors combined their understanding of Sloves and Peterlin's (1994) work with time-limited play therapy and Knell's (1997) cognitive-behavioral play therapy to create the three stages of structured play therapy model: opening, working-through, and termination. These stages begin with a low intensity before increasing that intensity to its highest point during the working-through stage and then decreasing it as the termination stage approaches. The directive or structured activities and techniques are selected to create the desired level of intensity for each session. These levels are defined as (a) evoke anxiety, (b) challenge to self-disclose, (c) increase awareness, (d) focus on feelings, (e) focus on the here and now, and (f) focus on the threatening issues (Jones et al., 2003). Therefore, as the counselor plans for each session, he or she determines the level of self-exploration or intensity needed and then assesses the direction of the session, activities, and materials (Jones et al., 2003)

TOYS AND MATERIALS

Children use toys and materials to express their thoughts and feelings symbolically through the language of play. These are used to (a) express emotions, (b) learn new coping skills, (c) increase self-esteem, (d) recognize and develop responsibility, (e) improve decision-making skills, and (e) increase self-control (Ray et al., 2013). There are differing perspectives about which toys and materials are required to supply children with the opportunity to express their thoughts and feelings. Nash and Schaefer (2011) point out that the selection of toys and materials will vary depending on a number of issues, including the counselor's theoretical orientation, personal ideas and values, space, and budget.

Landreth (2012) provides broad guidelines within three categories of toys and materials used for both directive and nondirective play therapy: real-life toys, acting-out/aggressive-release toys, and creative expression and emotional release toys. Real-life toys allow direct expression of feelings and include toys and materials such as dolls, dollhouses, puppets, cash registers, cars, trucks, and boats. The acting-out/aggressive-release toys and materials offer a means to convey intense pent-up emotions, such as anger, hostility, and frustration. These include a Bobo or bop bag, an alligator puppet, soldiers, wild animals, and rubber or play weapons. Other useful items are egg cartons, Popsicle sticks, and Play-Doh (useful for both aggressive and creative categories).

Finally, the creative expression and emotional release toys and materials make available the opportunity for clients to be spontaneous, expressive, and constructive or destructive. These may include sand, water, paints, and blocks (Landreth, 2012). For Kottman (2011), there are five specific categories of therapeutic values applicable across theoretical orientations. The toys are selected to represent each of the categories. These categories are: (a) family/nurturing toys, (b) scary toys, (c) aggressive toys, (d) expressive toys, and (e) pretend/fantasy toys (see Table 1.1).

Nash and Schaefer (2011) point out that a selection of basic items should be consistently useful.

> ...animal families, baby doll (with bottle), dishes/plastic silverware, doll families, doll house or box with furniture, puppets, toy soldiers, blocks and other building materials, clay, art supplies (markers, crayons, large paper, tape, blunt scissors), small pounding hammer, two telephones or cell phones, doctor's kit, small soft ball, playing cards, small box with lid, and transportation toys (cars, airplane, ambulance, etc.). In addition to these items, such items as masks, mirrors, rope, dinosaurs, plastic tools, cardboard bricks, Lincoln Logs, books, board games, a magic wand, dress-up clothes, and a sandtray and miniatures can also be beneficial. (p. 17)

Furthermore, Nash and Schaefer recommend predictability and consistency in these as the most important features for children. They

TABLE 1.1 KOTTMAN'S TOY CATEGORIES

Family/ Nurturing	Scary	Aggressive	Expressive	Pretend/ Fantasy
Baby doll Dollhouse Baby clothes Baby bottles Cradle People puppets Animal families	Plastic snakes Toy rats Plastic monsters	Bobo or bop bag Small pillows	Easel and paints Watercolor paints Crayons Markers Colored pencils Newsprint Sequins	Doctor kit Human figure puppets Animal puppets Blocks Magic wand Pieces of fabric
Small rocking chair Soft blanket Families of dolls Stuffed toys Pots, pans Dishes, silverware	Dinosaurs Dragons Sharks Insects	Soldiers Military vehicles Foam rubber bats	Play dough Pencils Glue Scissors Tape Stickers Pipe cleaners	Big pillows Iron and board Two telephones Animals, zoo and farm Puppet theater Knights & castles
Sand in sandbox/ tray Kitchen appliances (wooden or plastic) Empty food containers Family miniatures	Alligator Puppets of dangerous animals	Weapons (rubber) Handcuffs Plastic shield	Needles and thread Beads Construction paper Poster board Butcher paper Magazines Paper bags Sock puppets	Hats and purses Dress up clothes Costumes Fantasy puppets Toy vehicles & cars

Adapted from Kottman (2003); Ray (2015).

point out that this allows the clients to know that the toys and materials they need are available and how to locate them. Without consistency and familiarity, clients will spend time exploring the things rather than playing with them (Kottman, 2001 as cited in Nash & Schaefer, 2011).

Jones et al. (2003) support those ideas shared by Nash and Schaefer, stating that a variety of resources and theoretical orientations contribute to directive activities, toys, and materials. Therefore, in addition to those already listed, other materials could also include: (a) books and stories; (b) collages; (c) role-play; (d) checklists and worksheets; (e) games; and (f) self-composed songs, poems, and stories. For counselors working out of play bags, play kits, and/or rolling boxes, additional considerations must be given to portability. Limiting the number of toys and materials does not stifle the range of messages and feelings that children can communicate (Landreth, 2012). The limited play materials recommended are: crayons, newsprint, blunt scissors, clay, Popsicle sticks, tape, baby bottle, doll, plastic dishes and cups, doll family, dollhouse and furniture, face mask, rubber knife, dart gun, handcuffs, toy soldiers, car, airplane, puppets, two telephones, rope, and costume jewelry (Landreth, 2002).

The key to the selection and use of toys and materials in directive play therapy is the need of the client. Thought and deliberation on what the focus of the therapy is and what each session should provide the client should dictate these choices. If the focus is for the client to identify an object in the playroom that represents his or her problem, then toys and materials from varied categories must be available. "Look around at the things here, can you find something that looks like the _____ you have been talking about?" This process of externalizing the problem allows the client to select from an assortment of items. Likewise, when the focus is on a single event or time in the client's life, a sole specific toy, activity, game, or object may be used. If a client is struggling with anxiety in anticipation of riding a bus to school or an extended stay in a hospital, the use of a toy school bus or miniature hospital dollhouse would be items specifically required. Ray (2011) encourages counselors to ask these three questions about the selection of toys and materials: (a) What therapeutic purpose will this serve for the child? (b) How will this help the child express his- or herself? and (3) How will this help me build a relationship with the child? As a result, although these lists of toys and materials are notable, they are only a starting point. The needs and issues of the client make the final decision.

Settings for Directive Play Therapy

The general setting for play therapy is in an office with intentional playrooms or play areas specifically designed for the use of toys in therapy. Bratton, Ray, Rhine, and Jones (2005) shared the findings that play therapy is effective in a number of settings. These findings support the notion that toys can be taken anywhere the child is. Peterson and Boswell (2015) explain the ways creative counselors use to find settings where play therapy can take place. Creative settings for play therapy develop as counselors begin using play bags, play kits, and rolling boxes to carry a collection of toys to locations outside the traditional playrooms. Unique locations for such counseling sessions include schools, homes, hospitals, prisons, and shelters (Bratton et al., 2005; Peterson & Boswell, 2015). Peterson and Boswell go further, listing converted old school buses, portions of or empty rooms, sections of cafeterias or stages, and even outdoor natural settings (Landreth, 2002; Peterson & Boswell, 2015).

Attention and thought must be given to each setting selected for play therapy. Confidentiality is always important and should be secured with our clients. However, use of a nontraditional setting may compromise confidentiality; therefore, additional consent or confirmation of consent may be required. The comfort of the client should also be addressed as necessary. Certainly, the selection of toys and materials must also be mindfully considered. The availability to travel allows counselors to bring toys, materials, and service to a client in a multitude of settings (Peterson & Boswell, 2015).

PLAY THERAPY SKILLS

There are various therapeutic mechanisms within play that help clients. Some therapists and counselors are primarily interested in the use of their preferred theory, whereas others seek to understand and apply multiple agents in play therapy (Drewes & Schaefer, 2014). The following chapters introduce, describe, and illustrate the application and nature of play within various therapeutic approaches and illustrate their application. Yet the personal qualities of play therapists facilitate the therapeutic relationship. These key qualities include empathy, genuineness, and unconditional acceptance of the client. Axline (1947) suggests that successful counseling begins with the counselor. The use of consistency, courage, confidence, and relaxation are essential to this therapeutic relationship (Axline, 1947).

The basic skills shared in counseling with all populations include nonverbal and verbal skills. The nonverbal core skills include leaning forward to demonstrate openness; appearing interested, relaxed, and comfortable; and showing expression and tone congruent with the client. The verbal skills used for counseling with children require a different cognitive level and more limited vocabularies than those used with adults (VanVelsor, 2004). Ray (2004) describes the basic verbal skills as: (a) verbal responses, (b) tracking behavior, (c) reflecting content, (d) reflecting feeling, (e) facilitation of decision making and creativity, and (f) esteem building. Although these are expected in most play therapy sessions, the extent would depend on the theoretical orientation of the counselor (Ray, 2004). Along these lines, there are additional and varied skills to consider that may be specific to directive play; therapy to consider; clarity of a goal; open and closed questions; using metaphor; and the directive or prompt given to the client to move him or her toward the identified goal.

Nonverbal Skills

Leaning Forward. Leaning forward with an open body posture helps the counselor create a warm and accepting environment for the client. This small mindful action can impact the client's perception of the counselor and counseling. Therefore, as the client moves about, the counselor should be squarely facing the client. This also applies to the positions of the counselor's arms and legs (Giordano, Landreth, & Jones, 2005; Ray, 2004). This may require the counselor to shift or swing around in his or her seat to maintain a position that faces the client throughout the session while providing the space needed for the client to move about.

Appearing Interested, Relaxed, Comfortable. Interest in the client ought to be communicated throughout the session. The counselor should not be preoccupied with other matters. This can be demonstrated with the counselor's body postures, facial expression, and accurate responses (Giordano et al., 2005; Ray, 2004). The counselor's level of comfort will bring a sense of calmness and establish emotional availability. This can also increase the ability of the client to remain relaxed throughout the session (Giordano et al., 2005; Ray, 2004).

Expression and Tone Congruency. The counselor strives to be congruent with the client's expression. Matching the affect of the client should appear genuine and be reflected in the counselor's tone. Although the tone ought to reflect the affect, it should not end on a high note. This might communicate a question to the client where there is not one (Ray, 2004).

Verbal Skills

A counselor communicates with a client to convey an understanding of the material explicitly expressed. When working with adults, this communication translates into reflecting the verbal messages shared. Children share these messages through play and action. Therefore, a counselor must consider his or her verbal skills when working with young clients (VanVelsor, 2004).

Verbal Responses. Within verbal responses, there are two skills to consider: succinct interactive responses and rate of response (Ray, 2004). Children do not remember lengthy responses and may not internalize the meaning of the response. A lengthy response can be disruptive to a client's focus and interfere with the progress of the play or activity. With this in mind, the length of responses should be short, succinct, and focus on the client. Succinct, interactive responses reduce client confusion and communicate the counselor's understanding (Landreth, 2012). Rate of responses is the frequency of the verbal response, and the rate of the counselor's interactions or responses should match those of the client. Therefore, the counselor should be slow in his or her responses if the client is quiet. Likewise, the responses and interactions should increase if the client is highly active (Ray, 2004). It should be understood that silence is an added ingredient to the rate and succinct nature and rate of responses. Silence can often be overlooked and underutilized in the desire to provide clear and focused responses.

Tracking Behavior. When tracking behavior, the counselor is simply reflecting what the client is doing at any particular time: "You're drawing something." "You decided to pick that one." Behavioral tracking expresses the counselor's attentiveness to the client as he or she is engaged in play or activities instead of the traditional conversation (VanVelsor, 2004). When clients first experience a counselor's verbal tracking of their behavior, they may be confused because they are more accustomed to answering a question. A client could feel threatened if he or she does not feel safe around the adult (VanVelsor, 2004).

In directive play therapy, there may be some variations not generally found in nondirective therapy. Also, new counselors can find tracking a client's behavior awkward. Common questions about tracking might be: (a) How often do I track? (b) Can I ask questions about what the client is doing? and (c) Can I talk about other things while the client is playing or doing something? It can be hard when first starting out to determine how often to track a client's behavior. Landreth (2012) shares some ideas that are helpful for understanding this skill. He states that if the counselor sits quietly during the client's play or focus on an activity, the client may feel the counselor is not interested and could experience anxiety. However, if tracking is overdone, it can make the client feel self-conscious. Tracking should not follow the client's activity too closely (Landreth, 2012). When tracking with an older child or adolescent, it may be helpful to track less. Oftentimes, a client may initially feel scrutinized or judged by this skill until he or she is more comfortable and understands the counselor's intent. Keep in mind that tracking responses should not label items, objects, or colors. It should be putting into words what the counselor sees and observes the client doing. It is important to begin these responses with "You're" or "You are" rather than "I see. . . ." This keeps the focus on the client, provides validation, and empowerment (Landreth, 2012).

With directive play therapy, questions often fill the session. The nature of this approach, following its theoretical orientation, includes the use of open and closed questions. For some new counselors there can be confusion about when to track and when to ask questions. It might seem that while a client is playing, creating, or engaging in an activity (such as drawing or completing a task) it is an opportunity for the counselor to ask questions rather than track actions. However, this could cause the client to lose focus on what he or she is experiencing in the play or creation. An example of this would be for a counselor to direct a client to draw a picture and then begin to ask questions about the drawing while the client is still focused on drawing. The young client may be confused about what should be taking place at this time and wonder if he or she should be drawing or answering questions. In order to respond to the questions about the drawing, the client must stop synthesizing his or her thoughts about what should be included in the picture to answer the questions. This can slow the counseling process and effectiveness of the session. Therefore, when a counselor gives the client a directive or prompt it should be followed by time, space, and tracking of behaviors.

Reflecting Content. Reflecting content in directive play therapy is similar to counseling with adults. The counselor paraphrases the verbal utterances of the client. Landreth (2012) describes these reflections as: (a) short; (b) succinct; (c) interactive with the client's activity; (d) verbally descriptive; (e) reflective of content; (f) demonstrating of the counselor's understanding and acceptance; and (e) providing an opportunity for the client to unfold his or her story from his or her perspective.

Reflecting Feelings. Reflecting the client's affect serves to make the feelings explicit to the client. A child, much like an adult, may avoid the verbal expression of feelings. Many times it is difficult for a child to confront these feelings, but more specifically he or she lacks the vocabulary to express these feelings or affects (VanVelsor, 2004). Furthermore, Kottman (1995) maintains that it is unproductive to ask a child how he or she feels because he or she often lacks the self-awareness or language to answer the question. Landreth (2012) points out that reflecting a client's feelings leads to: (a) demonstration of the counselor's understanding and acceptance, (b) trust and acceptance of his or her feelings, (c) validation, and (d) creation of empathy.

A child may express his or her feelings in a variety of ways. These expressions are not limited to verbal communications. A young client may not have the words or self-awareness to communicate his or her feelings; however, he or she may share these with the use of play, or role-playing, or puppets. It is the counselor's role to reflect the feeling. This can also deepen the client's experience. Consideration should be given to how cultural, gender, and development levels affect the way a young client expresses feelings. In addition, the counselor should demonstrate patience with a child who may be experiencing an open communication and affirmation about feelings that the family may have been hiding (VanVelsor, 2004).

Both the reflection of content and feelings should be done with statements beginning with *you*. "You got to spend the weekend with your dad." "You just drew on there." "You look frustrated because you can't get that to stay." "You're angry your mom didn't stay with us."

Facilitating Decision Making and Creativity. When the client asks questions or asks for help from the counselor, it is an opportunity to return the responsibility back to the client. The counselor's role is to encourage the client to make his or her own decision and to take responsibility for the current concern. Another opportunity to facilitate decision making is recognizing when a client takes charge of a situation in the counseling session and makes a decision about what he or she wants to do or how he or she wants to do it. These occurrences help the client learn to be more autonomous, independent, and more comfortable with his or her own initial ideas (Giordano et al., 2005). Facilitating creativity and spontaneity helps a client experience a sense of uniqueness. This can be encouraged by responses that allow the client to develop flexibility in thought and action (Ray, 2004). "You can create the sand tray however you want." "You changed your mind about the color."

Facilitating decision making and creativity in directive play therapy can be a thin line because many times a directive or prompt is given to the client. The decision regarding how to respond to the directive would be for the client to make, thus providing him or her with the responsibility. If the counselor asks the client to "Draw a picture of a time when you had a good day in Ms. Smith's class," it should be the client's decision to choose the tools to use, colors, size of the drawing, and so on. The counselor responses that facilitate the decision making or return the responsibility to the client might be: "You decided to use the paint." "You know just what you want to draw." "You can spell that name any way you want." Additional caution is needed here for counselors to stay away from giving the client suggestions or comments that include rigid instructions. A counselor should refrain from proposing how the client might draw the picture: "You can use the pencils there." "Remember to include your friend in the picture." "I can tell you how to spell his name." These comments direct the client to create the drawing from the counselor's perspective rather than the client's. Allowing the client to facilitate decision making and to create spontaneously provides the opportunity for him or her to learn how to make a decision, take responsibility, become self-directed and self-motivated, and have a sense of control in his or her life (Giordano et al., 2005).

Esteem Building and Encouragement. Using esteem-building statements and responses helps a client experience and recognize his or her capabilities. These statements recognize when a client achieves something he or she may have struggled with, such as getting the top off of a container: "You didn't give up, you got it!" At times, counselors can struggle between encouraging a client and praising the client. A praise statement encourages the client to perform for the counselor. This reinforces an external locus of control (Ray, 2004): "I like the way you built that." "Your drawing is pretty." An esteem-building statement encourages the client to develop an internal locus of control: "You are proud of the way you built that." "You drew that picture just the way you wanted." When a client is encouraged to value the effort and work he or she put toward a task, he or she develops an internal source of evaluation. Then, instead of seeking approval from others, the client is able to applaud his or her own effort and accomplishment (Giordano et al., 2005).

CULTURAL SENSITIVITY

The *Association for Multicultural Counseling and Development* (AMCD) has established a framework for training mental health professionals. These guidelines include: (a) counselor awareness of his or her own cultural values and biases, (b) counselor knowledge of a client's world view, and (c) counselor implementation of culturally appropriate intervention strategies (Arredondo et al., 1996). In addition, the *Association for Play Therapy* (APT, 2000) requires that play therapists provide interventions that demonstrate an understanding of the diverse background of their clients, as well as be aware of how their own cultural/ethnic/racial identity may influence their work with their clients. These standards suggest that counselors can provide effective intervention strategies when they have self-awareness, cultural knowledge, and a commitment to play therapy (Chang, Ritter, & Hays, 2005). The therapeutic relationship is especially important and effective in contributing to positive outcomes in counseling. It is also a critical component in multicultural counseling (Swan, Schottelkorb, & Lancaster, 2015). Roaten (2011) advocates that counselors cannot treat young clients like *mini adults*, but rather must implement strategies that meet their developmental level. Furthermore, she maintains that young clients need to have control in sessions and feel valued and respected. The use of strategies such as sandtray, art therapy, and play therapy have been deemed best practices for working with young clients (Roaten, 2011).

However, challenges still remain and call for self-evaluation and awareness as the clients served by play therapy grow in diversity. In 2008, Homeyer and Morrison's review of practices, issues, and trends in play therapy shared Kao and Landreth's words of concern. These authors described the challenges between some of the common play therapy goals that come into conflict with particular cultural beliefs (Kao and Landreth, as cited in Homeyer & Morrison, 2008).

An example of this might occur when a play therapist offers a response to *return the responsibility* to the client: "You can decide how to do that" is often used to facilitate decision making. Yet it demonstrates an individualistic perspective common in Western values. Therefore, when working with a client with a collectivist viewpoint, the approach or wording should be different. An example of a different approach might be: "You're wondering if it is okay for you to decide how to do that. In here it is okay for you to decide." Play therapists must be responsive to their clients' culture (Homeyer & Morrison, 2008).

REFERENCES

Arredondo, P., Toporek, R., Brown, S., Jones, J., Locke, D. C., Sanchez, J., & Sandier, H. (1996). *Operationalization of the multicultural counseling competencies.* Alexandria, VA: Association for Multicultural Counseling & Development.

Association for Play Therapy (2000). *Standards of practice.* Fresno, CA: Author.

Axline, V. M. (1947). *Play therapy* (rev. ed.). New York, NY: Ballantine Books.

Bratton, S. C., Ray, D., Rhine, T., & Jones, L. (2005). The efficacy of play therapy with children: A meta-analytic review of treatment outcomes. *Professional Psychology: Research and Practice, 36*, 367–390. http://dx.doi.org/:10.1037/0735-7028.36.4.376

Chang, C. Y., Ritter, K. B., & Hays, D. G. (2005). Multicultural trends and toys in play therapy. *International Journal of Play Therapy, 14*, 69–85.

Costello, E. J., Angold, A., Burns, B. J., Erkanli, A., Stangl, D. K., & Tweed, D. L. (1996). The Great Smoky Mountains study of youth: Functional impairment and serious emotional disturbance. *Archives of General Psychiatry, 53*, 1137–1143.

Department of Health and Human Services. (2000). *Report of the surgeon general's conference on children's mental health.* Washington, DC: Author.

Drewes, A., & Schaefer, C. E. (2014). Introduction: How ply therapy causes therapeutic change. In C. E. Schaefer & A. Drewes (Eds.), *The therapeutic powers of play: 20 core agents of change* (pp. 1–8). Hoboken, NJ: John Wiley & Sons.

Frost, J. L., Wortham, S., & Reifel, S. (2001). *Play and child development.* Upper Saddle River, NJ: Merrill/Prentice Hall.

Giordano, M., Landreth, G., & Jones, L. (2005). *A practical handbook for building the play therapy relationship.* Lanham, MD: Jason Aronson.

Hambidge, G. (1955). Structured play therapy. *American Journal of Orthopsychiatry, 25*(1), 601–617.

Homeyer, L. E., & Morrison, M. O. (2008). Play therapy practice, issues, and trends. *American Journal of Play, 1*, 210–228.

Jones, K. D., Casado, M., & Robinson, E. H. (2003). Structured play therapy: A model for choosing topics and activities. *International Journal of Play Therapy, 12*, 31–37. http://dx.doi.org/10.1037/h0068870

Kenney-Noziska, S., Schaefer, C., & Homeyer, L. (2012). Beyond directive or nondirective: Moving the conversation forward. *International Journal of Play Therapy, 21*(4), 244–252. http://dx.doi.org/10.1037/a0028910

Knell, S. M. (1997). Cognitive-behavioral play therapy. In K. J. O'Connor & L. M. Braverman (Eds.), *Play therapy theory and practice: A comparative presentation* (pp. 79–99). New York, NY: John Wiley & Sons.

Kottman, T. (1995). *Partners in play: An Adlerian approach to play therapy.* Alexandria, VA: American Counseling Association.

Kottman, T. (2003). *Partners in play: An Adlerian approach to play therapy* (2nd ed.). Alexandria, VA: American Counseling Association.

Kottman, T. (2011). *Play therapy: Basics and beyond* (2nd ed.). Alexandria, VA: American Counseling Association.

Landreth, G. L. (2002). *Play therapy: The art of the relationship* (2nd ed.). New York, NY: Brunner-Routledge.

Landreth, G. L. (2012). *Play therapy: The art of the relationship* (3rd ed.). New York, NY: Brunner-Routledge.

Levy, D. M. (1939). Trends in therapy III: Release therapy. *American Journal of Orthopsychiatry, 9*, 713–736.

Nash, J. B., & Schaefer, C. E. (2011). Play therapy: Basic concepts and practice. In C. E. Schaefer (Ed.), *Foundations of play therapy* (2nd ed., pp. 3–14). Hoboken, NJ: John Wiley & Sons.

Peterson, D., & Boswell, J. (2015). Play therapy in a natural setting: A case example. *Journal of Creativity in Mental Health, 10*, 62–76. http://dx.doi.org/10.1080/15401383.2014.935545

Rasmussen, L. A., & Cunningham, C. (1995). Focused play therapy and non-directive play therapy: Can they be integrated? *Journal of Child Sexual Abuse, 4*, 1–20.

Ray, D. (2004). Supervision of basic and advanced skills in play therapy. *Journal of Professional Counseling: Practice, Theory, & Research, 32*, 28–41.

Ray, D. (2011). *Advanced play therapy: Essential conditions, knowledge, and skills.* New York, NY: Routledge.

Ray, D. (2015, September). Play therapy: Counseling in the child's language [Webinar]. In Chi Sigma Iota Play Therapy Series. Retrieved from https://www.csi-net.org/certifications/default.aspx?id=7319

Ray, D., Lee, K., Meany-Walen, K., Carlson, S., Carnes-Holt, K., & Ware, J. (2013). Use of toys in child-centered play therapy. *Journal of Play Therapy, 22*, 43–57.

Roaten, G. K. (2011). Innovative and brain-friendly strategies for building a therapeutic alliance with adolescents. *Journal of Creativity in Mental Health, 6*, 298–314.

Roberts, R. E., Attkisson, C. C., & Rosenblatt, A. (1998). Prevalence of psychopathology among children and adolescents. *American Journal of Psychiatry, 155*, 715–725.

Sloves, R. E., & Peterlin, K. B. (1994). Time-limited play therapy. In K. J. O'Connor & C. E. Schaefer (Eds.), *Handbook of play therapy: Advances and innovations* (pp. 27–60). New York, NY: John Wiley & Sons.

Swan, K. L., Schottelkorb, A. A., & Lancaster, S. (2015). Relationship conditions and multicultural competence for counselor of children and adolescents. *Journal of Counseling & Development, 93*, 481–490.

VanVelsor, P. (2004). Revisiting basic counseling skills with children. *Journal of Counseling & Development, 82*, 313–318.

CHAPTER 2

Post-Jungian Directive Sandtray in Play Therapy

ELAINE WITTMANN

Without this playing with fantasy, no creative work has ever yet come to birth. The debt we owe to the play of the imagination is incalculable
—Read, Fordham, and Adler (1991, para 93)

This chapter comes from an integrative/holistic approach to play therapy. Although the foundation is influenced by the work of Carl G. Jung, it is integrative because the author draws on practices from many other schools of psychotherapy as well. This chapter concentrates on directive approaches of using trays of sand and small figures as a therapeutic tool in the play therapy room.

JUNG'S PSYCHOLOGY

Jung's psychology, also known as analytical or depth psychology, is not a tool, methodology, or even a group of techniques, but a way to gain insights that can influence psychic healing. The goal is *individuation,* that is, a drive toward *wholeness*, finding balance, and ultimately discovering the true *Self* that is unique to each individual (Jung & Jaffé, 1989; Singer, 1994). This journey toward wholeness is accomplished by exploring layers of consciousness: to the depths of the unconscious, through the collective unconscious that is connected through time and to all of nature and mankind, and bringing those jewels to a conscious level. Unlike the personal unconscious, which is made up of an individual's personal memories and personality, the collective unconscious holds the experiences of all humanity's past and present (Figure 2.1).

Jung proposed that *archetypes* are inherited from the collective memory and are accessed through the collective unconscious (Jung & Jaffé, 1989). These themes or patterns of energy are imprinted on our psyche and influence our everyday thinking and behaving. Shadow aspects of the personal and collective unconscious are activated in times of crisis and delight. These unknown, unclaimed, or rejected parts of the psyche are unintentionally projected onto others and other situations in negative and/or positive ways. The job of the ego, the conscious, is to recognize how these archetypal energies are being played out and understand how to use them. In accessing of the unconscious and bringing light to the ego, the unconscious and conscious are integrated and are now able to bring balance, bring together fragmented elements of the psyche, and ultimately lead to psychic healing. The unconscious reveals new aspects of ourselves in symbols, metaphors, and images through dreams, active imagination, myths, fairy tales (Bettelheim,1986), legends, folks tales, and creative endeavors. This in term empowers the ego. In this process, Jung states that old ideas renew again, and then connections with contemporary situations are initiated (Jung & Jaffé, 1989). Jerry Wright suggested that the unconscious needs the conscious as much as the conscious needs the unconscious (Wright, 2012–2013).

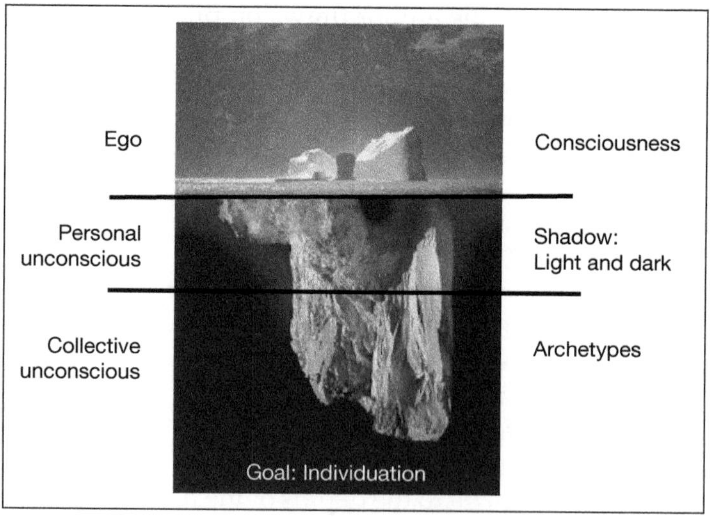

FIGURE 2.1 Model of depth/analytical psychology.
Source: Adapted from Jerry Wright's—Jung's model of the psyche.

Individuation is a lifelong process most often considered in the midlife of the individual (Campbell, 1988; Johnson, 1993; Jung, 1968; Jung & Campbell, 1976; Jung & Franz, 1964; Jung & Jaffé, 1989; Jung & Sabini, 2002; Singer, 1994; Turner, 2005).

> There is a thinking in primordial images, in symbols which are older than the historical man, which are inborn in him from the earliest times, eternally living, outlasting all generations, still make up the groundwork of the human psyche. It is only possible to live the fullest life when we are in harmony with these symbols; wisdom is a return to them. (Jung, 1933, p. 113)

JUNG PSYCHOLOGY AND CHILDREN

Ego–Self axis refers to the relatedness between the ego and Self. The ego emerges from the Self and begins to develop in early childhood at the time the child learns the concept of *I-ness*, when he or she distinguishes him- or herself from the others and the world, becoming more aware of the child's own thoughts, feelings, memories, and perceptions. Fordham (1994), a follower and contemporary of Jung, suggested that parts of the ego are present from birth. This process of ego–Self separation, according to Fordham, is defined by deintegration that reintegrates with adequate parental care, and later in life with the alignment of ego and self (Figure 2.2).

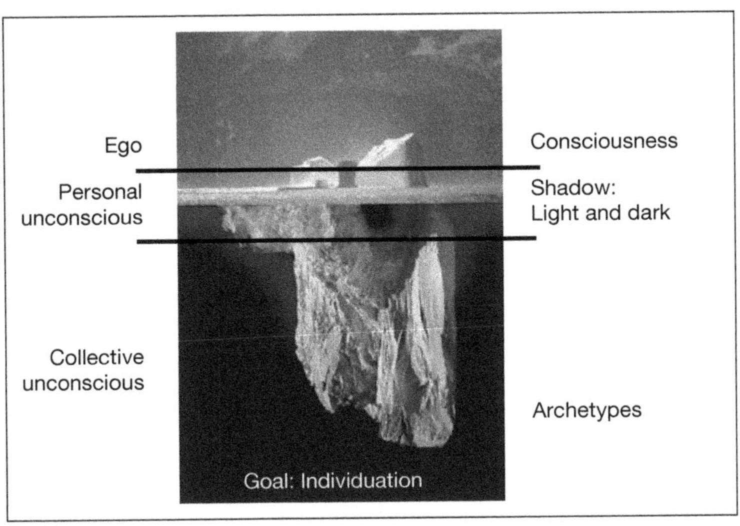

FIGURE 2.2 Model of the psyche for children.

> The first half of life is devoted to forming a healthy ego, the second half is going inward and letting it go. (Jung, 1958, p. 46)

The child will not have developed the ego defenses or unconscious strategies to cope when experiencing trauma or inadequate care in the early years of life. Green described Jung's concept of dissociàtion (Green, 2014, p. 57) as a way in which the child's psyche "trick's itself into cutting off the harmful, unbearable external elements of the trauma and suppresses it into the unconscious." Fragile egos may not be able to deal with a traumatic event, and psychic disintegration temporarily protects the child from being overwhelmed. Integrating the dissociation will be the task.

Jung's original work with children specifically was limited, but his concept was not that childen were "blank slates." Rather, Jung saw the child in the framework of products of a collective unconscious and many generations of family history. Jung appeared to be optimistic for the child and his or her "potential future" (Fordham, 1994; Green, 2014; Jung, 2008; Jung & Campbell, 1976).

> As the son of his father, he must, as is often the case, re-enact under unconscious compulsion the unlived lives of his parent. (Jung, 1938, para 307)

JUNGIAN PLAY THERAPY

As the child enters the *sacred space* of the play therapy room, the therapist begins to build a relationship of respect, acceptance, and trust, and without judgment allows the child's own personal and collective unconscious to guide him or her. Green (2014), in *The Handbook of Jungian Play Therapy With Children and Adolescents*, described that the goals in Jungian play therapy are for the child to connect symbolically with the unconscious and draw on the archetypes that are present. The psyche remembers the ancient and ancestral stories of the archetypes, and the child then creates them in play, in creative arts, and in the sand through active imagination. The story becomes the child's own and the individuation process is activated. Self-nurturing is realized through connection with the *good enough mother/father* and internalization of the positive self-image.

Marie Von Franz (1994) offered that characters or situations in a dream are not puzzles to be solved, but are valued in the intensity through which the individual engages with the object. This can also be true in the stories presented in play therapy.

With an *analytic attitude* for both the child and the therapist, the child is able to self-direct in the play and the therapist patiently allows and facilitates freedom in the play. The role of the Jungian play therapist is to create an environment of safety, build rapport, and allow the child to lead. The therapist creates a container for the process and helps the child remain on a feeling level. The therapist is mindful of transference and its reparative qualities, then within the therapeutic relationship helps the child ground, move from the symbolic, and return to more conscious realizations (Green, 2014).

Jung offered a four-part template for interpretation of dreams that can be applicable to considering the stories that children tell in their play: *the Locale*, the place and time of the story; *the Exposition*, the situation at the start of the story, beginning of plot; *Peripetcia*, how the plot develops, where it goes, and what changes; and *Lysis*, the result, solution, closure, and how it ends (Bulkeley, 2012; Jung, 2008). It is wise to consider the personal experience for the child in the play as well. Conflicts are illuminated in the story of the play, and transformation is possible. Themes are noted in the play and are considered as *guideposts* to follow in the treatment.

> The creation of something new is not accomplished by the intellect but by the play instinct acting from inner necessity. The creative mind plays with the objects it loves. (Jung, 1954, para 197)

Directive approaches can be successfully integrated to give the child a very full experience toward healing and growth. Cues for direction are made, but an analytical attitude is maintained in which the child is the storyteller and the leader. Clarification questions will give the child and therapist greater insights and direction.

ORIGINS OF SANDTRAY PRACTICES

Sigmund Freud and Carl Jung were contemporaries, friends, and intellectual pioneers in psychological theories and practice. Freud was also a mentor and a father figure for Jung, so when their theories collided over approaches to psychology, Jung lamented. Jung struggled with Freud's explanation of pathologies of repressed or frustrated sexual desires that often lived in the unconscious mind. Jung focused on the process of individuation and psychic healing through connection and balance in unconscious and conscious states. Jung brought religion and art into his theory while Freud rejected this.

In the uncertainty of parting ways with Freud, Jung reported having a "state of disorientation" (Jung & Jaffé, 1989, p. 170). As he pondered finding his own new *myth*, and examining his dreams, Jung "consciously submitted to the impulses of the unconscious" (Jung & Jaffé, 1989, p. 173). He remembered with great emotion the play of his childhood in which he first built with blocks and then stones, and then as an adult began to build again on the lakefront. Over and over again, towns of cottages, castles, and cathedrals emerged and his thoughts were clarified (Jung & Jaffé, 1989). In this creative effort, he was discovering his own new myth. Children, like Jung, build by lakes, in the woods, on the floors of their rooms, and in the sand boxes in our therapy rooms. Their connection to the unconscious, and inner worlds, is accessible and made visible in their conscious worlds.

Floorplay

H. G. Wells observed his children creating complex scenes and games with miniatures and toys and recorded their play (Turner, 2004; Wells, 1911, 1913). Wells inspired others with documentation of the richness of the play. At times, young children or children who are not ready to use the sand play with figures on the floor or on the tabletop in the play room. Figure 2.3 is an example of a 5-year-old creating links from his inner and

FIGURE 2.3 Floorplay by a 5-year-old.

outer world. *Good guys* and *bad guys* are common themes, and this youngster is integrating living in the two homes of his divorced parents.

In the 1920s, Margaret Lowenfeld (Amatruda & Helm, 2007; Boik & Goodwin, 2002; Lowenfeld, 2007; Turner, 2005), a child psychiatrist and pediatrician in London, considered Wells's observations and recognized that children think differently than adults (Lowenfeld, 2007; Turner, 2005, p. 691). Lowenfeld pointed out that "children have many ideas and experiences 'in their heads' which won't go into words" (Lowenfeld, 2007, p. 5). With this concept of "picture thinking" (Lowenfeld, 2007, p. 5), Lowenfeld introduced a box of sand, water, and miniature toys to her playroom and called this the "Wonder Box" or "The World." This eventually evolved into the development of the "World Technique" as a psychotherapeutic tool with children (De Domenico, 1988; Lowenfeld, 2007; Turner, 2005). Lowenfeld observed this nonverbal interaction between the child and the figures in the sand, and noted that children could express their inner thoughts through the images, as well as find relief emotionally and behaviorally (De Domenico, 2002; Lowenfeld, 2007).

Other therapists soon followed and explored the medium of sand and miniatures as an assessment and psychotherapeutic technique for healing and growth. Swiss Jungian analyst Dora Kalff studied with Margaret Lowenfeld in the 1950s and developed what is known as *Sandplay* (De Domenico, 2002; Turner, 2004). Using the Jungian theory coupled with Eastern philosophy, the child uses symbols and images in the sand that are derived from an unconscious need to move toward wholeness and healing. Archetypes emerge from cultural and collective experiences and a story is formed (Kalff, 1980; McNally, 2001; Turner, 2005). In an attitude of receptivity and acceptance, the therapist is conscious of creating a "free and protective space" or "temenos" for the client (Kalff, 1980). There is an awareness of transference and countertransference between the client and the therapist and the goal is for the transference to be made to the sandtray. Individual sandtray Worlds are tracked over time, symbols are interpreted by the therapist, and connections are made between the unconscious and conscious in the move toward individuation (Kalff, 1980).

Neurobiology researchers support nonverbal sensory experiences like Sandplay that bring the unconscious into consciousness (Kestly, 2014). Kestly discussed the progression of the intuitive right brain that operates out of the unconscious and the left brain operating out of consciousness. Both are activated in the right-left-right progression (Kestly, 2014, p. 124) as the child plays, moving from being grounded in the play or "wordless story" (Kestly, 2014, p. 132) to where words and language tell the story, and then to integrate in the right brain (Kestly, 2014).

Dr. Gisela Schubach De Domenico studied the teachings of Lowenfeld, Kalff, and others, then developed her own approach to using the sandtray. Growing out of her personal "phenomenological, hermeneutic research" (De Domenico, 2002, p. 31) and her work with children, adults, families, and couples, De Domenico developed Sandtray-Worldplay in the early 1980s (De Domenico, 1988). In De Domenico's approach, the psyche reveals itself as the builder illustrates his or her story in the sand. Objects become real when placed in the sand; they are no longer symbols or representations. These formations are defined by the builder of the story in the sandtray and not interpreted by the therapist. Transference is recognized in Sandtray-Worldplay, but the transfer is with the *World* and is not the therapist. The therapist is actively involved in the process as the observer who is also reflecting and jointly experiencing the World of the builder (De Domenico, personal communication, 2008).

It is real. It's just shrunken. It is really real!

—6-year-old of her story in the sand

THE PROCESS OF SANDTRAY-WORLDPLAY

The child's psyche leads the process in Sandtray-Worldplay. Symbolic images become concrete as they bring powerful insights into consciousness. The builder and the witness travel together through four stages in Sandtray-Worldplay: (a) building and observing, (b) experiencing and reflecting, (c) joint experiencing, and (d) photographing. The builder is simply directed to "Put the World in the tray." They are encouraged to "let the figure choose you," and are given time to place the objects in the sand and experience the World that they created (De Domenico, 1988, 1992, 1998). The World becomes tangible and can be touched, experienced, moved, pondered, changed, and discussed. Internalized material becomes conscious as the symbolic becomes alive in the here and now (De Domenico, 1988, 1992, 1998). De Domenico described several different types of "Sandtray-Worldplay sessions," including "free and spontaneous sand play" and "therapist-directed sand play," in which the witness suggests a topic for the builder, such as "Show me what it is like when depressed in the morning" (De Domenico, 2002, pp. 30–31).

The sandtray process is led by the builder and facilitated by the witness/therapist. The witness holds an important role in Sandtray-Worldplay as an empathetic and fully attentive companion who not only observes the creation of the World, but is also able to *hold* the outer aspects while the builder holds the inner space. De Domenico (1988, pp. 50–59) described powerful "observational modes" that can be "simultaneously tapped during witnessing." The witness's personal responses, conscious or unconscious, have the capacity to influence the builder's World on many levels.

SANDTRAY MATERIALS

Sandtrays

Typically, sandtrays are made from wood or plastic, measure 57 × 72 × 7 centimeters or approximately 20 × 30 × 3 to 4 inches in depth, and are half-filled with sand. A tray of 5 inches deep may be useful for younger children or those who need to *go deeper*. In this psychic *container* the whole World may be seen at a glance by the builder. Slightly smaller trays are used by clinicians who travel. Round trays may be useful to decrease anxiety or for groups.

Sand

There is a tradition for using sand in healing rituals across cultures and time in religious practices, in traditional ceremonies for collective renewal, and in personal healing. Ancient and sacred traditions of sand paintings, similar to mandalas, are found in both Navajo and Tibetan Buddhist cultures, and the Dogon people of Mali use sand divination ritual rights. African traditional healers and religious advisors are also reported to use sand in healing ceremonies. In Mexico and Japan, sand is applied to the body for healing and Zen gardens soothe (Gold, 1994; Iroegbu, 2010; Jongeward, 1990; London & Recio, 2004; Sabini, 2008; Stevenson, 2006).

The healing power of sand is observed as children play at the beach: pouring, molding, patting, constructing, destructing, and reconstructing. As children play with the sand, they are developing motor skills and coordination, and as they create and recreate, they tap into their own collective unconscious and develop new stories and personal myths. Being in touch with their senses (Ackerman, 1990), and connected to others and the natural world across time and space, they are healing themselves and the world. Children may *turn off* their senses to survive in traumatic situations. The introduction of tactile experiences may reawaken the senses, and memories and feelings may be stimulated.

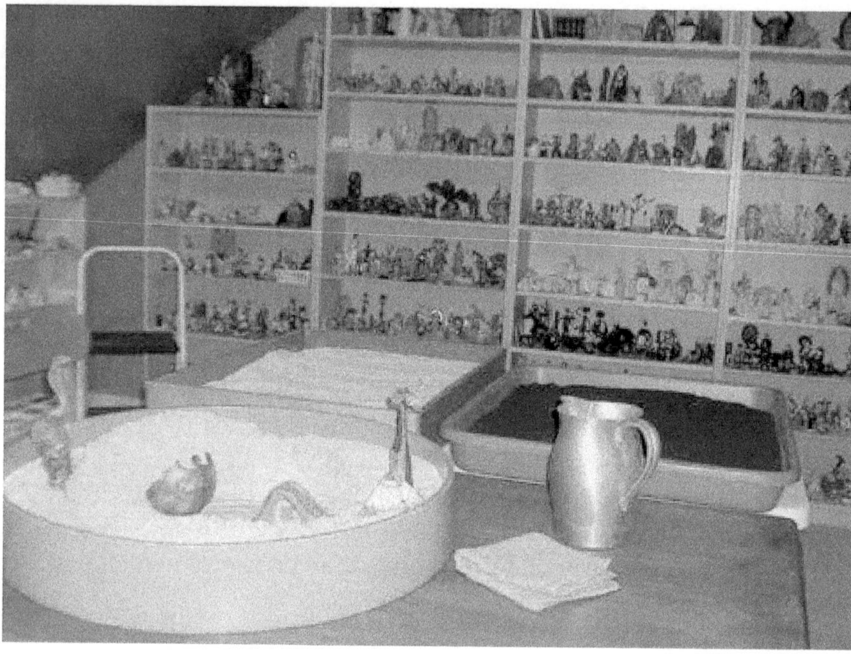

FIGURE 2.4 Different types of trays, different textures and colors of sand, and figures on shelves.

> Most people think of the mind as located in the head, but the latest findings in physiology suggest that the mind...dwells in the whole body. (Ackerman, 1990, p. xix)

In a society where children may often be identified with a "nature deficit disorder" (Louv, 2008 p. 36), playing with sand, a component of nature, the child has the potential to *be born*. *Nature* comes from the Latin word *natura:* birth, constitution, character, course of things, and *nasci:* to be born (Ackerman, 1990; Charles, Louv, Bodner, Guns, & Stahl, 2009; Louv, 2011; Reynolds, 1995).

> Natural life is the nourishing soil of the soul. (Jung & Adler, 1972, para 300)

Thirty to sixty grade sanitized/dustless play sand is used in sandtrays and is available at building and supply stores. Figure 2.4 illustrates primary sand colors of natural, black and white sands, but other colors, such as blue, garnet, coral, and so on, are available and may elicit different memories or emotions. Two trays, one with dry sand and the other with moist sand, offer children greater possibilities.

Water

Water is available to moisten sand, to create bodies of water, to cleanse, and to nurture as in cooking. An additional deep clear tray of water may be beneficial especially when the child has the need to use large amounts of water or to *flood* the tray.

Figures

Miniatures used in sandtray therapies are organized on shelves, in drawers or cabinets, and behind curtains so that the builder has the ability to access and use them as the psyche desires (Figure 2.4). The objects, natural and manmade, are chosen with intention and reflect diverse experiences, time periods, ethnicities, and emotions, and would include humans and nonhumans, fantasy and reality, mineral and vegetation, transportation, and housing. De Domenico organized her vast collection in colors. Hoss (2005) proposed that colors offer subliminal emotional associations, so choosing from groups of colors on a shelf may elicit feelings and draw a builder in. Each figure speaks to the builder in a metaphor (De Domenico, 2002; Hegeman, 2001; Hoss, 2005).

Camera, Paper, and Pencil

The sandtray process is documented in several ways: from the verbalizations of the builder, in the written journey of the movement of the process, and with photographs. In the sandplay model, photographs are not taken in view of the client, but tracked by the therapist, and are reviewed at the end of the process. In Sandtray-Worldplay, pictures may be taken with the client present and are often given to the client to process between sessions.

DIRECTIVE SANDTRAY

Mindfulness in the Sand

Higgins-Klein reminds us of "Meditative/Deeper Awareness" in the process of mindfulness (Higgins-Klein, 2013, p. 28). As the therapist remains in the present, open and receptive, the child senses the attitude and is invited into that space as well. Children can be taught to calm through

Mindfulness teachings. In order to be fully present in the moment and to experience the sandtray, the child uses Mindfulness techniques such as conscious breathing (Kotler, 1996; Nhat Hahn, 1996).

> We are mindful, deeply in touch with the present moment, our understanding of what is going on deepens, and we begin to be filled with acceptance, joy, peace, and love. (Nhat Hahn, 1996, p. 4)

Touching and playing with sand has the potential to be centering for some children. In this tactile, kinesthetic experience, the child may explore the sand and the senses, and some children with sensory difficulties appear to benefit from the experience of playing with sand. Guided imagery, scripted or unscripted (Berkowitz, 2005; Hall, Hall, Stradling, & Young, 2006), may be used to facilitate calming. This is then incorporated into the preparation for building in the sand as the visualizations help move the client from the everyday stressors into a space for readiness in the sand. Music can be added to the process, either selected by the therapist or by the client. Adolescents have clear choices of music. Relaxation music, classical or with different rhythms, are used, as well as music for specific moods.

CASE EXAMPLES: SAFE PLACE

Put Your Safe Place in the Sand: Cecily

Early in therapy, a child may be asked to create his or her *safe place*. After facilitation of conscious breathing, and direction on the awareness of the senses, the child is asked to clear his or her mind and imagine a safe place, a place of security, where distracting thoughts are cleared.

Cecily was referred for play therapy with excessive anxiety and a negative self-concept. Both parents brought her to the first appointment. Despite their reported animosity toward each other and long-term divorce, these parents were clear that they wanted the best for their 8-year-old daughter. Cecily appeared frightened on her first appointment and expressed to both parents that she did not want to come in the building, and then sat close to her parents in the waiting room. After Cecily was shown around the play therapy room, she asked when she could return.

(*continued*)

Cecily chose to use sand and was asked to create a *safe place* on her second session (Figure 2.5). Tentatively, Cecily explored the trays and the sand: moving the damp sand, flattening, and using brushes to smooth. "If I couldn't be in my house, I would have a place to live," and a miniature tent was placed in the sand. Cecily then placed a drink and food, a campfire, and a horse, and explained that she never rode a horse, but loved to look at them. A phone was placed last, hidden behind the tent, "In case something bad happened." Cecily looked surprised when she realized that she forgot herself in the scene and included a figure of a mature regal queen. A fence separated the wild animals (horses and cows) and a bridge connected the two sides. The queen and her horse visited and brought food for the other animals, but did not stay long. "It is a little scary here. You never know what can happen." "Wild animals can't come over the bridge. They only like the sand so they won't come over." The tamed horse and the queen had the ability to move between the areas, but were safe because the wild animals were contained. In finishing, Cecily stated, "I can go over there since I am getting used to it."

Cecily could imagine a safe place with herself as a powerful figure. She introduced her fear of the future to the therapist as well as a cautious resolution. Cecily found the sand and figures as a way to express herself in a safe environment with a therapist who was

FIGURE 2.5. A safe place in the sand for an 8-year-old female.

(*continued*)

(*continued*)

welcoming, understanding, and open. As Cecily risked crossing the bridge to her *wild side* in the sandtray, she also risked coming to the play therapy and engaging with the counselor. Her first experience with sandtray therapy appeared to be positive.

Cecily retuned the next week with her mother and wanted to recreate her *safe place*. The figures and theme were very similar, but with some significant differences. Cecily now included her self-figure as a "princess" and a "princess's friend" to join her. The princesses were able to move freely between the places of the "wild animals" and the animals were free to join them across the bridge. "Ruby slippers" were placed on the bridge. Food was included for the people and the horse and a glass jar of a "potion" was included. A small hole was burrowed into the sand behind a fence, "They don't know about this little area."

Cecily seemed to be moving in the sand and in the process of therapy in a short time. She had the support of a friend on this heroine's journey and the ruby slippers. "Click your heels together three times and say 'There's no place like home' and you'll be there" reminds Glinda in the Wizard of Oz. The ruby slippers came from the defeat of the Wicked Witch of the East and had great power. Dorothy did not realize that, but Glinda informed her, "You've always had the power, my dear, you just had to learn it for yourself." Cecily's safe place continued to evolve. She was the one who led the therapy and found that she did have the power, and was ready to cross the bridge and go down her own *yellow brick road* (Bunch, 2006; Fleming, 1937).

The directive to "Put your safe place in the sand" safely led this girl to a place where she could begin to trust and gave her the courage to travel there. Cecily drew on archetypes of feminine power, as well as a secret to be discovered later that remained to be answered in the *hole*.

Put Your Safe Place in the Sand: Memphis

Memphis also used the directive "Put your safe place in the sand," but the result was very different. This 10-year-old presented as a very anxious child who had periodic panic attacks. Memphis identified

(continued)

a frightening incident during summer vacation as a "four" on a scale of one to ten. After instruction, Memphis and his father used a relaxation breathing technique, and the child was instructed to "Put your safe place in the sand."

Exercises for relaxation can take the form of breathing techniques, muscle tension relaxation, guided imagery, or movement. The breathing exercises for reducing anxiety and bringing calm for Memphis included instructions to first find his diaphragm with his hand and watch his hand move up and down, then breathe through his nose and out his mouth. Once Memphis completed three deep breaths, he was directed to find his own comfortable breathing pace and then visualize a balloon in which he could blow any worries. Memphis could imagine the balloon as large as was necessary, and when it was full, he could—let it go! Memphis could let go of any worries and let them disperse into the air. Memphis and his father were told that they could practice the exercise so that Memphis could be prepared to use the relaxation anytime he needed.

Memphis appeared methodical as he silently placed figures in the sand. Two trays were filled with objects of protection (Figure 2.6). When asked, Memphis described different areas of safety: (a) gates

FIGURE 2.6 A safe place in the sand for a 10-year-old male.

(continued)

(*continued*)

surrounding the perimeter; (b) a medieval army who could not get past the gate; (c) "Ironman" who stood tall protecting "My Kingdom"; (d) magic powers to bring "bad people" to jail; (e) ancient places to keep evil spirits from the past; and (f) weapons and places to hide. Memphis reported that the safest place in his kingdom was in his home, and the magic crystals around him. The most frightening, for Memphis, was the gate that needed protection. There was much protection needed in this World! Memphis showed his father the tray when he was done, and photos were taken and printed to show his mother as well. Memphis stated that this sand play "was the most fun ever!"

Memphis was an anxious child who needed protection from fears and his own negative inner dialogue. He now had the physical and visceral experience of creating a safe place. Instinctually, Memphis had his answers, given to him from his unconscious. His father told Memphis that he would frame the photo and now this safe place built in the sand became another layer as a transitional object of safety for him.

Put Your Feelings in the Sand: Lacy

As De Domenico described in Sandtray-Worldplay, the therapist/witness to the play may direct and request the child to show a feeling in the sand (De Domenico, 2002). At times, a feeling elicited from a sandtray is amplified and explored in another tray (De Domenico, 2002).

Mandalas in the Sand

In times of stress, Jung found peace and a sense of wholeness in sketching a series of mandalas. This practice is used by many cultures as a form of self-expression. Mandalas are sketched or painted symbols drawn in a circular frame for the purpose of personal development and spiritual transformation. Reflecting on these drawings, Jung wrote: "In them I saw the self that is, my whole being actively at work" (Jung & Jaffé, 1989, p. 196). Jung's personal story of being lost and found is described in his journaling, and a succession of mandalas are documented in Jung's *Red Book* (Jung, 2009).

(*continued*)

Before a child is invited to paint or draw a mandala on paper or any other surface, the therapist instructs the child on how to ground or center himself or herself by creating a still place, breathing, and centering. This is true when a child is requested to put the *mandala in the sand* (Otto, 2005).

> I live my life in widening circles that reach out across the world. I may not complete this last one but I give myself to it. (Rilke, 1996, p. 45)

Lacey was 10 years old when she started using the "finger Labyrinth" in the play therapy room. She walked a labyrinth with her counselor and found the circles soothing. Coloring pages of labyrinths and mandalas were selected by Lacey on a regular basis. She then moved to creating her own mandalas when she was 11 years old. The sandtray gave Lacey a way to expand and amplify the experience in the third dimension.

Lacey's mother died when she was 2 years old and she had few memories of her mother. She struggled with blending into her new family after her father remarried. Lacey now grieved and longed for the idealized version of her biological mother. Following one particularly stressful week, Lacey was asked to put the mandala in the sand. There is a tradition of *painting in the sand* in Tibetan Buddhist, Navajo, and Malian cultures, and Lacey was to create her own. Lacey used a round sandtray to create her mandala with figures and centered a large circular mirror surrounded by smaller mirrors. In the center was an article used by this child in the past: a large clear "jewel" often associated with her mother. Lacey placed other items of comfort around as well: dogs, cats, and trees. Finally, she added angels that were placed atop the small mirrors; Lacey made the connection that the angels were her connection to her mother, who was watching over her and giving her strength (Figure 2.7).

Lacey chose a round sandtray for her mandala, hence doubling the circles. Golden threaded beads circled the edges of the tray again. She broke the circle with stones in quadrants: a series of four lines of stones, much like Jung's. Without being aware of Jung's concept of *sacred geometry*, the mirror and the jewel were centered in the

(*continued*)

(*continued*)

FIGURE 2.7 A mandala in the sand.

mandala and created a space in which everything was related. The unconscious was instinctually tapped and balance was created with the conscious. Pathways from all sides lead to the "good mother"; the image is "mirrored" in a jewel, and the angels encircled the jewel. Jung saw the mandala as an archetypal image of the "wholeness of the self" (p. 335) and the circular pattern of the mandala as the "likeness of the God-image"—the light that may emerge from the darkness (p. 334) (Jung & Jaffé, 1989).

> In the products of the unconscious we discover mandala symbols, that is, circular and quaternity figures which express wholeness, and whenever we wish to express wholeness, we employ just such figures. (Jung, 1989, p. 324)

Put Your World in the Sand: Annalisa

Annalisa, at 13 years old, was referred for difficulties in attending and focusing. She was given a diagnosis of attention deficit disorder with hyperactivity and currently was not taking medication after several attempts with unwanted side effects. Annalisa presented

(*continued*)

as a bright, physically mature young adolescent, but struggled with peer interactions. Her father and psychotherapist mother were supportive of expressive arts counseling and understood the value for their daughter. Annalisa expressed an interest in the figures and sand and was invited to "Put your World in the sand."

Annalisa was observed taking great care in her choice of figures and their placement. When she appeared ready, the therapist asked, "Could you take me down into your world, as if I were a tourist in a new land?" Annalisa responded, "Hop on Pegasus with me and I will show you around." From there Pegasus brought Annalisa and the counselor to each figure and told them what each could teach: "The dancer will teach us to dance." "The fairies holding the jewel will teach us to share." "The angels are praying for us," and so on. The glass ball is "peace... they all want to go there." Annalisa continued the tour around the World and came to the large dark "Garuda" figure. Garuda is a large bird creature in Buddhist mythology that is a combination of god and animal. The golden-winged Garuda's heart radiates light and is very powerful when alive; however, after death, the flesh and bones disintegrate and return to the four elements. The heart does not decay, but remains whole and intact, and

FIGURE 2.8 Glass ball of "peace" and "Garuda" are circled.

(*continued*)

(*continued*)

FIGURE 2.9 Opposite view of Figure 2.8.

continues to glow brilliant light. It is considered a spiritual treasure. Annalisa defined the dark bird that faced the clear shining globe of peace as the "evil" in the tray. At first, she proclaimed that the evil would have to be removed from the World, then reconsidered, and concluded, "There needed to be some evil because without evil, the world would go crazy" (Figures 2.8 and 2.9).

The heart of Garuda still shone and Annalisa was unconsciously aware of the treasure and the need for both peace and evil to coexist in the same world. Annalisa needed to *hold* both in her own life and tapped into the archetypal, spiritual collective. She took us into a world of learning: jealousy, power, joy, and then confronted "evil." Her wisdom was shining.

Put Your World in the Sand: James

After a honeymoon period in the foster home, 7-year-old James was having difficulties adjusting, and seemed to resist any attachment to his foster parents. His foster parents planned to adopt James, but had concerns about his future in their home. His behavior became more oppositional and defiant. With James's frustrated foster mother in the room, he was instructed to "Put your World in the sand," and as his caregiver described his problematic behavior, James created. The therapist was curious about how her discourse impacted James.

(*continued*)

"They are fighting about the jewel." The counselor did not see the jewel that was placed in the tray. James later said, "It is buried under the mountain and the dragon is trying to get it." When speaking about three warrior figures on another dragon, James stated, "They are fighting the other dragon to get the jewel" (Figure 2.10). It was noted by the counselor that James used the same warriors in the past and they seemed to represent James and his two foster parents. After dramatic fighting between the dragons, the battle was won. The warriors on the dragon were the conquerors and they unearthed the treasure—a mirror (Figure 2.11).

FIGURE 2.10 Fighting for the jewel.

FIGURE 2.11 Finding the treasure.

(*continued*)

(*continued*)

James had a long series of broken attachments with his biological family and other foster homes and was ambivalent about attaching to this family. He appeared to be fearful of further abandonments and was pushing the adults away before he could be hurt again. His foster mother grew to love James in their 6-month relationship and wanted the adoption finalized, but was apprehensive. Given her own issues of loss, she feared rejection by James. The counselor and James's foster mother watched James create his story and heard his narrative:

Counselor:	The warriors fought hard to win the jewel, James. They were up against a powerful dragon!
James:	(agreed, and was able to speak for the dragon) He (the warrior's dragon) had even more power and the warriors were helping.
Counselor:	Imagine for the warriors now, James.
James:	They are a team and they worked together.
Counselor:	(after noticing that James's foster mother had tears in her eyes, and keeping with the metaphor) What do they see in the jewel?
James:	They see everything.
	James and his mother hugged.

The jewel/mirror was buried under a mountain of painful experiences for James and his foster mother, but could be found with the teamwork of three and a strong and powerful force. James's unconscious knew where to find his power and the power of the family. They fought the opposition together and won. The mirror reflected this and "everything" could be seen. James and his mother were then able to talk about how this reflected their lives together and how they best could move forward as a "team." James would develop a new myth for himself and his new family.

> Slight shifts in imagination have more impact on living than major efforts at change. (Moore, 1994, p. viii)

(continued)

Put the Problem in the Sand: Jeremy

The direction "Put the problem in the sand" increases the specificity of the prompt by the therapist when used thoughtfully and with caution. In this presented case, Jeremy often took responsibility for his family's actions. He began the session giving examples of the struggle in the relationships in the family during the previous week. The hope for the cue was to gain greater insights for both the child and therapist.

At 6 years of age, Jeremy was the youngest in his family, and his family was in crisis. His 8-year-old sister, Emma, was initially identified as the client because of her oppositional, defiant, and aggressive behavior, particularly toward her mother. Their parents' relationship was in jeopardy. They were polarized in their roles as parents with their father as disciplinarian. He often screamed and yelled at his children and at times became harsh in his parenting. The mother typically took a passive role and was frustrated with the conflict and chaos in the family. The children ran to her for protection from their father's anger. They often exhibited sibling rivalry and aggressive conflict.

After this, the counselor worked with the family for some time with limited success. Emma and the family were referred to an intensive home-based therapy program. Jeremy continued play therapy with the counselor to provide a safe space to assess the impact of the family dynamics, express his feelings, and to give him coping tools.

Jeremy exhibited great creativity as he used a variety of play therapy tools. He enjoyed playing with clay and created animals, people, transportation items, and his favorite—tractors, his symbol of power. After a particularly stressful week for the family, Jeremy was asked to "put the problem of your family into the sand." Jeremy was familiar with the sandtray room and immediately chose coarse black sand in a deep tray. Actively using military figures of opposing colors, Jeremy stated, "This is me and Emma" and aggressively fought with weapons (Hegeman, 2001). Sand was flying. Jeremy stated, "We are fighting about the couch," and who would use the space. "I'm buried.... She killed me" and he buried his self-figure. "Daddy comes in and kills her (Emma)" and then Jeremy

(continued)

(*continued*)

buries his sister. He then played, "Mommy comes in: 'Daddy you are a bad boy!" and Daddy is buried. The in-home counselors were also included in the sandtray, "Jack and Mary comes in" . . . "All the family gets buried." "Mary kills Jack" and Jack then gets buried. "A stranger comes in and kills Jack and Mary and then kills himself. He lights a cannon and BOOM he kills himself. They all died. The end."

After sitting with the story for a few minutes, the counselor reflected on the events and asked, "Is there any hope for this family? Is there any hope that things will be different?" After solemnly considering, Jeremy answered, "I don't know. I hope so." The counselor asked, "Is there anyone who could help?" and Jeremy answered, "Maybe Jack and Mary could tell them to stop fighting," and he dug up the figures of the counselors. The intensive home-based counselors were consulted after this session. The problem was certainly a family problem and a 6-year-old felt his world disintegrating. He felt little control in this scenario as he demonstrated the succession of events and cumulative effect on the family. Perhaps the in-home counselors could help make changes in the family.

Several months later, based on the family's progress, the sandtray counselor considered moving Jeremy's sessions to every other week. The plan was changed when this little boy answered questions about what he did this summer and what was his favorite. Jeremy responded, "Coming to see Elaine." When asked about the best thing in coming to see Elaine, Jeremy answered, "Playing. Sometimes when I am not here I picture it in my head." Jeremy carried the burden of his family's "unlived lives" but had images from his play to express his World. In the sand he was able to connect with the archetypal and the reality of his world and bring himself peace and healing; he was also able to use the images in his head as transitional objects.

Put Your Dream in the Sand: Sara

> Play for a child is a gift from the imagination when the child is awake that is projected from the unconscious as a drama onto toys and activities that give us hints into insights, clarification, and potential. (Wittmann, 2009)

(*continued*)

> A dream is a gift from the imagination as we sleep that is projected from the unconscious as a drama onto a dream-screen to give us hints into insights, clarification, and potential. (Wittmann, 2009)
>
> Children's conceptions of dreams are an important component of their developing understanding of the mind. (Woolley, 1992, p. 365)

Dreaming is a kind of play (Bulkeley, 2012; Saarinen, 2003)! Woolley noted that Carl Jung reported vivid dreams as a child and came to rely on his dreams and fantasies to find solace and solutions to his problems. Jung did not work with the dreams of children directly, but looked at the childhood memories of dreams reported by adults and the impact on their lives. Childhood dreams, according to Jung, originated in depths of the personality and were of the highest importance. Dreams could give hints of what was to come in a lifetime (Beudet, 2008; Bulkeley, 2012; Jung, 2008). For Jung, dreams came directly from the collective unconscious in symbolic forms as messages for the conscious. In the spirit of dreams telling the ego what the unconscious already knows, Jung, his students, and colleagues used the metaphors of these traditions to interpret the dreams remembered by adults. Although the power of the dream's message may not need interpretation (Jung, 2008), Marie-Louise Von Franz stated that in looking at these symbolic messages, the ego is able to remember and use the images to influence everyday life.

> Significant dreams are often remembered for a lifetime, and not infrequently prove to be the richest jewel in the treasure house of the psyche. (Jung, 1974, p. 78)

Sara was seen in a residential setting. This streetwise 15-year-old appeared older than her chronological years, but emotionally appeared to be stuck several years younger. Her needs for acceptance and family connection made her an ideal candidate for the play therapy room. Sara described her history: "Everyone in my family uses drugs and has been in jail." Sara followed in their footsteps and started using drugs at 12 years old. Her mother was currently in a rehabilitation center and she had not seen her father since she was 10 years old since he was sent to prison for murder. It was

(*continued*)

(*continued*)

unlikely that she would see him again. Pregnant at 14 years, Sara lost her baby to domestic violence by her boyfriend.

Sara presented the following dream in a therapy session: "There were horrible creepy things that would not stop screaming," but could not give any further details. One of Sara's strengths was writing, and she was asked to *amplify* the dream in a poem. The dreamer is able to augment the dream by amplification (De Domenico, 2002, pp. 1–6; Pando-Mars, 1998, pp. 16–18). By recreating the dream or images of the dream in the sandtray or other expressive/creative methods, the dreamer is able to explore feelings connected to those images. This examination can lead the dreamer to archetypal meanings of the dream. The dream is then allowed to continue in a conscious experience toward increased meaning making (De Domenico, 1998; Hall, 1983; Van de Castle, 1994). Sara created a poem that connected her own drug use to the "horrible creepy things" and to her losses and needs. She used the poem to express her feelings in several sessions, and then she was asked to further amplify the dream in the sand (Figure 2.12).

> One does not become enlightened by imagining figures of light, but by making the darkness conscious. (Read et al., 1991, para 113)

FIGURE 2.12 Horrible creepy things in the sand.

(*continued*)

From a sentence in a dream, to words in a poem, now presented and experienced visually and viscerally, Sara and the counselor had a richer picture of her world. Babies crawled toward the danger of drugs; compulsively drawn and knowing the danger, but unable to fight the power of the pull.

Behind and to the side of the most prominent danger in the tray resided Sara's parents; her mother holding her child and her father protecting her. A prayerful figure kneeled in front of a damaged baby (Figure 2.13).

Kalsched (2003) quoted Jung and others as he explored *daimonic* elements of unconscious when personal *divine archetypal defenses* were symbolized and served as a container for self-care. In this sandtray, Sara included both symbols of evil and benevolent daimonic features. In the presence of an empathetic witness, the builder creatively played in the sand. Sara was integrating the unconscious and the conscious. Sara confronted her greatest losses and fears and grew from this experience and many others. The therapist did as well (Green, 2014; Kalsched, 2003).

> The meeting of two personalities is like the contact of two chemical substances: If there is any reaction, both are transformed. (Jung, 1933, p. 113)

FIGURE 2.13 Love and protection in the sand.

(*continued*)

(*continued*)

Put Your Dream in the Sand: Maddie

Maddie was diagnosed with developmental delays and attentional difficulties. Attempts were made to decrease the anxiety that she experienced. Maddie and her mother reported significant repetitive "bad dreams" that frightened this 9-year-old on waking, altered her sleep habits, and increased daytime fears. Side effects of the new medication appeared to be the culprit, and the dreams stopped after the medication was changed, but the fears continued. Maddie enjoyed the sand and was encouraged to "put the dream in the sand." Maddie demonstrated how she could protect herself in the dream by changing the ending of the story in the play. In doing so, Maddie was reminded of the support she had with family and friends, with her faith, and with therapy. A photo was taken of the sandtray story and Maddie's power and control over her fears; this was printed for Maddie to take with her. The experience was relayed to Maddie's mother, who reminded and supported Maddie in her experience. Fears associated with this dream no longer had power over Maddie, and the mastery of this play was continued for this child.

> *When I went to my dream…*
>
> —6-year-old female

For young children, the dream happens in their room and only later in their development is the dream experienced as in their mind. Dreams, as in play therapy, present themselves in metaphor; in symbols, signs, and motifs. Metaphors offer dynamic and dramatic views beyond the surface to deeper significant hidden material. After hearing a *therapeutic story* adapted from a fairy tale, a child responded, "That's like my life, but not like my life." This 9-year-old clearly understood the meaning of metaphor.

Symbols in dreams and play are not rational thoughts, but give us even more meaning through their metaphor. An example is the American flag, a familiar symbol in daily life that possesses obvious and great meaning. Signs point to something, such as red and green traffic lights, whereas motifs are recurring ideas, concepts, symbols, themes, or objects. In dreams and play, there may be unconscious

(continued)

reactions to conscious situations, or the conscious situation may be followed by a reaction of the unconscious in the form of a play or a dream (Beudet, 2008; Bulkeley, 2012; Haden, 2010; Hudson, 2000; Jung, 1968; Taylor, 2009).

Conflict Management in the Sand: Anna and Joslyn

These 10- and 11-year-old sisters competed for the basics in life and for the attention of their biological mother. After a long history of abuse and neglect, they were transitioning from foster care to adoption. They were well cared for, but the severe sibling competiveness continued.

After treating the girls individually and conjointly for several months, Anna and Joslyn were asked to use the sand to solve the problem of their relationship. The girls were each given a tray of natural-colored sand and the same items to create (Figure 2.14). At first, the girls watched each other for cues and then built independently and uniquely. Each girl described her efforts to the counselor and each other. The counselor coached listening skills and respect for the other's work. The girls were then told that they could add objects to their trays with the same goal: problem solving about their conflicts.

With little discussion, it was obvious that there was significant tension in their relationship: shells pierced into each other's

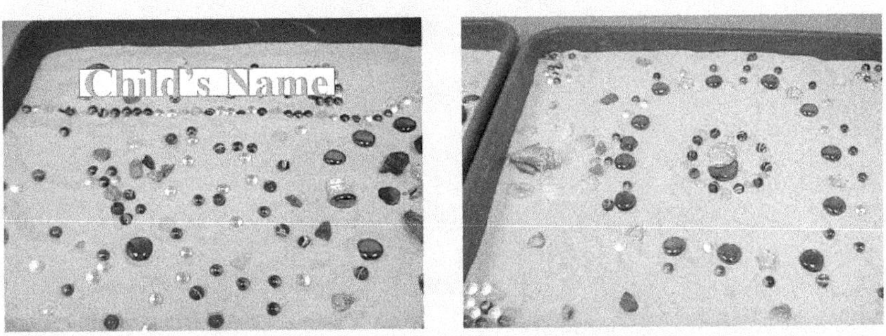

FIGURE 2.14 Siblings using the same items to create in the sand, but creating very different scenes.

(continued)

(*continued*)

space, a witch was added at the boundary (Figure 2.15), and a volcano erupted into red-hot lava. The girls then worked together cooling the fire with blue stones, and finally "angel" hands soothed the explosion (Figure 2.16). What they could not imagine or say in words, they could say in the sand. We were able to use that image and metaphor as we continued to work on their relationship. The new parents also had a vocabulary they could use to address the behaviors.

> Often the hands know how to solve a riddle with which the intellect has wrestled in vain. (Jung, 1972, p. 171)

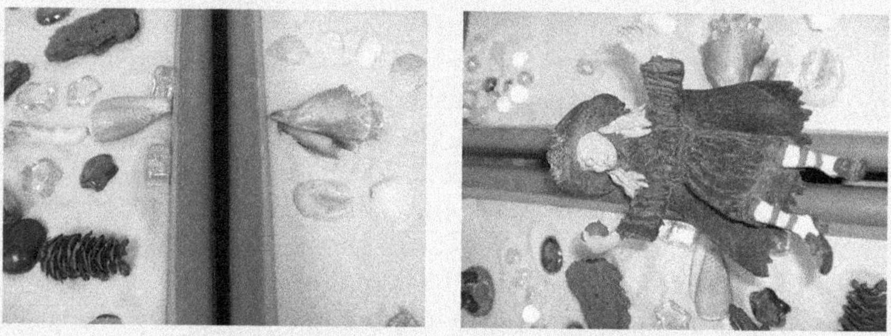

FIGURE 2.15 Siblings' sandtrays interconnecting.

FIGURE 2.16 Working toward resolution in the sand.

(continued)

Momma's House and Daddy's House in the Sand: Kendra and Carlos

With the increased frequency of children living in two homes of divorced parents, the directive to use two trays to illustrate the child's experience in both homes was introduced. A 9-year-old and his 7-year-old sister were struggling since their father left to live with his girlfriend and her 8-year-old daughter. Daddy's house in the sand included a large tiger looming over two small cubs. The children described that they felt that the other child in the home was favored and that they were often blamed by their father. When asked how it felt in this home, the children responded, "Not protected." The illustration of Mommy's house in a second tray included a "party" with balloons and cake. The children reported that they wanted to give their mother a party, because "she stayed." In between the trays stood a figure of a police officer, "to protect us." The children told their mother their feelings, but did not talk to their father, because, "He would get mad." They could not risk the relationship with their father at this time.

Momma's House and Daddy's House in the Sand: Kenisha

For the 5 years of shared custody, Kenisha changed living arrangements weekly between her mother and father. This 10-year-old composed sandtrays of Mommy's and Daddy's houses and included her parents' new partners, significant others, animals, and favored items in the homes. It was a surprise to Kenisha's mother that this child continued to fantasize about her parents' reconciliation and remarriage in the trays.

Momma's House and Daddy's House in the Sand: Jenny

Jenny put a figure of herself between the trays of her mother's and father's homes and explained that she continued to feel pulled in

(continued)

(*continued*)

each direction. These visual constructions gave the parents better understandings of the impact of their relationships.

Trauma in the Sand: Eli

Kestly (2014) reported, "Neurobiological research supports the fact that emotional memories and traumatic sensory experiences are stored in the limbic system and right hemisphere of the brain, along with nonverbal, sensory experiences such as images, body sensations, and emotions." Using sensory experiences in the sand, creating a container in the tray as well as a container in the supportive relationship, then may help in reconnecting the fragments in the unconscious and returning to ego consciousness.

The local Department of Social Services referred Eli for therapy describing the neglect and abuse in the family as one of the "worst" cases they investigated. Eli was now in a caring foster home with a knowledgeable and committed family. Scores on a variety of assessments were significantly high for traumatic events, reexperiencing, avoidance, and increased arousal, as well as difficulties with focusing, attention, and impulsivity, indicating a diagnosis of posttraumatic stress disorder.

Eli's third grade teachers reported that he was significantly behind in most academic areas, and he was having difficulty with attendance and focusing in class. Eli needed direction from adults at school as he interacted with his peers, as appropriate boundaries were an issue. Eli's foster mother and the therapist consulted with teachers and the school counselor on a regular basis. His school provided support and accommodations to help Eli succeed academically and socially—and he did! Eli proved to be a bright youngster who, with encouragement and help, moved quickly toward grade level with a more positive image of self-worth. He was referred to a pediatrician and psychiatrist who prescribed medication and monitored his physical health, moods, and behavior. His foster parents provided safety and gave Eli unconditional love. They taught and modeled respect and Eli was learning to reciprocate. Eli's foster parents were actively

(continued)

involved in the therapeutic process and were consulted before and after sessions, engaged in family play therapy, supported in their roles, and brainstormed parenting interventions with this counselor.

This 9-year-old presented as an attractive child with wide blue eyes and quick disordered physical movements as he investigated everything in the room. Eli explored the play therapy room, the toys, and the relationship with the counselor. Stress management skills were created as play and Eli responded. Muscle tension and relaxation were played as "gorillas" and "slugs" (Eli's interpretation). Breathing was played with bubbles: "biggest bubble wins" (which meant blowing slowly), "get the bubble through the hoop," "let's imagine where the bubble is going" (best played outdoors), and "send a message in a bubble to each other" (M. Davis, personal communication, May, 2009). Yoga poses were imitated and laughing proved to be a needed release. Eli was able to teach his foster parents Mindfulness practices and they helped Eli practice the skills.

Law enforcement and judicial officials wanted information from Eli, but was Eli ready? It was a delicate balance. Eli was invited to talk about what happened at his biological parents' home and he tentatively shared some information, but he was clearly anxious in his reporting. After a short time, and beyond Eli's "window of tolerance" (Siegel, 2010), he was invited into the sandtray room with the prompt, "Show me your World." Eli enjoyed playing in the sand, and jumped in immediately. He set up battle fields in two trays and invited his therapist into the play. Eli appeared to build methodically, using exactly what was needed in the trays and directed this counselor on the figures to use. He gave instructions on how the figures were to battle, where they would move, who would die, who would live, who would be saved, and how the battle would progress. Eli identified his "team" as the "bad guys" and the counselor as the "good team." The war was fierce and when the prompt for ending the session was given, the "bad guys" won. The therapist did not question Eli about his abusive past, and the battle in the sand continued for several more sessions. Eli, as member of the "bad guys," continued to win: "Bad guys always win." The counselor continued to play the given role in the battles with trust and

(continued)

(*continued*)

hope that Eli would find what he needed. Verbalizations were made for the "good guys" who protected babies in the play. "Bad guys are more powerful" was the environment in which he lived in his birth home and Eli was showing his World in the most powerful way he could, not in his words, but in metaphor. Babies were not protected in the home of his birth.

Family Sandtray

Eli's foster father did not typically bring him to the session, but did so several weeks into the battle of "good" and "bad." Eli excitedly invited his foster father into the sandtray room and instructed him to join the "good team" with the counselor. Eli fought enthusiastically, was observed to be perspiring despite the cool room, and directed the father on how to fight. At one point, Eli aimed his weapons at his foster father's figure and challenged. The father hesitated at first, stating that he did not want to hurt his charge's figure. The therapist encouraged the father to acquiesce and use his weapons despite his discomfort. He was asked, "How would you fight to protect Eli if someone wanted to hurt him?" and this father responded that he would fight "with all my might" and did so in the sand. It was the "good enough father" fighting against evil. As the session was ending, Eli stood in the middle of the two trays and stated, "We won!" and declared that he would be on the "good team" with his foster father. Periodically, particularly when the foster father was attending, Eli tested his foster father's commitment for his safety in a variety of play activities. Eli was able to give us a picture of his inner World as well as to correct cognitive distortions about his abuse in his play. His unconscious knew what he needed and led the therapist into his World via the sand. Eli followed the "Hero's Journey" (Campbell, 1988) from "the resistance" to "departure," "the adventure," and finally to "the return home." When ready, Eli did talk about his abuse, but not when the adults requested. In fact, months later, Eli appeared eager to give information and demonstrate the power of his words.

> I am not what happened to me, I am what I choose to become.
> (Paraphrased from Jung & Jaffé, 1989)

Groups in the Sand: Adolescent Girls

A small group of adolescent girls chatted enthusiastically in the waiting room. They waited to enter the group room where they were to reconvene for their weekly group session. Seven 13- to 15-year-olds were all referred after traumatic events in their lives. The experiences were somewhat different, but their age-appropriate psychosocial tasks were similar: to connect with peers and form a group identity rather than achieve a personal identity. One problem was that their personal identity was stunted by the traumas. These girls often felt different than their peers and their self-image appeared to be misshapen by their experiences. Friendships in this age group contributed to an adolescent's sense of well-being and assisted in the development of a positive self-image (Cobb, 2010). The peer group connection was important in this group. The events were different, but the girls could connect emotionally and spiritually. They were not alone.

The girls knew the structure of the group and respected the continuity and safety that it provided. Soothing music played in the background, and it was a time for calming and their quiet check-in with the group. The sandtray was available. Keeping in the present, the girls considered and placed a figure in the tray based on how they were feeling at that moment. The nonverbal communication was honored with silence and awareness of the process. Figures were added and moved, and when the introduction was completed, the facilitators requested a sentence from each girl; then the next segment of the group began.

The dynamics and stages of the group were evident in the check-in process. The trays were photographed and the progressions were noted: Who placed their figure first, who was last, and how did the figures interact? How did the process reflect the stages of the group? As the figures moved and the flow of interactions continued, the facilitators were able to visually appreciate the growth of the group as it became more cohesive, or, on the other hand, see problems to which they could respond appropriately.

This psychotherapeutic group provided the container for the group with an *analytic attitude* and the girls were free to lead as the facilitators provided and modeled appropriate boundaries. The facilitators *held the field* (of consciousness) and the sandtray continued to hold that space.

A younger children's group mirrored the adolescents' in a more developmentally relevant version. These 5- to 8-year-olds were referred for problematic sexual behaviors. Their non-offending parent attended a parallel psychoeducation group in which they learned the dynamics of abuse, behavior management and parenting skills, how to respond to their problematic behaviors, and how to protect the children who often had difficulties with physical and emotional boundaries.

The children were often described as disruptive as they waited with their parent, so the facilitators began the session in the waiting room. A line was formed and the boys and girls followed "in their bubbles." Mindfulness teachings influenced the start of the group with soothing music as each child silently took his or her place on a carpet square. A box with previously selected stones, "precious jewels," was given to each child as a reminder of his or her own preciousness. The children then held their stones in silence until they were ready to join the group. At that point, one by one, the children placed their stones in the sandtray in the middle of the circle. When all the stones were placed, the group officially began with a story, told by the clinicians in segments each week, that followed the quests of a band of children and the stones.

The children were responsible for their own behavior and had the power to lead the group opening with their behavior. Given these boundaries and their own authority, they experienced success and were empowered.

Clinician Wisdom and Self-Care

I must ask myself periodically, "Who is my client and what is my job?" Am I the therapist whose job is to provide a therapeutic relationship and space of healing? Then the child is my client. Sometimes, the parent or family or teacher is my client. Am I requested to find out "what happened?" Then law enforcement or social services are my clients, but I must always remember that the child is primary! I cannot be the therapist and forensic interviewer at the same time. If I am confused about the answer, then I must ask: "Who is my client and what is my job?" again or the "client" will not benefit.

The concept of "Depth psychology" allows the unconscious to be available for our clients and for ourselves (Singer, 1994, p. 25). A wise teacher and Jungian analyst once asked how our clients went to those deep places. Her answer resounds with me today.

> Our clients are able to go to those deep places because they sense that we have been there and returned. They trust that if we went there and returned, they can as well. They trust that if we went there and returned, we will not be afraid to walk with them to those deep places and return. (L. Craig, personal communication, October, 1992)

Jung and Jaffé (1989) stated in *Memories, Dreams, Reflections,* "Only the wounded physician heals" (p. 134). As wounded healers, our clients go to those dark places and return. Psychotherapists need "mother or father confessors" (Jung & Jaffé, 1989 p. 134) and even seasoned clinicians need supervision! As Jung said, we must always be open to our own psychic process and how it impacts on our lives and how we sit across from our clients.

> Stories move in circles. They don't go in straight lines. So it helps if you listen in circles. There are stories inside stories and stories between stories, and finding your way through them is as easy and as hard as finding your way home. And part of the finding is the getting lost. And when you're lost, you start to look around and listen. (S. Bender, 1995, p. 10)

REFERENCES

Ackerman, D. (1990). *A natural history of our senses.* New York, NY: Vintage Books.

Amatruda, K., & Helm, P. (2007). *Sandplay: The sacred healing: A guide to symbolic process.* Taos, NM: Trance-Sand-Dance Press.

Bender, S. (1995). *Everyday sacred.* New York, NY: Harper Collins.

Berkovits, S. (2005). *Guided imagery with children: Successful techniques to improve school performance and self-esteem.* Duluth, MN: Whole Person Associates.

Bettelheim, B. (1986). *The use of enchantment.* New York, NY: Random House.

Beudet, D. (2008). *Dreamguide: Open the door to your child's dreams.* Charlottesville, VA: Hampton Roads Publishing.

Boik, B. L., & Goodwin, E. A. (2000). *Sandplay Therapy: A step-by-step manual for psychotherapists of diverse orientations.* New York, NY: W. W. Norton.

Bulkeley, K. (2012). *Childrens dreams: Understanding memorable dreams and nightmares of childhood.* Lanham, MD: Rowman and Littlefield.

Bunch, C. K. (2006). *The Wizard of Oz: Symbolic quest to find your inner heroes, face your worst enemy, and attain wholeness. This timeless movie in cinematherapy for the soul.* New York, NY: iUniverse.

Campbell, J. (1988). *Campbell, Joseph: The power of myth.* New York, NY: Random House.

Charles, C., Louv, R. D., Bodner, L., Guns, B., & Stahl, D. (2009). *Children and nature network: A report on the movement to reconnect children to the natural world.* Santa Fe, NM: Children and Nature Network. Retrieved from http://www.parkerriver.org/docs/CNNMovement2009.pdf

Cobb, N. (2010). *Adolescence: Continuity, change and diversity* (7th ed.). Sunderland, MA: Sinauer Associates.

Cornell, J. (1994). *Mandala: Luminous symbols for healing*. Wheaton, IL: Quest Books.

De Domenico, G. S. (1988). *Sand tray world play (volume three). Theory and practice: How to introduce sand tray to the client and the art of observing sand tray play*. Oakland, CA: Gisela.

De Domenico, G. S. (Producer). (1992). *Introduction to sandtray worldplay: Teaching video #1*. (Video). Oakland, CA: Vision Quest.

De Domenico, G. S. (1998). Sandtray-Worldplay amplification process techniques. *Sandtray Network Journal, 2*(3), 1–6.

De Domenico, G. S. (2002). Sandtray-Worldplay: A psychotherapeutic and transformational sandplay technique for individual, couples, families and groups. *Sandtray Network Journal, 6*(2).

Fleming, V. (Producer). (1937). *The Wizard of Oz*. (Motion Picture). United States: Lowes.

Fordham, M. (1994). *Children as individuals*. London, UK: Free Association Books.

Gold, P. (1994). *Navajo & Tibetan sacred wisdom: The circle of the spirit*. Rochester, VT: Inner Traditions.

Green, E. J. (2014). *The handbook of Jungian play therapy with children and adolescents*. Baltimore, MA: Johns Hopkins University Press.

Haden, R. L. (2010). *Unopened letters from God: A workbook for individuals and groups*. Flatrock, NC: Haden Institute Publishing.

Hall, E., Hall, C., Stradling, P., & Young, D. (2006). *Guided imagery: Creative interventions in counselling & psychotherapy*. London, UK: Sage Publications.

Hall, J. A. (1983). *Jungian dream interpretation: A handbook of theory and practice*. Toronto, ON, Canada: Inner City Books.

Hegeman, G. (2001). *The sandplay collection. Journal of Sandplay Therapy, 1*(2), 101–106. Retrieved from http://www.sandplay.org/symbols/index.htm

Higgins-Klein, D. (2013). *Mindfulness-based play-family therapy: Theory and practice*. New York, NY: W. W. Norton.

Hoss, R. J. (2005). *Dream language: Self-understanding through imagery and color*. Ashland, OR: Innersource.

Hudson, J. (2000). *Natural spirituality: Recovering the wisdom tradition in christianity*. Danielsville, GA: JRH Publications.

Iroegbu, P. E. (2010). *Healing insanity: A study of Igbo medicine in contemporary Nigeria: Studies in endogenuous medical system, culture and development*. Bloomington, IN: Xlibris Corporation.

Johnson, R. (1993). *Owning your own shadow: Understanding the dark side of psyche*. New York, NY: Harper Collins.

Jongeward, D. (1990). *Weaver of worlds: From Navajo apprenticeship to sacred geometry and dreams*. Rochester, VT: Destiny Books.

Jung, C. G. (1933). *Modern man in search of a soul*. Orlando, FL: Harcourt.

Jung, C. G. (1938). *Collected works of C.G. Jung* (Vol. 6, para. 307). Princeton, NJ: Princeton University Press.

Jung, C. G. (1958). *Collected works of C. G. Jung: Psychology and religion* (Vol. 11). Princeton, NJ: Princeton University Press.

Jung, C. G. (1968). *Man and his symbols*. New York, NY: Dell Publishing.

Jung, C. G. (1972). *The transcendent function: Jung's model of psychological growth in the Collected Works of C. G. Jung* (p. 171). Princeton, NJ: Princeton University Press.

Jung, C. G. (1974). On the nature of dreams. In R. F. C. Hull (Ed. & Trans.), *Dreams*. Princeton, NJ: Princeton University Press.

Jung, C. G. (2008). *Children's dreams: Notes from the seminar given in 1936–1940*. Princeton, NJ: Princeton University Press.

Jung, C. G. (2009). *The red book*. New York, NY: W. W. Norton.

Jung, C. G., & Adler, G. (1972). *Collected works of C. G. Jung: The structure and dynamics of the psyche* (Vol. 8). Princeton, NJ: Princeton University Press.

Jung, C. G., & Campbell, J. (1976). *The portable Jung: A compilation*. New York, NY: Penguin Books.

Jung, C. G., & Franz, M.-L. (1964). *Man and his symbols*. New York, NY: Dell Publishing.

Jung, C. G., & Jaffé, A. (1989). *Memories, dreams, reflections*. New York, NY: Vintage Books.

Jung, C. G., & Sabini, M. (Eds.). (2002). *The Earth has a soul: The nature writings of C. G. Jung*. Berkley, CA: North Atlantic Books.

Kalff, D. M. (1980). *Sandplay*. Boston, MA: Sigo Press.

Kalsched, D. (2003). Daimonic elements in early trauma. *Journal of Analytical Psychology, 48*, 145–169.

Kestly, T. A. (2014). *The interpersonal neurobiology of play: Brain-building interventions for emotional well-being*. New York, NY: W. W. Norton.

Kotler, A. (Ed.). (1996). *Engaged Buddhist reader: Ten years of the engaged Buddhist reader*. Walking meditation. Berkley, CA: Parallax Press.

London, E., & Recio, B. (2004). *Sacred rituals: Creating labyrinths, sand paintings, and other traditional arts*. Gloucester, MA: Fair Winds Press.

Louv, R. (2008). *Last child in the woods: Saving our children from nature-deficit disorder*. Chapel Hill, NC: Algonquin Books.

Louv, R. (2011). *The nature principle: Human restoration and the end of nature deficit disorder*. Chapel Hill, NC: Algonquin of Books.

Lowenfeld, M. (2007). *Understanding children's sandplay Lowenfeld's world technique* (2nd ed.). Portland, OR: Sussex Acedemic Press. (Original work published in 1979).

McNally, S. P. (2001). *Sandplay: A sourcebook for play therapists.* Campbell, CA: Universe.

Moore, T. (1994). *Soul mates: Honoring the mystery of love and relationship.* New York, NY: Harper Collins.

Nhat Hahn, T. (1996). *The long road turns to joy: A guide to walking meditation.* Berkeley, CA: Parallox Press.

Otto, D. (2005). *Lecture: Healing the world, healing the self: Comparing Tibetan Buddhist mandalas to Navajo sandpaintings.* Meadows Museum, LA: Centenary College.

Pando-Mars, K. (1998). Clearing the path: Using amplification. *Sandtray Network Journal, 2,* 16–18.

Read, H., Fordham, M., & Adler, G. (Eds.). (1991). *The collected works of C. G. Jung* (Vol. I). New York, NY: Routledge.

Reynolds, R. (1995). *Bring me an ocean: Nature as teacher, messenger, and intermediary.* Acton, MA: VandreWyk & Burnham.

Rilke, R. M. (1996). *Rilke's book of hours: love poems to God.* (A. Barrows & J. Macy, Trans.). New York, NY: Penquin Group.

Saarinen, P. (2003). Dream screen phenomenon in psychotherapy process and artistic work. *Nordic Journal of Psychotherapy, 57*(5), 383–388.

Sabini, M. (Ed.). (2008). *C. G. Jung on nature, technology & modern life.* Berkley, CA: North Atlantic Books.

Siegel, D. (2010). *Mindsight: The new science of personal transformation.* New York, NY: Bantam Books.

Singer, J. (1994). *Boundaries of the soul: The practice of Jung's psychology.* New York, NY: Random House.

Stevenson, J. (2006). *Ceremonial of Hasjelti dailjis and mythical sand painting of the Navajo Indians.* Project Gutenberg. Retrieved from http://www.archive.org/stream/ceremonialofhasj19331gut/19331-pdf_djvu.txt

Taylor, J. (2009). *The wisdom of our dreams: Using your dreams to tap into your unconscious and transform your life.* New York, NY: Penguin.

Turner, B. A., & Unnsteinsdottir, K. (2011). *Sandplay and story telling: The impact of imaginative thinking on children's learning and development.* Cloverdale, CA: Temenos Press.

Turner, B. A. (2005). *The handbook of sandplay therapy.* Cloverdale, CA: Temenos Press.

Turner, B. (Ed.). (2004). *H. G. Wells floor games: A father's account of play and its legacy of healing.* Cloverdale, CA: Temenos Press.

Van de Castle, R. (1994). *Our dreaming mind.* Boston, MA: Random House.

Von Franz, M.-L. (1994). *Dream.* Boston, MA: Shambhula.

Wells, H. G. (1911). *Floor games.* New York, NY: Arno Press.

Wells, H. G. (1913). *Little wars: A game for boys from twelve years of age to one hundred and fifty and for that more intelligent sort of girl who likes boys' games and books.* Stockbridge, NJ: HardPress Publishing.

Wittmann, E. (2009). Hide and seek in the play therapy room. *Play Therapy, 4*(3), 10–12.

Woolley, J. W. (1992). Children's conceptions of dreams. *Cognitive Development,* 365–380.

CHAPTER 3

Solution-Focused Play Therapy

ELSA SOTO LEGGETT

Solution-focused brief therapy (SFBT) principles have been advocated for children, adolescents, and adults. SFBT states that the client brings strengths and capacities to access and develop to make life more satisfactory (Corcoran & Stephenson, 2000; Leggett, 2009). The counselor demonstrates confidence in the client's ability to make positive changes in his or her life by accessing and using inner resources (Davis & Osborn, 2000; Lewis & Osborn, 2004). This creates an atmosphere where strengths move from the shadows to the foreground and strengths are found in the spaces between problems (De Shazer, 1985; Hall, 2003). The client is the expert, and the counselor is responsible for developing a collaborative context and helping the child or adolescent articulate desired changes. This process magnifies strengths, resources, and past successes, which leads to the construction of solutions (Walter & Peller, 1992). The counselor and client create a cooperative context within which solution building ensures information is collected in order to understand what will be different once the problem is solved. Language and techniques address how problems will be solved rather than what caused the problem (Corcoran & Stephenson, 2000; Leggett, 2009).

SOLUTION-FOCUSED BRIEF THERAPY

In *Becoming Solution-Focused in Brief Therapy,* Walter and Peller (1992) provide 12 assumptions that guide solution-focused (SF) thoughts and actions, and provide meaning and guidelines to the SF approach.

1. *Advantages of a positive focus.* Change in the desired direction is facilitated by focusing on the positive, on the solution, and on the future. Therefore, solution-oriented talk becomes the focus rather than problem-oriented talk.
2. *Exceptions suggest solutions.* Exceptions to every problem can be created by the counselor and the client, and can be used to build solutions.
3. *Nothing is always the same.* Change is occurring all the time.
4. *Small change is generative.* Small changes lead to larger changes.
5. *Cooperation is inevitable.* Clients are always cooperating; they are showing the counselor how they think change takes place. As the counselor understands what the clients are thinking and act accordingly, cooperation is inevitable.
6. *People are resourceful.* People have all they need to solve their problems.
7. *Meaning and experience are interactionally constructed.* Meaning is the world or medium in which people live. People apply meaning onto their experience and it is their experience at the same time. Meaning is not imposed from without or determined from outside of them. People inform their world through interaction.
8. *Reclusiveness.* Actions and descriptions are circular.
9. *Meaning is in the response.* The meaning of the message is the response a person receives.
10. *The client is the expert.* Therapy is a goal or SF endeavor, with the client as the expert.
11. *Unity.* Any change in the way clients describe a goal (solution) and/or what they do affects future interactions with all others involved.
12. *Treatment group membership.* The members in a treatment group are those who share a goal and state their desire to do something about making it happen. (Walter & Peller, 1992, pp. 10–24)

These assumptions provide a counselor with the freedom to roam and to be creative with the assurance that his or her actions are being guided while intensifying the intervention with play. Solution-focused play therapy (SFPT), therefore, expands the basic SF model to provide both verbal and nonverbal tools for expression. It allows adjustments according to the developmental level of the client. Furthermore, it increases the communications between the counselor and the client while facilitating the relationship (Leggett, 2009).

SFBT Basic Concepts

SFBT uses signature questions to help focus on how the client can change. The questions are designed to allow counselors to listen to the client's words and absorb the meaning. The formulation of the next question is connected to the key words and phrases that the client has shared. This exchange leads the client to establishing new thinking and co-constructing new and/or alternative meaning. This new thinking creates an avenue toward change and solutions (Leggett, 2009; Trepper et al., 2008). The various components of SFBT have been built over time. The description of the problem invites the client to tell his or her story. Although little time is devoted to the exploration of the problem, this allows the counselor an opportunity to (a) reorient the client to the problem; (b) search for clues to how others perceive the problem situation; and (c) notice changes (Gillen, 2011). With this exchange, clear goals are articulated. The miracle question helps the client to look beyond the present, beyond the problem, and into the future. The client opens up his or her imagination to a time when the problem is gone. Relationship questions reveal who and what is important to the client. They add clarity regarding what the miracle looks like, what is different, and who notices these differences; this helps the client to visualize the future without the problem or when the situation is better. The exploration for exceptions to the client's problem or situation is another key component. Exceptions are those moments in the past when the miracle was already happening or already taking place in the client's life. These are moments when the problem did not occur or occurred less frequently. To help a client recognize these exceptions, Murphy (1994) suggests these five methods: (a) elicit times when the problem was absent; (b) elaborate on the features and circumstances of these times; (c) expand the exception to other contexts; (d) evaluate the exception based on the goals and details of the miracle; and (e) empower the client to maintain that change over time.

Another important technique of SFBT is the scaling question. The scaling question provides a tangible demonstration of achievements; it measures client success, as well as proximity to an identified goal or miracle picture. The client can put her or his observations, impressions, and predictions on a scale from 1 to 10, with 1 meaning *no success, the problem is in control,* or *no chance,* and 10 meaning *success, the client is in control,* or *there is a chance.* This technique can produce motivation and confidence in a client. The solution message then follows. This final step can include three basic parts: compliments, a bridge, and a task or suggestion for the client (De Jong & Berg, 2009). Compliments are designed to affirm what is important to the client and to affirm successes and strengths. The bridge connects these successes and strengths to the task or suggestion given to move the client into future action toward the goal.

SOLUTION-FOCUSED PLAY THERAPY

SFBT is a "talk therapy," which many times does not always work well with a child's or an adolescent's tendencies to express him- or herself best through nonverbal means. Furthermore, the young client may not be capable of cognitively understanding such abstract concepts as "miracles" and "goals." In fact, SFBT questions alone may be too difficult for some children to grasp even after therapists concretize the wording of the questions (Selekman, 1997). Additionally, the ability of a young client to respond to therapeutic interventions may be found in the context of his or her level of developmental function. The counselor should not push a young client beyond this current developmental level. A counselor working with a young client, while searching how to best serve this population, oftentimes makes the client's needs fit his or her particular counseling model. To facilitate a young client's verbal and nonverbal expression of thoughts, feelings, and behaviors, it becomes necessary to consider therapeutic approaches designed especially for children and adolescents and the use of a combination of talk and play. By expanding on the basic SFBT model with a more therapeutic flexibility, the needs of a young client can be adequately managed (Leggett, 2009; Nims, 2011). The use of an SFPT provides an effective integration to meet the needs of a young client. By considering the flexibility of SFPT, the counselor can recognize how the signature components of SFBT can be successfully integrated with play. Table 3.1 demonstrates a small range of the SFPT but offers a starting place for counselors seeking to wander into this approach. The breadth of SFPT is limited only by the counselor's imagination.

SFPT PROCESS

SFPT uses signature SFBT questions and experiential activities to help focus on how a client can change. The experiential activities basic in play therapy include books and literature, drawing, prescribed selection of

TABLE 3.1 SOLUTION-FOCUSED PLAY THERAPY

Solution-Focused Play Therapy	Describing the Problem	Miracle Question	Exploring Exceptions	Scaling Questions
Books	✔	✔		
Art and drawings	✔	✔	✔	✔
Toys and puppets	✔	✔		
Sandtray	✔	✔	✔	✔

toys, puppets, and a sandtray to serve as the medium of this dialogue (Leggett, 2009; Nims, 2011). This process helps the client establish the groundwork for new thinking while co-constructing with the counselor new and alternative meanings that move toward change and solutions (Trepper et al., 2008). SFPT should be crafted with the client's specific details in mind: needs, situation or problem, developmental level, and culture and diversity. Following are a few demonstrations of the ideas presented in Table 3.1 that have been helpful to this author. Keep in mind the counselor is only limited by his or her own imagination.

Describing the Problem and Establishing Goals

"What brings you here today?"

This initiation step invites the client to tell his or her story. The client identifies what he or she wants different or to change, which leads to establishing a goal. This goal should: (a) fit the young client's needs; (b) be relevant, meaningful, and specific to the situation; and (c) be concrete, behavioral, and measurable (Leggett, 2009). At times, a young client has difficulty explaining or expressing the problem he or she is facing. The use of either books or drawings can be very useful at this stage. These added strategies help to normalize the situation for the client as well as externalize the problem.

Books

Books selected for this strategy are generally picture books. It does not have to be a therapeutic book and should be easy to read. The topics of the books can either focus on feelings or match the needs of the client's situation. There are various picture books that describe feelings and could be used to help a young client to identify his or her feelings. *The Way I Feel* by Janan Cain (2000) is a good selection if there is some uncertainty about getting started. With this book, or any other book that describes feelings, a young client can understand and identify various feelings. Begin by reading the book to the client, taking time to enjoy the book's content and illustrations. Then ask the client to identify three feelings he or she is feeling or has felt recently. Explore these feelings:

"What tells you that you are/were feeling____?"

"What do you say when you feel ________?"

"When you are feeling ______ how do others know?"

Follow this with the identification of one feeling the client would most like to change: "Is there one of the feelings you talked about that you would like to change?" This strategy allows the client to select the issue most important to him or her and the counselor to understand the situation from the client's perspective.

Drawings

Drawing materials can consist of simple supplies, such as plain paper or drawing paper and crayons or colored pencils. The client may be more comfortable drawing the situation he or she wants to change. Begin by providing the client with materials and time to draw a picture of the situation that is most troubling him or her. It is important to allow the time needed for the client to add details to the drawing that will provide important information and details of the client's situation. Tracking the client's actions during this drawing time would let him or her know that you are still engaged. Following this time of drawing, the client should feel comfortable to describe the details of the picture. The client should be given time to express and describe these details. The use of relationship questions and "not-knowing" questions during this stage will allow the counselor to gather important information about what and who is important to the young client.

Selected Toy

Toys can be used not only to help identify the client's problem or situation but also to externalize it. A variety of toys, puppets, and/or stuffed animals should be available for the client to select from. Initiate this session by allowing the client to describe a problem he/she is currently having. Then ask the client to select a toy that could represent the problem or situation described: "I was wondering if you could find a toy that matches the problem you were describing." A name can be given to the toy selected that would be used for future conversation about the problem or situation. To further externalize the problem or situation, have the client remove the selected toy from his or her presence, even by removing it from the room. Once the toy is gone from sight, the exchange would then change to what life will look like without the problem. "Now that [problem's name] is gone, how do you feel? What will your day look like now that [problem's name] is gone?" Furthermore, this creates a smooth introduction to the miracle question of a day without the problem.

Miracle Question

"If a miracle happened tonight while you were asleep and you woke up tomorrow and the problem that brought you here today was solved by magic, what would be the first small thing you would notice that told you this miracle has happened?"

The miracle question is intended to help the client look beyond the present into the future. It helps the client to visualize how life will be different when the goal is achieved. This step can prove to be the most difficult for the youngest of clients due to the various developmental levels of each client. Sometimes a change of wording or question format is sufficient, for example, "Imagine that tomorrow was a perfect day and the problem you are having today was gone. What would that perfect day look like?" Moreover, either books or drawings may be used to contribute to the facilitation of this stage.

Books

There are various picture books that describe *a perfect day*. The use of one of these books will help the young client grasp the idea of the miracle question. Begin by reading the book to the client followed by a discussion of the elements described in the book as a *perfect day*. Explore the details of the character's perfect day. Then allow the client to imagine what his or her *perfect day* would be like, including enriched details. Suggestions for books include, but are not limited to: *A Day in the Sun* by Frank Berrios (2014); A *Perfect Day* by Remy Charlip (2006); *Brave, One Perfect Day* by Steve Purcell (2012); *It's a Perfect Day* by Abigail Pizer (1990); and *Ruby's Perfect Day* by Susan Hill (2006). Include a follow-up of relationship questions that will expand the features to others in the client's world.

Drawings
The client may again be more comfortable drawing. Allow the client to draw a picture of his or her miracle or perfect day. Provide the young client with materials and time to draw a picture. The details in the drawing should be discussed and enriched with relationship questions and not-knowing questions.

Exploring for Exceptions

"Can you think of another time when you did not have a problem with ______?"

The exploration for exceptions includes the search for times when the problem is not happening or is less severe. It can also include times in the past similar to the miracle picture. Additional questions provide insight to whom did what to make the exceptions happen. The use of art therapy allows the client to carefully examine even the smallest exception.

Drawing
The client should be encouraged to consider exceptions. Allowing the client to draw the exception may allow him or her to contemplate the actions or behaviors that contributed to it. Begin by asking the client to consider a time in the recent past when he or she may have experienced a small part of his or her perfect day or miracle. For some young clients it may be simplest to concentrate on only one exception rather than the exploration of several. "Can you draw a picture of the time you were talking about, that time when the problem wasn't so bad?" Once more, it is important to allow the client time to both draw the picture of exception with details and to describe those details to the counselor.

Scaling Questions

"On a scale of 1 to 10, with 10 meaning you have every confidence that this problem can be solved and 1 meaning no confidence at all, where would you put yourself today?"

These questions allow the client to evaluate his or her own progress. These visual representations of the scaling question can make this step concrete. The format of the question may be altered to fit the selection of the visual scaling question. An example of such a rewording might be: "On a scale of 1 to 10, with 10 being your miracle, picture-perfect day, and 1 being the worst day, where would you say you are today, right now?"

Pictures
Visual pictures also provide concrete methods for a young client to evaluate his or her progress. Consider such pictures for visual scaling questions.

Reprinted from Davis and Osborn (2000).

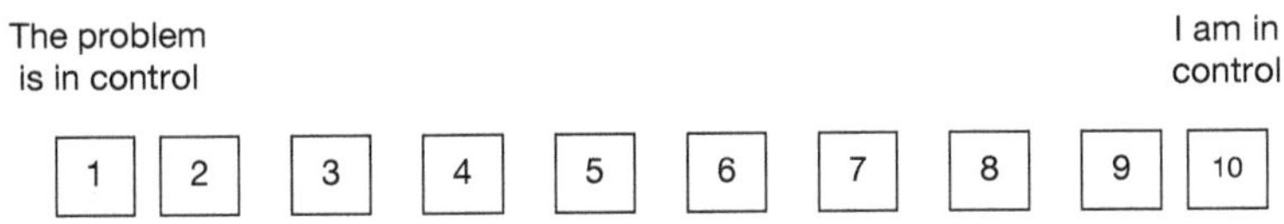

Source: Shapiro (1996).

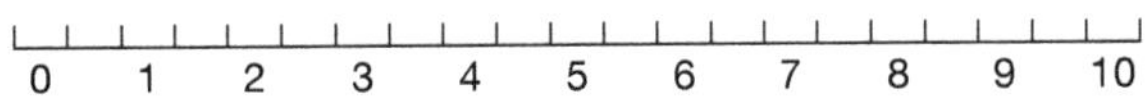

Even a simple number line can create a visual tool to allow a client a more concrete format to scale his or her position or progress.

Drawings
The young client may believe it is easiest to draw his or her place on the scale. Nims (2007) suggests that a drawing may work as well for this stage. Begin by asking the client the scaling question. Then ask the client to draw a picture of what the number *looks like* (Nims, 2007).

Physical Response
With clients of all ages, a physical response to the scaling question can provide a unique format. On the floor, designate a location for a number line marking off the locations for 0, 5, and 10. Then, when asking the young client the scaling question, ask him or her to stand on his or her place on the number line. Follow this up with questions about how

this decision was made and what needs to be different to be closer to 10. Always use small increments to encourage small changes: "What needs to be different for you to move from a 6 to, say, 6 ½?"

Solution Message

The final step of the SFPT process is the solution message. This time offers the opportunity to summarize the details of the session in a way that is meaningful for the young client. There are three parts to this message: compliments, the bridge, and the task or suggestion. The compliments are affirmations of strengths about the client that were revealed in the participation and efforts communicated through play in the session. Past successes, exceptions, and attempts at reducing the problem or changing the situation are acknowledged. For the young client, it may be helpful to create a list of these. A drawing of one such intentional act could also be created by the client. The client could keep either of these so that he or she can recall his or her thoughts, feelings, and actions that contributed to the outcome. This is followed with the bridge that connects the past success or exception to the task or suggestion. Therefore, the bridge acts as an explanation for the task or suggestion that the counselor will offer. The solution task or suggestion should be something small and simple that the client can aim for in the near future. For a young client, the task should also be directly relevant to the goal and something that the client has already had some success with. Therefore, the solution task might easily come off of the compliments list or drawing. Keep in mind that with SF the notion is that small tasks lead to experiencing more success and small changes lead to big changes.

Additional Considerations

This SFPT approach may be used with children and adolescents and has at times even been used with adults. It allows the counselor to make the selection to use one or more of the techniques described as appropriate to the client's needs and the counselor's comfort level. However, the amount of time it takes for a client to progress through the counseling process may vary. The amount of time needed to discuss the details of a book or create a detailed drawing followed by discussion will vary. Therefore, it would not be unusual to have a young client to progress through the session slowly, sometimes only progressing through one or two steps during one session.

RESEARCH SUPPORT

SF principles have advocated for children and adolescents, maintaining that clients have strengths and capacities that can be accessed and developed to give life more hope (Leggett, 2009). Corcoran and Stephenson's (2000) use of an SF approach resulted in notable change in pretest and posttest scores on the *Conner's Parent Rating Scale* along with positive improvements on the *Feelings, Attitudes, and Behavior Scale for Children*. Frels, Leggett, and LaRocca (2009) established how the use of creativity and SF counseling with a chronically ill child restricted to a hospital setting was able to provide laughter and hope. While a 7-year-old client was waiting to receive a heart, her counselor was about to help her find a place between sadness and happiness by visualizing a time when things would be different. This case underscores how children can tap into spontaneity, imagination, and the freeing aspects of play for confidence and hope in the future.

Additional studies in school settings purport SF techniques with children and adolescents to be successful. In 2007 and 2008, this author's studies in schools used a creativity integrative SF counseling approach. Each of these demonstrated notable changes for the clients in the groups. In 2007 (Leggett, 2007), students displaced in the aftermath of hurricanes Rita and Katrina received group counseling in a small school setting. Nineteen students participated in 12 small-group counseling sessions using an SF integrative approach. The students reported an increase in hope as measured with a pretest and posttest as on the *Children's Hope Scale* (Snyder et al., 1997). In another study in 2008 (Leggett, 2008), SF classroom guidance curriculum provided empirical support for the theorized notion that the systematic delivery of age-appropriated preventative SF guidance concepts facilitates a ripple effect to cultivate a positive classroom environment. Following the application and the participation of 11 classroom guidance sessions, the *Classroom Environment Scale* (Trickett & Moos, 2002) calculated, pretest and posttest, a positive change in the classroom environment. The principles and practice of solution-focused counseling (SFC) seek to activate the core ingredients of change through a positive, strength-based approach, which is culturally responsive, empowering, and developmentally considerate (Murphy, 2015).

CASE EXAMPLE: DANIEL'S STORY

I began work at an elementary school in midyear. This small rural elementary school held just less than 400 students, grades kindergarten to 4, with 40% of parents on active military duty with the navy. As the school counselor, my duties included meeting the counseling needs of special education students and addressing any Individual Education Program (IEP) requirements for counseling as a related service. This is how I came to work with Daniel. He was a tall African American boy, the oldest child in an active military family. His primary identification for special education services was emotionally disturbed (ED) with a secondary diagnosis of learning disabled (LD) with a treatment plan for weekly counseling sessions to help cope with stressors in his life. His family history revealed that he lived with his mother and stepfather. He was the oldest in a blended family: he and his brother from his mother's first marriage and two additional siblings from her current second marriage. His mother reported that Daniel responded well to his stepfather, accepted his role as father, and was excited at the birth of his younger siblings. His stepfather was absent from time to time due to his active duty status with the navy. The family was also subject to reassignment to other navy bases, a common occurrence among the students of the active military families.

Daniel's teacher, Ms. Zepeda, had been with him for 2 years in a unique teaching arrangement that was designed so that teachers could serve the same students through two grades. This arrangement was structured for kindergarten and first grades as well as second and third grades. In this case, Ms. Zepeda had been his teacher for both kindergarten and first grade. I met him in the midyear of first grade. Her concerns for Daniel began in kindergarten. She noticed instances when he withdrew from interaction with the other students, pulled away from small groups, and even avoided instructional activities. She indicated that he would begin by becoming disengaged from those around him. In more intensified episodes, he might crawl under the tables or desk, refusing to respond to any requests. During these more intense moments of withdrawal, Ms. Zepeda found that Daniel would respond only to his mother's voice. It was this behavior that spurred her to begin

(*continued*)

the referral process for special education services. Daniel's mother agreed to this referral. Additional important details about this client's history revealed that these episodes seemed to occur during times when his stepfather was absent due to his duties. It was also suspected that Daniel might have been sexually abused earlier in his life but that it had not been fully confirmed.

My treatment plan for Daniel, as dictated by his IEP, was to meet with him on a weekly basis with a blend of both individual and small-group counseling. Therefore, one week he would participate in individual counseling and the following week group counseling with a small group of other first graders with a prescribed requirement for counseling as a related service on their IEPs. This case study will focus on the content of his individual SFPT sessions. The goals for the individual sessions were fundamental goals compatible with his IEP and the school setting: (a) to enable the child to deal with stressful issues; (b) to enable the child to feel good about himself; and (c) to enable the child to function comfortably and adaptively within the school setting. However, with SFPT the goals should also be clear and concrete and fit Daniel's individual need. This would also be an overarching guide to the goals as well.

SFPT, like SFBT, is an idea for brief counseling arrangements. The process and format conform to a counseling situation where brevity is paramount. However, it can also be drawn out into pieces and chunks. In my work with children and adolescents I have become comfortable adapting to the flexibility of SFPT to meet the development needs of the client. Therefore, as needed, my sessions can be smaller pieces of a full counseling session.

Session One

It was important to begin our counseling relationship by creating a safe and accepting environment for Daniel and to allow him to build his trust in me. It was also important to begin exploring his perspective of his world. With this in mind, following my introduction to my office, how confidentiality would be applied, and what

(*continued*)

(*continued*)

our time would be like, I began by asking Daniel to draw a picture of anything he would like me to know about him. I made sure he had the materials he needed; I also gave him room and time to feel comfortable with the task. While he drew I sat quietly and tracked some of his actions and feelings. This would give Daniel the chance to tell me about himself and who and what was important to him. Once he had completed the drawing, we spent time exploring the details of it. I allowed Daniel to describe what he had chosen to include in the drawing and what it meant to him. In addition, relationship questions were incorporated to expand his details and to add clarity. Some of the SF statements and questions used were:

"Tell me about what you have drawn here."

"That is something important to you. Hmm, what tells you it is important? How do you know?"

"Do you think your family, say your mom or brother or sisters, know how much you like that?"

"What about your friends here at school? Do they know?"

"Is that something you told them or did they hear you talking about it?"

In a school setting, counseling sessions can be subject to time constraints. In order to not keep the client out of class too long, I chose to limit our session to this one activity. Before ending the session, I summarized for Daniel what we had done and what he could expect from our future individual sessions. I also took a moment to ask if there was anything else he would like to share or talk about and to check his comfort with our time. He reported that he did not have any additional concerns and was comfortable with our time. I ended with one scaling question about how likely he was to return to counseling. I used a pictorial example with a range of expressions with a frown for 1, indicating not likely, to a big smile for 10, very likely. Daniel selected an expression equivalent to a 6 or 7.

(continued)

Session Two

Daniel was content to return for another counseling session, which I took as an indication that a level of trust and comfort had been met. This session would follow the same format as the first. My hope was to continue the development of our counseling relationship and increase his level of trust and comfort. Furthermore, I wanted to expand my understanding of Daniel and his point of view; therefore, I asked him if he would be comfortable drawing again. On his agreement I asked him to draw a picture of his family. Again, I provided him with materials, time, and room, and quietly tracked his actions and feelings. I wanted to notice for myself who was included in his drawing and where each person was placed. Sometimes I also noted the sizes of the persons included if they were varied. This was not the case for Daniel. He turned his focus to drawing his blended family of six. His affect appeared calm and comfortable as he attended to the details of what and who were important to him. It seemed he was becoming comfortable with our relationship. Again, relationship questions were included while he described his drawing. Coping questions and the search for times when things were easiest were also integrated into the session. "It sounds like it is hard for you when your stepfather is gone." "Do you think your mom or brother know how you feel about those times, when your stepfather is gone?" "How do you think they know that?" "What do you do to make it easier?" "Sounds like you have been trying to figure this out."

Before Daniel left the session I summarized the content of our session. Intentional attention was given to the times when things were easier or better and to the things he had tried. This was a smaller edition of a solution message. I wanted to make sure he heard these repeated and began to recognize his strength and successes. I ended with the same scaling question I had asked in the previous session: *"Using these faces, how likely are you to want to come back to counseling again?"* Daniel selected an expression equivalent to an 8 or 9.

(continued)

(*continued*)

Session Three

I felt comfortable enough with the progress we had made in our sessions to begin moving in a different direction with this third session. Daniel seemed comfortable and receptive to something different as well. I decided for this session to read *The Way I Feel* by Janan Cain (2000). I took my time to read it slowly to allow Daniel time to process the content of each of the feelings described in the book and to enjoy the drawings as well as the colors used to amplify the content. Once the reading was completed, I asked for his thoughts about the book and the content:

"Do you think the artist did a good job of drawing the feelings?"

"Did the colors used match the feelings?"

Then a shift was made toward his feelings and outlook:

"Hmm, what about your own feelings? Can you think about a time when you felt some of these same feelings?"

"Thinking about those, are there maybe two or three you have felt recently? Today or yesterday?"

"What told you you were feeling_____?"

Each of the feelings he identified was explored in search of rich details. Next I asked Daniel to identify one feeling he would like to change or have different:

"Can you find one of these feelings you wish you did have or maybe wished was different?"

"Hmm, so you don't want to feel so sad anymore."

"Do you know what makes you sad?"

"So, if you weren't feeling sad anymore, what would you feel instead of sad?"

Along with these questions is the affirmation and validation of his feeling. It is important for him to understand that the feeling is not wrong but rather should be recognized and not allowed to overcome him or stop him from engaging with what is around him.

With this session Daniel was able to identify a goal for himself, to change or modify his feeling of sadness. The following solution

(*continued*)

message was designed to help him appreciate his strengths and resources. His suggestion or task was then to identify a time when he might have been sad but was not. When we were together again we would talk about that time. We would look at the situation, his thoughts, his feelings, and did he choose, deliberately, not to feel sad or did it just happen? As we were ending the session, he pointed to the facial expressions used for scaling questions, specifically the expression equivalent to a 10 to indicate he would be very, very likely to want to come to counseling again.

Session Four

Daniel continued to demonstrate comfort with our counseling sessions. He had identified a goal, something he would like different. With this in mind, it seemed a good time to share the miracle question. This would help him to visualize how his life would be different when his goal was achieved. To help him with this abstract question, I decided to use the book *Just Josie and the Perfect Day!* by Emily Gale (2010). I read the story to him, again taking my time. He enjoyed the adventure of the main character and the outcome of her perfect day. We discussed this character's situation, her choices, and her end result of a perfect day. After that, the discussion swung to Daniel with conversation about what his perfect day might look like. "If this were your perfect day, what would that look like?" "What would you be doing?" "Who would be a part of that day?" "What about your feelings, would there be any sadness?" "What would you be feeling instead of sadness?" Although the collection of elements of this perfect day are key to the client's visualization of his own miracle, it is also important to keep in mind the client's developmental level. Therefore, it was helpful to zone into one aspect of his miracle and focus on it. This would help it seem more realistic and obtainable. It began to center around controlling or coping with his feeling of sadness. "What is one small thing you would notice about this day that would tell you you were less sad or not sad at all if this was perfect?"

Relationship questions were sprinkled in to again add clarity and expand the perfect day, the miracle. "How would your mother

(*continued*)

(*continued*)

act differently with you?" "What about your teacher, what would she say about you on this day?" "What do you think your friends would notice?" These details help the client recognize how close he is to his goal, how likely it is to happen or already be happening. The solution message that followed was a reflection of the elements of the perfect day, the miracle that he was able to identify for himself. Daniel left the session with the suggestion to notice when this element of his perfect day, his miracle, was already happening.

Session Five

During this session, we would begin by talking about the miracle day he had described in our last session. I began by asking Daniel what he recalled from our last time together. What details of his perfect day, his miracle, could he remember. I find it more therapeutic for the client to share his recollections first and for me to add in pieces as we go along. When he finished recalling his miracle, we moved to the task he was asked to do: "Did you notice a time when you might have been sad but for some reason you weren't or maybe not so sad?" Daniel described an event that occurred in school one day in the previous week when things had not gone his way. We spent some time talking about the details of the event as well as his thoughts, feelings, actions, and choices. The idea was to focus on what had happened to make him less sad. This would be the exception that would allow us to move forward with this goal.

At this point, I decided to ask a scaling question in a new format. First, I marked a spot on the floor on the far side of the room that would represent the one on the scale, then around the middle of the room I marked a spot that would represent a five, and at the far end of the room I marked a spot on the floor for a 10. I explained to Daniel that the 10 would represent his perfect day, his miracle, all that he described to me. The one would be his worst day ever. "Use the floor as a scale. Show me, on a scale of 1 to 10, how close are you today to your perfect day?" With some thought and sliding up and down the scale, Daniel was able to find his spot. This number gave us a lot to discuss. "How did you do that, get to that number?" "What is happening here at the 5 that told you, this is your spot?"

(*continued*)

"What did folks around you see about you that looked like you should be here [at the 5]?" I followed up with more coping and relationship questions. At that time, I was ready to move in another direction. "What about the 6, how can you get there? What needs to happen to move to the 6?" Time was given to explore what intentional actions he would need to take to move up the scale. This activity set the tone for Daniel to be physical, participatory, spontaneous, and prepare to plan for the future.

With the time that was left, we were able to draw a picture of what his five looked like. I used his description of his drawing to build his solution message. We closed our session with the suggestion that he do more of the same. He should find another time when he could be sad and use this experience, this exception, to make it less sad or not sad at all.

Follow-Up Sessions

The sessions that followed these began with remembering the goal. We spent time discussing what happened differently or better since our last session. Coping and relationship questions were always sprinkled in to create a clearer understanding and to expand the content. Scaling questions were used to establish progress and to let Daniel see for himself where he was and what he could do to move up the scale. From time to time, the miracle question was asked to create new goals if needed or if it seemed it would be helpful. I incorporated toys, drawings, books, puppets, and a sandtray to give him language and tools to communicate his ideas, thoughts, and feelings.

We met for two-and-a-half years. During that time, his episodes decreased in frequency and intensity. Unfortunately, at the end of his third-grade year his mother pulled him and his siblings out of school before the end of the school year. Her husband had been transferred to another naval base. She had decided to tell her children they would be moving at the end of the summer but her actual plans were to move them earlier without notice. We were not able to have any terminating sessions; instead, we shared a quick good bye as he was swept out of the school.

REFERENCES

Berrios, F. (2014). *A day in the sun*. New York, NY: Random House.

Cain, J. (2000). *The way I feel*. Seattle, WA: Parenting Press.

Charlip, R. (2006). *A perfect day*. New York, NY: Greenwillow Books/Harper Collins.

Cook, D. R. (1998). *Solution-focused brief therapy: Its impact on the self-concept of elementary school students* (Doctoral dissertation, Ohio University, 1998).

Corcoran, J., & Stephenson, M. (2000). The effectiveness of solution-focused therapy with child behavior problems: A preliminary report. *Families in Society, 8*, 468–474.

Davis, T. E., & Osborn, C. J. (2000). *The solution-focused school counselor: Shaping professional practice*. Philadelphia, PA: Accelerated Development.

De Jong, P., & Berg, I. K. (2009). *Interviewing for solutions* (3rd ed.). Belmont, CA: Brooks/Cole Cengage Learning.

De Shazer, S. (1985). *Keys to solution in brief therapy*. New York, NY: W. W. Norton.

Frels, R. K., Leggett, E. S., & LaRocca, P. S. (2009). Creativity and solution-focused counseling for a child with chronic illness. *Journal of Creativity in Mental Health, 4*, 308–319.

Gale, E. (2010). *Just Josie and the perfect day*! Bath, UK: Parragon Book Service.

Gillen, M. (2011). Solution-focused therapy. In S. Degges-White & N. L. Davis (Eds.), *Integrating the expressive arts in counseling practice: Theory-based interventions* (pp. 29–33). New York, NY: Springer Publishing.

Hall, A. S. (2003). Expanding academic and career self-efficacy: A family systems framework. *Journal of Counseling & Development, 81*, 33–39.

Hill, S. (2006). *Ruby's perfect day*. New York, NY: Harper Collins.

Leggett, E. S. (2007). Hope after the hurricane. In D. Coy (Ed.), *Children of promise: Investing in our legacy* (pp. 101–112). Addison, TX: Ron Jon Publishing.

Leggett, E. S. (2008). The effects of solution-focused classroom guidance on classroom environment. *New York State School Counseling Journal, 5*, 45–54.

Leggett, E. S. (2009). A creative application of solution-focused counseling with children's literature and visual arts. *Journal of Creativity in Mental Health, 4*, 191–200.

Lewis, T. F., & Osborn, C. J. (2004). Solution-focused counseling and motivational interviewing: A consideration of confluence. *Journal of Counseling and Development, 82*, 38–49.

Murphy, J. J. (1994). Working with what works: A solution-focused approach to school behavior problems. *School Counselor, 42*, 59–68.

Murphy, J. J. (2015). *Solution-focused counseling in schools*. Alexandria, VA: American Counseling Association.

Nims, D. R. (2007). Integrating play therapy techniques into solution-focused brief therapy. *International Journal of Play Therapy, 16*, 54–68.

Nims, D. R. (2011). Solution focused play therapy: Helping children and families find solutions. In C. Schaefer (Ed.), *Foundations of play therapy* (2nd ed., pp. 297–309). Hoboken, NJ: John Wiley & Sons.

Pizer, A. (1990). *It's a perfect day*. New York, NY: J. B. Lippincott Junior Books.

Purcell, S. (2012). *Brave, one perfect day*. New York, NY: Disney Press.

Selekman, M. D. (1997). *Solution-focused therapy with children: Harnessing family strengths for systemic change.* New York, NY: Guilford Press.

Shapiro, L. E. (1996). *The kid's solutions workbook.* Kings of Prussia, PA: The Center for Applied Psychology.

Snyder, C. R., Hoza, B., Pelham, W. E., Rapoff, M., Ware, L., Danovsky, M., . . . Stahl, K. L. (1997). The development and validation of the children's hope scale. *Journal of Pediatric Psychology, 22*, 399–421.

Trepper, T. S., McCollum, E. E., De Jong, P., Korman, H., Gingerich, W., & Franklin, C. (2008). *Solution focused therapy treatment manual for working with individuals.* Retrieved from http://www.sfbta.org/Research.pdf

Trickett, E., & Moos, R. (2002). *A social climate: Classroom environment scale manual: Development, applications, research* (3rd ed.). Redwood City, CA: Mind Garden.

Walter, J. L., & Peller, J. E. (1992). *Becoming solution-focused in brief therapy.* New York, NY: Brunner/Mazel.

CHAPTER 4

Eye Movement Desensitization and Reprocessing and Play Therapy

KAREN SULLIVAN AND GAEL THOMPSON

Children heal through play; it is their work (Landreth, 2000). With posttraumatic stress, however, a child can be so shutdown and isolated within himself or herself that even the safe, welcoming environment of the play therapy room is not enough to unlock her chains. Such a child has lived in an atmosphere of threat, fear, uncertainty, and self-protection, often not knowing what will trigger the next emotional or physical attack. Such an environment creates a fear of self-expression (Gomez, 2013). These behaviors and feelings have been documented by many who have researched posttraumatic stress disorder (PTSD) in children (Gil, 2012; Fleming, 2012). The *something more* that is needed is Eye Movement Desensitization and Reprocessing (EMDR) therapy. Through the combination of nondirective and directive play therapy with EMDR, an evidence-based therapeutic protocol, traumatized children can process their type 1 and type 2 traumas and regain their freedom and new views on self and life (Ahmad, Larsson, & Sundelin-Wahlsten, 2007). Type 1 traumas can be referred to as "big T" traumas and are characterized by large events from which a person cannot escape, that is, life-threatening events such as war, crimes, or natural disasters. These stressful events overwhelm a person's coping abilities and create a sense of helplessness and loss of control (Shapiro & Forrest, 2004, pp. 14–15). Type 2 traumas, which can be referred to as "small t," are upsetting events of daily life that vary in impact depending on the individual but may have long-term consequences on a person's life or functioning (i.e., teasing by classmates, derogatory comments by a parent or coach, not making a team, hypercritical relationships, failures in school; Shapiro & Forrest, 2004).

Traumatic events are stored in our minds on all levels, emotionally, physically, mentally, and conceptually (Shapiro, 2001). All this content goes underground but does not stay silent. It is often displayed in pathology because the experience is stored in a dysfunctional manner in the nervous system (Shapiro, 2001; Soberman, Greenwald, & Rule, 2002). How can a child access this maladaptive stored information, for which she may not even have words, concepts, or safety for expressing, and then reprocess it so it becomes integrated and useful in life? EMDR therapy addresses these questions and provides meaningful resolution. Francine Shapiro (Shapiro, Kasko, & Maxfield, 2007), creator of EMDR therapy, said,

> In its 20 year history, [EMDR] has evolved from a simple technique into an integrative psychotherapy approach with a theoretical model that emphasizes the brain's information processing system and memories of disturbing experiences as the basis of pathology. The eight-phase treatment comprehensively addresses the experiences that contribute to clinical conditions and those that are needed to bring the client to a robust state of psychological health. (p. 3)

EMDR therapy includes the Adaptive Information Processing (AIP) model, memories, the neurological processes, and a distinct eight-phase integrative treatment approach using bilateral stimulation (BLS). Dysfunctional stored memories of events contain emotions, physical sensations, and beliefs that can become intrusive and result in hyperarousal and avoidant behaviors. They are stored as implicit rather than explicit memories. EMDR therapy facilitates reprocessing the implicit to become explicit and useful. The therapy uses integration of mind, heart, and body at its core. For a child, we can talk about processing memories like eating food. We chew up pieces and gradually swallow and absorb it into our bodies so that the good becomes useful to us (Gomez, 2007).

Shapiro made her initial observations about eye movements helping to process memories in 1987, but the therapy was not officially introduced until 1989 with a published randomized controlled study that evaluated one-session treatment effects with traumatized individuals (Shapiro, Kaslow, & Maxfield, 2007). Through additional studies in 1991 and 1994, it was discovered that bilateral taps and tones were also effective in reducing fear and anxiety resulting from the trauma (Fleming, 2012). Eventually, Shapiro discovered that the whole process of desensitization was only a by-product of a comprehensive reprocessing of the experience. Shapiro's original Accelerated Information Processing model morphed into the expanded AIP model (Shapiro, 2001) that better describes its broader applicability. She hypothesized that we have an inborn information processing system that accesses the many aspects of experience so that it becomes useful to us as learning takes place. She conceptualized that memory is stored in linked networks (i.e., emotions, physical sensations, beliefs) that are organized around the earliest-related event of trauma. If the information related to a distressing or traumatic experience is not fully processed, the initial perceptions, emotions, and distorted thoughts will be stored as they were experienced at the time of the event (implicit memory). Children are not only egocentric, but also lack the perspective of life experience with which to assess the events of their lives. Shapiro argued that such unprocessed experiences become the basis of current dysfunctional reactions and are the cause of many mental disorders. Shapiro proposed that EMDR therapy successfully alleviates the components of the distressing memory by targeting the memory and linking it with other more adaptive information. When this occurs, learning takes place, and the experience is stored with appropriate emotions able to guide the person in the future. The implicit memory becomes explicit, conscious, useful, and no longer destructive (Gomez, 2007).

A truly thorough understanding of how and why EMDR therapy works continues to be a work in progress as more is learned and understood about how the human brain functions. Research in the fields of neurophysiology, rapid eye movement (REM) sleep (reconsolidation of information), working memory, and parasympathetic response all are informing a better understanding of EMDR therapy. It is a unique therapeutic approach that differs from psychodynamic therapy, which views the foundation problem to proceed from intrapsychic conflicts; and from cognitive behavioral therapy (CBT), which addresses dysfunctional beliefs and their resulting behaviors. EMDR therapy uniquely addresses transforming implicit memories into useful explicit memories. The alternating BLS shifts the child's focus from traumatic material to external stimuli, such as the wand moving or the puppet tapping her knees, which disrupts all the ways the trauma is stored, chewing it up, and allowing learning to occur (Gomez, 2007).

Play therapists, such as Goodyear-Brown (2010), have recognized that children dealing with PTSD need a blended approach of nondirective and directive play therapy to fully address their issues. Goodyear-Brown's Flexibly Sequential Play Therapy model uses a phase approach: (a) establishing emotional safety; (b) physiological soothing and emotional modulation; (c) gradual exposure to the traumatic material; and (d) sense of self in light of the trauma (Goodyear-Brown, 2010). Her approach blends well with the phase approach to EMDR therapy with children (Table 4.1). Therapists using EMDR therapy begin with a thorough client history and preparation phase, including coping skills and resources for self-care in handling disturbing content (Table 4.1). In the assessment phase, counselors identify the most disturbing image related to the event, the negative belief about self that has formed as a result of the event, the desired positive belief one would choose to have once the memory becomes integrated, as well as the positive associated emotions and physical sensations. Negative beliefs are categorized as ones having to do with personal defectiveness, responsibility for actions, vulnerability and safety, and control or choices. These beliefs can be simply presented to children through a child-friendly list of suggestions or similar means. As each belief is identified it is also rated for the level of *emotional disturbance* that it causes (ranked by subjective units of disturbance [SUDS] on a scale of 1 to 10, with 10 being the most distress). Children can note this by describing how big it is—as big as the office, a building, or the universe—cutting a piece of ribbon, using a measuring scale with their hands, and so forth (Adler-Tapia & Settle, 2008; Gomez, 2007, 2013). The positive outcome belief is also rated for how *true it feels* (validity of cognition [VOC] on a scale of 1–7, with 7 being the most valid and believable). The same kinds of measurement scales can be used for this with children.

Once these first three phases have laid the foundation, the desensitization process can begin. This phase uses BLS to activate memory processing. The BLS method is preferably eye movements but other BLS methods, such as taps or tones, can also be used. For children, one can use gently vibrating tappers either held in the hands or creatively tucked into pockets, socks, or shoes; tones played through headphones or speakers positioned by the sandtray; a bouncing puppet or favorite stuffed animal; a magic wand; the beating on a drum; and so on. The important thing here is that the child chooses the method. The desensitization is a dynamic process that is unique to each client. Our brains are amazing and adaptive. It is as if the brain knows how all these memories and processes work and how to unwind the twisted ball of thoughts, feelings, and sensations to bring the individual to the point of insight and healing. As EMDR therapists, we have watched this process in its uniqueness with each client, child, and adult, with great awe. The therapist continues to follow and guide the client through all the many interconnections until the memory no longer holds a significant level of disturbance, preferably a SUD rating of 0. The work continues through past events and memories into present manifestations of symptoms and beliefs and on into future scenarios. The process is not complete without also increasing

TABLE 4.1 OVERVIEW OF EMDR ADAPTIVE INFORMATION PROCESSING MODEL

Phase	Description	Integration of Play Therapy Techniques
1. Client history	Background information Discern suitability for EMDR Identify positive and negative events in child's life	Sandtray, writing/drawing, puppets, role-play, timeline, self-portrait, toys
2. Preparation	Educate about emotions, body awareness, and coping skills Educate about EMDR process and identify bilateral stimulation (BLS) options	Feeling charts, emotion faces, body pictures, bibliotherapy, drawing, sculpting, guided imagery, sandtray, deep breathing exercises, movement exercises, music, puppets, toys
3. Assessment	Identify specific key events, feelings, and beliefs that are disruptive Assess for dissociation	Movement exercises, drawings, puppets, feeling charts, emotion faces, toys, sensory objects
4. Desensitization	Process experiences to a resolution of SUD 0	Toys, sandtray, music, guided imagery, storytelling, puppets
5. Installation	Incorporate and strengthen connection to positive experience and awareness	Toys, puppets, bibliotherapy, sandtray, drawing
6. Body scan	Check for and address any residual physical disturbance	Toys, self-portraits, movement exercises
7. Closure	Review and reinforce resources for emotional stability between sessions or for completion of therapy	Guided imagery, drawing, sandtray, toys
8. Reevaluation	Evaluate treatment effects between sessions and over time Assess for any newly surfaced concerns	Sandtray, puppets, drawing, self-portrait, toys

EMDR, Eye Movement Desensitization and Reprocessing; SUD, subjective units of disturbance.
Sources: Adler-Tapia and Settle (2008); Gil (2012); Gomez (2013); Landreth (2012); Lovett (1999); Shapiro (2001); and Waldon (2004, 2007).

connections to positive beliefs and networks. There is an ongoing dance and movement through desensitization, installation, body scans, and reevaluation. Often a single session ends with unfinished work, so the counselor uses established resources to contain the remaining work and ensure client stability between sessions. Containers of all sizes and shapes, either real or imagined, are created by the child for this part of the work (Gomez, 2013). One of our favorites is the library because it allows for the gradual engaging of the traumatic material (Table 4.2). Work continues until the client no longer reports or experiences negative disturbance and exhibits integration of the memories/incident.

As in any therapeutic intervention, the rapport of counselor and client has been shown to be the most powerful component for healing (Goodyear-Brown, 2010). Therapists are trained in two levels of basic training (20 hours each: 10 of lecture and 10 of practicum) and then use 10 supervised hours of continued clinical training. This is not a *canned* therapy. There are additional critical areas of consideration such as dissociation, a coping skill that distances the client mentally and emotionally from the trauma. Knowing how to guide clients of all ages through staying present to the process and integrate their experiences requires training and experience. As you will see in our case example, there is a flow and dance of the therapist and client through the specific therapy process and using techniques originating in play therapy and other disciplines. As is often the case, once a therapist has completed graduate-level education with multiple professors, attended additional certification trainings, and completed multiple hours of continuing education courses, one can lose track of where a particular technique was learned. Additionally, many techniques become integrated into a therapist's own style and practice. It is our intent to reference techniques noted in this chapter, but we also acknowledge that we may have missed references due to our familiarity and routine use of them.

RESEARCH SUPPORT

In 1987, when Shapiro first discovered the effect of spontaneous eye movements and began developing procedures, the first controlled studies for PTSD were conducted. That same year, the first studies on prolonged exposure therapy, psychotherapy, and hypnosis for the treatment of PTSD were also conducted (Shapiro, 2001; Ironson, Freund, Strauss, & Williams, 2002). In 1990, eye movement desensitization (EMD) became EMDR and additional forms of BLS were introduced, such as tapping, tones, and so

TABLE 4.2 CONTAINER TECHNIQUE—THE LIBRARY

Step	Description
1. Invitation	The child is invited to envision and describe a library and all she knows about one. The child's story is stored within the library, but she does not have to go into the library until she is ready.
2. Entrance	There are steps leading up to the door. She may walk the steps, but not go in if she so chooses. Once she chooses to approach, walk up the steps, and enter, she walks through the library until she finds her shelf.
3. Choosing a book	On the shelf are book(s) containing her story. She may choose to have one book with many chapters. She may choose to have a book for each incident or aspect of the trauma. It is important for the therapist to let the child lead in creating the image.
4. Choosing the story	Once the book(s) are identified, the child can leave the library, stay, or take down a book at which to look. When the child is ready, she can open a book and choose a part of the story to process.
5. Processing the story	When this session of processing is ended (either due to the end of a session or resolution) the book can be returned to the shelf with a new ending or as a container until processing can continue.
6. Leaving	The child then leaves the library. Many like to lock the door on the way out; this is another way to contain and gain control of the traumatic memory. This empowers the child to walk away from the library (and her trauma) until she chooses to return.
7. Maintenance	Should a memory surface in-between sessions, the book drop can be used to contain the thoughts, feelings, or body sensations until the next session. The magical book drop knows where to shelve the material until the child chooses it.

This technique is creative because each therapist and child can add to it and make it uniquely his or her own.
Source: S. Packwood, personal communication, April, 11, 2013, Library technique used as a container.

on. More than 20 controlled studies have consistently found that EMDR effectively decreases and/or eliminates symptoms of PTSD for the majority of clients. These studies typically include three to six sessions, finding 77% to 100% remission of PTSD symptoms from a single incident, or 12 or more sessions involving multiple incidents (EMDR Institute, n.d). Component studies testing a variety of neurobiological hypotheses have supported theories of working memory, orienting response, reciprocal inhibition, and REM effect (EMDR Institute, n.d). A 2001 meta-analysis by Davidson and Parker and a 2002 study by Maxfield and Hyer validated EMDR as effective in treating PTSD. Additional meta-analysis studies have also shown an equal effect on PTSD with EMDR and exposure therapies. A major difference between EMDR therapy and exposure therapy is that EMDR uses no homework and exposure therapy requires 1 to 2 hours daily of imaginal and/or in vivo homework (Greenwald et al., 2015).

A summary of 15 studies encompassing both type 1 and type 2 traumas in children and adolescents showed EMDR therapy to be effective (Fleming, 2012). A 2009 study of children exposed to abuse and witnessing homicide, used assessment scales that showed a significant result in the reduction of symptoms achieved with EMDR therapy (Adler-Tapia and Settle, 2009).

One of the strongest indications for using EMDR with children is that troublesome behaviors may not stem from the most recent or obvious trauma. They may in fact be from early deep-seeded events (Greenwald, 2007; Lovett, 1999). EMDR therapy emphasizes encouraging and guiding the client to remember and feel back as far as possible to his or her earliest memory of the trauma feeling or thought. For example, Ann Beckley-Forest noted with her client Missy that her difficulties were not arising primarily from a car accident but from her adoption as a very young child (Beckley-Forest, 2015). A 2002 study by Soberman and associates considered adolescents diagnosed with conduct disorder. The use of EMDR therapy showed greater success because it identified traumatic events that precipitated the conduct. Once the trauma resolved, so did the disruptive conduct. For us, the authors of this chapter, one of the greatest motivators to use EMDR therapy with play therapy has been the heading off of ongoing difficulties into adolescence and adulthood by dealing with the earliest traumas at as young an age as possible (Lovett, 1999).

Researchers targeting single and multiple trauma incidents, phobias, behavior disturbances, and nightmares, as well as the use of EMDR therapy, have shown significant improvement in resolution of symptoms, improved self-esteem, the ability to reassign meaning to the events, and new perspective (Ahmad et al., 2007; Lee & Cuijpers, 2013; Rodenburg, Benjamin, de Roos, Meijer, & Stams, 2009; Tufnell, 2005; Wander, Serra, & deJongh, 2006). In addition, the American Psychiatric Association gave EMDR therapy the highest level of recommendation in the treatment of trauma (American Psychiatric Association, 2004). The Department of Veterans Administration and the Department of Defense in 2004 assigned EMDR therapy a Category A ranking for the treatment of trauma. In 2005, the National Institute for Health Care Excellence (NICE) empirically supported trauma-focused CBT and EMDR treatment for adult PTSD. EMDR therapy is considered the treatment of choice according to the 2009 PTSD guidelines set out by the International Society for Traumatic Stress Studies (Foa, Keane, Friedman, & Cohen, 2009). In 2014, both the Substance Abuse and Mental Health Services Administration (SAMHSA) and the World Health Organization supported EMDR for treatment of PTSD.

Although some of the neurobiological underpinnings of EMDR are still undiscovered, research has shown that the greatest improvement occurs when trauma is processed in a more detached manner (Leeds, 2012). According to the EMDR Institute, multiple studies have shown that eye movements have effects on memory and the orienting response of working memory, as in REM sleep (EMDR Institute, n.d.)

INTEGRATING PLAY THERAPY AND EMDR THERAPY

Phase 1—Client History

Client history can be obtained creatively with children using many play therapy techniques, including art, sand, and puppets. Timelines are an effective way to gather information about both positive and negative happenings in their lives. One method has a child place positives above the timeline and negatives below it. This can be done with pictures or words depending on the child's age. With younger children, individual drawings can be used and placed in order of occurrence in a book, using parental assistance if needed. Another history-gathering technique for older children is to have them list the best and worst things that have happened in their lives. If children enjoy sand more than art, pictures of the best and worst things can be created in the sandtray and photographed for reference later. For any age child, puppets can be used to tell the story of what happened in third person, providing some distance for a sense of child safety.

Phase 2—Client Preparation

Preparing clients for EMDR therapy is a step that helps them to understand the process and feel more in control. Ana Gomez's book (2007), *Dark Bad Day Go Away*, is a great way to introduce children to EMDR therapy concepts. In the book, Ms. Gomez compared processing trauma memories to digesting food, a much easier concept for children to understand. In addition to the book, Ms. Gomez also uses analogies to talk about how the trauma affects the child. For instance, the use of "the pearl analogy" may "help children understand, identify, honor, and celebrate what they have used to protect and defend themselves from negative events" (Gomez, 2013, p. 49).

Client preparation also includes providing the children with various coping strategies. A peaceful place is used to help children tolerate affect. Children may draw, sculpt, use guided imagery, or do a sandtray of a place where they feel calm or could be themselves. There are often times when traumatized children cannot think of a real or imaginary place where they could feel peaceful. This is another time to get creative and playful and wonder about times when children have felt a moment of calm, when they have felt at their best, or focus in on how they feel when they do something that they enjoy. Once they have identified their peaceful place or moment, they can be taught how to effectively use this strategy using BLS.

In addition to a peaceful place, other resources and strategies for coping during the tough times are needed. Earth, Wind, Water, and Fire technique is one of those strategies (T. Becker-Fritz, March 14, 2012). For Earth, the children focus on the things around them in the room, especially those things touching their bodies, such as the sofa they are sitting on or the ground beneath their feet. For Wind, the children take two deep breaths, holding each for 4 seconds before slowly exhaling. For Water, the children swish around the saliva in their mouth, allowing for the engagement of the parasympathetic nervous system. For Fire, the children use the butterfly hug—arms crossed over the chest and taps their own shoulders back and forth—to provide BLS while imagining a protective fire surrounding themselves. Inside the ring of fire, the children imagine things that bring comfort; the negative or difficult things are outside of the protective ring of fire. Another strategy is to have the children imagine being surrounded by a circle of supportive friends, helpers, and family members. This guided imagery can also be made stronger by using short, slow sets of BLS.

Other skills are also taught during the client preparation phase, such as feelings identification and deep breathing. There are many well-known games that focus on feelings identification, but having children identify where in their bodies they feel the emotions is more challenging as traumatized children often describe their bodies as numb. To prepare for the EMDR therapy process, children can color an outline of their body with different colors to match their feelings. For instance, they may identify feeling anger in their heart and color that area of the outline in red. Movement games can also help children to identify these bodily sensations. Having children act like angry, scared, worried, or startled animals may help them to connect the emotions to their body sensations. To teach deep breathing, have children compete with the therapist to blow the biggest bubble with either gum or bubbles. In order to blow a big bubble, they have to take in a lot of air and release it slowly, thus teaching them the deep breathing skills. Another game is to have a ping-pong ball race across the therapy room floor. After a few tries, children will realize that taking a big breath and releasing it slowly moves the ping-pong ball in a more predictable line toward the goal. The breathing games also offer another chance to talk with the child about bodily sensations. How does the child's body feel after the games—tingly, energized, or calm?

Containment, both within the session and outside of the session, is another skill that will be critical to EMDR therapy success. Children often become overwhelmed when they begin working on the traumatizing material. Containment within the session can be metaphorical or tangible. An example of a metaphor would be imagining or drawing the child's library in which each issue, feeling, or incident is in its own separate book (see Table 4.2). At the beginning of the session, the child chooses which book he or she wants to work on and, at the end of the session, places the book back on the shelf before leaving and locking the library. Another metaphorical option would be to draw or create a box or vault in which to place all the negative thoughts, feelings, or memories. Children can draw locks, bolts, chains, or whatever is needed to keep their issues contained until the next session. Ana Gomez gave two examples of tangible containment within the session—a shy blanket and a cushion house—both of which provide a sensory experience of containing emotions and protecting oneself (Gomez, 2013). Children can use these skills both within and outside of sessions when their thoughts, feelings, or memories become overwhelming.

Finally, in the client preparation phase, the therapist teaches types of BLS and stop signs. BLS can be accomplished in a variety of ways—tapping machines, drumming, marching, swordplay with both hands, music, or following toys, magic wands, or hand puppet movements with their eyes. Exploration of different BLS options can be a playful way to engage children in play and the EMDR therapy process. Teaching children how to measure what they feel inside can be tricky. Ideas include using nesting dolls, number lines or rulers, bar graphs, or cups of sand; having them measure with their hands how big it is; using toys of differing sizes; or using movements to show how big it is. After preferences of BLS and measurement are decided, the final preparation is to identify a stop sign, which can be used during processing if the child becomes overwhelmed and needs to take a break. Some children prefer to hold up their hand while others prefer to use a toy police stop sign or to make one of their own.

Phase 3—Assessment

The assessment phase is when all of the previous phases begin to come together to form targets for treatment. The key goal in this phase is to identify negative cognitions resulting from the trauma and positive cognitions that the child would like to have about himself or herself. Examples of cognitions can be presented to the child in a variety of playful ways. One idea is to write them on a soccer ball, toss the ball back and forth, and wherever your thumb touches you speak about a time when you had that negative or positive thought. Another approach with older children is to write a variety of cognitions on index cards and allow the children to sort through and identify the ones they feel most often or that are most disturbing. For children who have told their stories in the history phase through pictures, timelines, or puppets, the therapist could have them reflect on what negative thought they have for each significant picture, event, or scene. Once cognitions are identified, the therapist helps the child identify emotions that are brought up when thinking about a particular picture of the disturbing event. Feeling charts and emotion faces are helpful to identify which feelings are triggered. The next step is to have the children use the body sensation identification skills they have learned to show where in their bodies they feel the emotions. Children can be engaged to draw their bodies with colors or symbols to identify where they are feeling things. For example, children may color the chest area blue to show sadness or they may draw squiggly lines to show nervousness felt in their stomachs. The final step in the assessment phase is to have the children measure the disturbance using the playful measurement strategies.

When children are processing traumatic information, dissociation should always be assessed. In her book, Ana Gomez presented a variety of techniques to assess dissociation, have children measure their level of dissociation, and help children to stay present during processing of the trauma. Ms. Gomez had children measure their level of dissociation using folding fans, hand signals, toys, and animals. To help children to stay present during processing, Ms. Gomez suggested using shapes, textures, scents, movement cards, and facial gestures to ground the child (Gomez, 2013).

Phase 4—Desensitization

This is the phase when BLS is used to process the trauma picture and associated negative cognition, feelings, and body sensations identified in phase three until the SUD is 0 or 1. Even though the child has already identified his or her preference of BLS (i.e., tappers, magic wand, finger puppets), the effectiveness should continue to be monitored during this phase. If there is no movement in the SUD (unit of measurement), then another type of BLS can be used to see if it generates more processing and reduction of distress.

There are often times when children do not want to sit still during this phase because of their normal energy level or because the distress is uncomfortable for them. A variety of playful interventions can be used if this is the case. The therapist can follow the children around the room as they play tapping on their shoulders or allow them to place the tappers in their socks or pockets. Another option is to have the child do a sandtray about the trauma picture and feelings while speakers placed on either side of the sandtray have music providing the BLS. Sometimes children prefer to tap on themselves, providing a level of control in the uncomfortable situation. For older children, imagery tends to work effectively to provide distance from the trauma. One example is to have the children watch the trauma like they are watching television with a remote control in which they can adjust the speed or sound, or stop the image. Another imagery solution is to have the children imagine watching what happened while they were in a safe train that simply passed by the trauma. Previously identified helpers and containment strategies can provide safety and support during the processing of the trauma.

Joan Lovett developed a storytelling technique that works well to help very young children or children who cannot verbalize to process traumas. Dr. Lovett advised that the therapist and parents work together to create a third person story. "The story should begin with everyone safe, lead up to the trauma, describe details, and end with positive cognitions and everyone safe" (Lovett, 1999, p. 226). The story is then told in conjunction with the BLS. After the story is told, the child can be asked to contribute to the story by adding details, feelings, and other cognitions. The story is repeated in future sessions until the posttraumatic behaviors and symptoms are reduced.

Phase 5—Installation

Even though a positive cognition was identified at the beginning of the EMDR process, it should be reassessed during this phase to ensure that it is still the best fit. Once the positive cognition is identified, slower and shorter sets of BLS are used to strengthen the connection. Therapists should look for pleasing and avoidance behaviors during this phase. Sometimes children have difficulty connecting to the positive cognition, but want to please the clinician. Blocking beliefs and additional traumas should be explored if the positive cognition cannot be strengthened. Children also become afraid of not being fearful any longer. The vulnerability of no longer being hypervigilant can be unsettling and should be explored further through play. Puppets and stories can be effective to help children understand their uncomfortable feelings when letting go of negative emotions and cognitions.

Phase 6—Body Scan

During this phase, children should examine their bodies to ensure that the negative body sensations are no longer troubling them. This can be done playfully by using a magnifying glass, feeling glasses, or a pretend x-ray machine to examine their bodies. Self-portraits can also be useful if one is done at the beginning of treatment and then again during this phase to identify changes to self-image. If there is any residual negative body sensation, BLS should target those sensations until they are resolved. Children will sometimes talk about the body sensations changing during the desensitization phase. For instance, one child expressed that the disturbing body sensation began as a knot in her stomach, moved to pain in her heart, and then became a lump in her throat before going away completely.

Phase 7—Closure

Ideally, closure would be done at the end of the process and would coincide with the end of a session. Realistically, this rarely happens, especially with children, due to the efforts that are needed to create a safe environment before they can begin processing the trauma. Therefore, closure can be done at the end of an incomplete session to transition the child back into his or her daily life. Imagery of putting the traumatic material in the child's containers while using BLS is an effective way to manage an incomplete session. Once the traumatic material is contained, other resources, such as peaceful place or circle of helpers, can be used to ensure that the child is in a calm state before leaving the session. A drawn or actual toolbox can be used as a reminder to the child about the coping strategies to use at home.

Phase 8—Reevaluation

In this final phase, the therapist will reassess for any residual thoughts or feelings or if there are any new concerns. It is not uncommon for a type 1 trauma to resolve and then a type 2 trauma to surface. If on reevaluation there are no concerns, it is important to assess how the negative cognition impacts present and future behaviors. The therapist would then move back through the eight phases to address each one. For instance, if the negative cognition associated with the trauma was *I'm not good enough,* this could affect current school performance and life goals in the future. The child and therapist explore and desensitize events that may trigger this negative cognition in the present and future by using *what if* situations.

CASE EXAMPLE: AMY'S STORY

When Amy was just 4 years old, her mother, Tracy, and her mother's new boyfriend, Tom, took her away from the only family she had known and moved to another state. Within a few days of the move, Tracy moved again, but chose to leave Amy with Tom and discontinued all contact. Tom initially provided and cared for Amy, but soon began to take out his frustrations with life on her. After about

(*continued*)

(*continued*)

4 months, the abuse escalated from scolding and isolation to beating Amy with extension cords, belts, and cables. The beatings would leave Amy with open wounds on her legs, torso, arms, and buttocks. Tom also made Amy hold heavy objects for long periods of time, do wall sits, and eat spicy foods for punishment. During the abuse, Tom's new girlfriend, Sarah, would occasionally wash and bandage Amy, but never intervened or sought any medical treatment until the last beating in which Amy almost lost her life. Amy remained in the hospital for a month before being moved through five different foster homes. During this time, Amy had only one phone call from Tracy, who had abandoned her months earlier. Fortunately, Amy's aunt, Missy, had been looking for her since Tracy had moved her out of state. Missy was able to work with Children's Protective Services to adopt Amy. Missy moved Amy back to her home state where she had extended family and friends to help love and parent her. Despite all of the support, Amy began having symptoms of PTSD—nightmares, poor peer relationships, fears of abandonment, clinginess, general anxiety, poor concentration, intrusive thoughts, sleep difficulties, mood swings, enuresis, and encopresis.

Amy, now aged 6 years, began sessions twice a week to see if EMDR therapy would alleviate the lingering posttraumatic symptoms. Being a play therapist, sessions began with nondirective play in a traditional play therapy room where Amy tentatively explored. As rapport was built, Amy began revealing an EMDR target. Amy was especially drawn to the sandtray where she would run her hands through the sand, hide toys for me to find, and try to build sand castles by adding water to the sand. Amy loved playing in the sand, but worried excessively about getting dirty and being in trouble. As sessions progressed, Amy would spend more time in the sand and, as a result, get dirtier and dirtier. Each week, she would come back into session with amazement that she was not in trouble for getting dirty or making a sand/water mess on the floor. Nondirective play therapy gave Amy the space to experience getting dirty without being in trouble, but the underlying negative cognition of "I can't do anything right" was still prevalent in her school work and daily life.

(*continued*)

To begin the EMDR therapy, we read a book, *Dark Bad Day Go Away*, to explain how EMDR therapy works and how it would help. Before working on the multiple traumas of her separation from extended family, abandonment by Tracy, and the severe physical and emotional abuse by Tom, the counselor strengthened Amy's internal resources.

The therapist taught Amy how to use a peaceful place and deep breathing as a way to ease negative emotions and anxiety. Bubble races and watching a stuffed animal rise and fall on her tummy made learning about deep breathing fun for Amy. Her peaceful place was easy to identify—cuddling with Missy, her adoptive mother, because this was when she felt the safest, happiest, and most comfortable. In later sessions, Amy and the therapist also used BLS to create a circle of support in which Amy imagined all of her support people, including social workers in the other state, the adoption worker, her previous counselor, and her family, standing in a circle around her protecting her and loving her. Despite using her peaceful place and circle of support, Amy continued to have difficulty at school. Transitions, such as changing classes, were especially dysregulating, but it was also hard for Amy to simply focus in class. Sometimes her curious peers would ask about her scars, which would take Amy back to thinking about what happened with Tom, whom she now called the "bad daddy." The therapist worked with Amy to identify smells that were soothing to her. The smell that worked best was her mother's perfume, which was placed on a cotton ball in a ziplock bag. Amy received permission from her teacher to keep the ziplock bag in her desk so that whenever she felt "yucky," she could pull it out, smell it, and calm herself down and then be able to focus in class. The perfume worked well, but when Amy was too dysregulated, she could also go to the nurse's office. There, Amy was given space to do her resource activity of Earth, Wind, Water, and Fire (T. Becker-Fritz, personal communication, March 14, 2012). This usually helped Amy, but occasionally, she would need a quick call to her adoptive mother that would serve to remind Amy that she was safe and loved. These strategies helped Amy to stay present in class, to handle the questions from peers, and to be able to focus.

(*continued*)

(*continued*)

Once Amy had some strategies to help her and was doing better at school, she began talking with the therapist more about the traumas she had endured. The pair worked together to draw a path, which we used as a timeline to chronicle where she had lived and where traumas had occurred. Because of the numerous incidents of trauma and abuse, the therapist and Amy decided that Amy would draw her story frame by frame. During each session, Amy would draw one or two pictures. For each picture, Amy shared her negative cognition, emotions, body sensations, and gave a SUD level. Amy had a difficult time initially providing a SUD level so the counselor used a set of 10 nesting dolls to show her level of distress. The EMDR protocol was used with each individual picture that Amy drew. The prominent negative cognition throughout Amy's book was "I can't be safe," but other negative cognitions included "I don't have any control," "I did something wrong," and "I'm not lovable."

When EMDR therapy began, the therapist reviewed with Amy the different types of BLS. Amy preferred the tappers, which vibrated back and forth in her hands. As therapy progressed, the therapist noticed times that processing would stall or slow down considerably. During these times, other forms of BLS were used and often reenergized the processing of the traumas. Other things that were used included following a turtle finger puppet that was placed on the end of a magic wand and listening to bilateral nature sounds. Finally, following a stuffed animal that jumped back and forth on her knees was effectively used when Amy was diagnosed with absence seizures, a condition in which the child loses awareness for a few seconds at a time. Even children with physiological disorders can use EMDR therapy, but we caution therapists to seek medical consultation and additional EMDR consultation before proceeding.

A container technique was used to help Amy function between sessions without reliving the traumatic material. At the end of each session, the therapist would provide BLS while Amy would imagine placing her difficult thoughts and feelings in a box she had decorated, securely taped, and glued and left in therapist's office. As sessions

(*continued*)

progressed to dealing with more traumatic material, Amy decided that the decorated box was not secure enough and instead envisioned using a "spikey, brick box," chaining and bolting the box closed and then leaving it in a secure place in the therapist's office. When troubling content would creep up during the time between sessions, Amy used the same technique and would imagine herself sending the thoughts and feelings to the box in the therapist's office.

As therapy progressed, the aunt, Missy, and the therapist noticed a pattern of behavior in which Amy would regress significantly when she became ill. Amy would sink into deep depressions and be unable to function for days after physically healing. Missy also noticed a similar experience when Amy was constipated. Being that this issue affected her daily life and was causing excessive school absences, the therapist did not have the luxury of working through it with nondirective play therapy. EMDR was used to target the negative cognition of "I'm not in control." Amy reported feeling sad and depressed like an empty hole in her stomach, which she gave an SUD of 10. The picture that represented these feelings was of herself in a dark pit that was impossible to escape. As the negative cognition was being desensitized, Amy talked about how she had been left alone with her injuries still bleeding. By the time the SUD reached a 3, Amy shared that this was in the past and that she was safe, loved, and cared for by her aunt, Missy. She also talked about having a voice. The SUD did not progress any further, probably due to the fact that the actual trauma of the beatings had not yet been processed. After EMDR therapy was done on each picture, the counselor revisited this target with Amy and she reported that it had moved to an SUD of 1.

On picture number 10, Amy drew a picture of Tom hitting her nude body with a large belt. She talked about how the buckle tore her skin in numerous places and no one helped her. Amy reported that she felt scared, helpless, and worried when she thought about this part of her abuse. Her negative cognition was "I can't be safe." She felt her emotions in her gut and gave an SUD of 10. BLS with the tappers was used to process this memory. Amy began the processing by reflecting on her helplessness in the situation and the fact

(*continued*)

(*continued*)

that Sarah never came to her aid until she washed her after the beatings. As processing continued, Amy's thoughts and feelings shifted to anger toward Tom and Sarah for injuring her and not protecting her. Amy had tremendous difficulty tolerating her feelings associated with this memory. While providing BLS, Amy was asked to watch the memory as if it was a movie, but she would have a remote control to make it more tolerable. Amy initially muted the sound and fast-forwarded through parts of the memory until, after many sets of BLS, she was able to tolerate thinking about the memory in its entirety. Processing ended when Amy reached an SUD of 0 and reported that the emotions she had previously felt in her gut moved during processing to her throat and then disappeared. After the last set of BLS, Amy stated that now she had a stronger voice, would know more about how to protect herself, and had family that would protect her. The positive cognition of "I have a voice" was then strengthened with slower and shorter sets of BLS. Amy was always drawn to the turtle finger puppet. After processing this trauma, she talked about how she used to be like the turtle who always wanted to be in her shell to stay safe, but now she could put her head out of the shell because she had a voice.

After treating the past belief of "I can't be safe," sessions focused on present and future templates. Amy shared that she didn't feel safe at school when people asked about her marks and scars. She also didn't feel safe when she was away from Missy, her aunt and adoptive mother. Amy reported feeling scared and worried in her heart and she gave an SUD of 7. The present examples were processed in the same way as the past traumas with the BLS until the SUD was 0 and all bodily sensations dissipated. For the future template, Amy imagined situations in which she might feel unsafe in the future and saw herself successfully handling the situations by being the changed turtle and having a voice. Even though Amy wished she could see Tracy again, she also realized that it could be unsafe to do so. As one of her future templates, Amy pretended to call Tracy on a play phone to tell her how she felt about her abandonment and that she did not want her around anymore. At this point in treatment, Amy wrote thank-you letters to all of her former foster parents and all the helpers

(*continued*)

in the state where she was abused. To Tracy, her biological mother, Amy wrote a letter of confusion about why she had left her with someone she did not know and who did not love her. Amy attached each note to a balloon and released them into the air, one by one.

Another pivotal moment in Amy's treatment occurred when she was 9 years old. In the beginning of the EMDR treatment, Amy was clear about Tom's responsibility and wrongdoing. She processed the incidents and gained some resolution. However, she always struggled to understand why Sarah was in jail because "she didn't do anything to me." Amy would talk about how Sarah cleaned her up after beatings, but how Sarah could not have stopped the beatings. When Amy was asked to write a victim impact statement concerning Sarah's role in her abuse, all the pieces came together for Amy, resulting in a deeper understanding of what she had processed years before this. She reflected on how she now had a voice and would be able to write a letter to the judge. Amy began dictating her statement during a therapy session and stated, "Sarah didn't do anything," and then she paused for a while before starting with conviction, "Sarah didn't *DO ANYTHING*." Amy processed how Sarah did have a voice as an adult; she worked outside the house and could have asked for help, but did not. Amy then proceeded to write a strongly worded victim impact statement about how Sarah's neglect was just as damaging as the blows she endured from Tom because that is what made her believe that people could not be trusted to help her. In that moment, Amy's maturity allowed her to have a deeper understanding of the earlier EMDR processing and her negative cognition that she was not safe.

EMDR therapy was able to help Amy get to the roots of her traumas and negative cognitions. When she began therapy with the therapist at age 6 years, Amy needed to attend sessions twice weekly and frequently call the therapist in order to be able to maintain daily functioning and progress in school. She was frozen with fear even though she was in a safe and nurturing environment with someone she trusted. Traditional play therapy helped her to maintain, but she continued to have debilitating and limiting thoughts that were rooted in her experiences of abuse and abandonment. Through using EMDR

(*continued*)

(*continued*)

therapy, Amy moved to weekly sessions; phone calls to the therapist were rare, and she made significant strides in school success, building and maintaining friendships, and playing freely. The therapist noticed that she increasingly used her voice to advocate for herself and she worried less about getting in trouble. In fact, she began to push boundaries with Missy that were typical and expected for a child her age. Amy continued to use the strategies of Earth, Wind, Water, and Fire, her peaceful place, and her circle of support to keep her strong during challenging times. Earth, Wind, Water, and Fire has become a morning routine done on the way to school each day along with her morning prayers and devotionals to get her day off to a good start.

While at a recent play therapy conference, I was talking with Evelyn Wright, a fellow play and EMDR therapist, about the value of using a combination of these therapies with children. She remembered hearing an analogy of play therapy being equivalent to sweeping up shards of glass after a vessel has fallen and shattered. She added that EMDR therapy is like taking the wet paper towel across the floor to pick up all the slivers that cannot be seen by the naked eye (Wright, personal communication, September 12, 2014).

REFERENCES

Adler-Tapia, R., & Settle, C. (2008). *EMDR & the art of psychotherapy with children: Treatment manual and text*. New York, NY: Springer Publishing.

Adler-Tapia, R. L., & Settle, C. S. (2009). Evidence of the efficacy of EMDR with children and adolescents in individual psychotherapy: A review of the research published in peer reviewed journals. *Journal of EMDR Practice and Research, 3*(4), 232–247.

Ahmad, A., Larsson, B., & Sundelin-Wahlsten, V. (2007). EMDR treatment for children with PTSD: Results of a randomized controlled trial. *Nordic Journal of Psychiatry, 61*(5), 349–354.

American Psychiatric Association. (2004). *Practice guideline for the treatment of patients with acute stress disorder and posttraumatic stress disorder*. Arlington, VA: American Psychiatric Association.

Beckley-Forest, A. (2015). Play therapy and EMDR: A conversation. *Play Therapy, 10*, 10–14.

Davidson, P. R., & Parker, K. C. (2001). Eye movement desensitization and reprocessing (EMDR): A meta-analysis. *Journal of Consulting and Clinical Psychology, 69*(2), 305–316.

EMDR Institute. (n.d.). Research overview. Retrieved from http://www.emdr.com/research-overview

Fleming, J. (2012). The effectiveness of eye movement desensitization and reprocessing in the treatment of traumatized children and youth. *Journal of EMDR Practice and Research, 6*, 16–26.

Foa, E. B., Keane, T., Friedman, M. J., & Cohen, J. A. (2009). *Effective treatments for PTSD: Practice guidelines from the International Society for Traumatic Stress Studies* (2nd ed.). New York, NY: Guilford Press.

Gil, E. (2012). *The healing power of play: Working with abused children.* New York, NY: Guilford Press

Gomez, A. (2007). *Dark, Bad Day .... Go Away: a book for children about trauma and EMDR*. Phoenix, AZ: Author. Retrieved from AnaGomezTherapy.com

Gomez, A. (2013). *EMDR therapy and adjunct approaches with children: Complex trauma, attachment, and dissociation.* New York, NY: Springer Publishing.

Goodyear-Brown, P. (2010). *Play therapy with traumatized children: A prescriptive approach.* Hoboken, NJ: John Wiley & Sons.

Greenwald, R. (2007). *EMDR within a phase model of trauma-informed treatment.* Binghamton, NY: Hayworth.

Ironson, G., Freund, B., Strauss, J. L., & Williams, J. (2002). Comparison of two treatments for traumatic stress: A community-based study of EMDR and prolonged exposure. *Journal of Clinical Psychology, 58*(1), 113–128.

Landreth, G. (2000). *Innovations in play therapy.* New York, NY: Brunner-Routledge.

Landreth, G. (2012). *Play therapy: The art of relationship* (3rd ed.). New York, NY: Routledge.

Lee, C. W., & Cuijpers, P. (2013). A meta-analysis of the contribution of eye movements in processing emotional memories. *Journal of Behavior Therapy and Experimental Psychiatry, 44*(2), 231–239.

Leeds, A. (Producer). (2012). *Can you tell us why EMDR works?* (Podcast). Retrieved from http://youtube.com/watch?v=sWyDWvMEl1E

Lovett, J. (1999). *Small wonders: Healing childhood trauma with EMDR.* New York, NY: Free Press.

Maxfield, L., & Hyer, L. (2002). The relationship between efficacy and methodology in studies investigating EMDR treatment of PTSD. *Journal of Clinical Psychology, 58*(1), 23–41.

Rodenburg, R., Benjamin, A., de Roos, C., Meijer, A. M., & Stams, G. J. (2009). Efficacy of EMDR in children: A meta-analysis. *Clinical Psychology Review, 29*(7), 599–606.

Rothschild, B. (2000). *The body remembers. The psychophysiology of trauma and trauma treatment*. New York, NY: W. W. Norton.

Shapiro, F. & Forrest, M. (2004). *EMDR: The breakthrough "eye movement" therapy for overcoming anxiety, stress, and trauma*. New York, NY: Basic Books.

Shapiro, F. (2001). *Eye movement desensitization and reprocessing: Basic principles, protocols and procedures* (2nd ed.). New York, NY: Guilford Press.

Shapiro, F., Kaslow, F. W., & Maxfield, L. (Eds.). (2007). *Handbook of EMDR and family therapy processes*. Hoboken, NJ: John Wiley & Sons.

Soberman, G., Greenwald, R., & Rule, D. (2002). A controlled study of eye movement desensitization and reprocessing (EMDR) for boys with conduct problems. *Journal of Aggression, Maltreatment and Trauma, 6*(1), 217–236.

Substance Abuse and Mental Health Services Administration's National Registry of Evidence-based Programs and Practices. (2015). *Eye movement desensitization and reprocessing intervention report*. Retrieved from http://legacy.nreppadmin.net/ViewIntervention.aspx?id=199

Tufnall, G. (2005). Eye Movement Desensitization and Reprocesscing in the treatment of preadolescent children with post-traumatic symptoms. *Clinical Child Psychology & Psychiatry, 10*(4), 587–600.

Waldon, A. (2004). *Goodbye yucky thoughts and feelings: An EMDR workbook for children*. Carrboro, N.C: Author.

Waldon, A. (2007). *Hello strength and bravery: A resource workbook for children*. Carrboro, N.C: Author.

Wander, F., Serra, M., & deJongh, A. (2006). EMDR versus CBT for children with self-esteem and behavioral issues: A randomized trial. *Journal of EMDR Practice and Research, 2*(3), 180–189.

World Health Organization. (2013). *Guidelines for the management of conditions specifically related to stress*. Retrieved from http://apps.who.int/iris/bitstream/10665/85119/1/9789241505406_eng.pdf?ua=1

CHAPTER 5

Directive Play Therapy Techniques in Trauma-Focused Cognitive Behavioral Therapy

EVETTE HORTON AND DONNA POTTER

One of the most widely known, researched, and disseminated therapeutic interventions for traumatized children and adolescents (aged 3–18 years; hereafter referred to as children) is trauma-focused cognitive behavioral therapy (TF-CBT; Child Welfare Information Gateway, 2012; Cohen, Mannarino, & Deblinger, 2006). The TF-CBT model being implemented today began when several clinical researchers combined their similar trauma-focused interventions (Cohen & Manniaro, 1993; Cohen et al., 2006; Deblinger & Heflin, 1996) into a single model with the most efficacious components. The new model combined well-established cognitive behavioral, learning, and family therapy theory and techniques with emerging research on childhood posttraumatic stress disorder (PTSD), neuroscience, and child development. The result was a relatively short-term (typically 12–18 sessions, each 60- to 90-minutes), manualized intervention that included both the child and the nonoffending caregiver in the treatment process and could be implemented in a wide variety of settings.

TRAUMA-FOCUSED COGNITIVE BEHAVIORAL THERAPY

TF-CBT is broadly designed to improve children's cognitive, emotional, and behavioral symptoms stemming from memories of traumatic life events (Cohen et al., 2006). These symptoms may originate from a single traumatic incident (such as a hurricane, car accident, or loss of a loved one) or from recurrent traumatic events (such as ongoing sexual abuse, child maltreatment, or domestic violence). TF-CBT contains specific goals for the child and the nonoffending caregiver. TF-CBT child-related goals include reducing children's negative emotional and behavioral responses to the trauma and correcting maladaptive or unhelpful cognitions related to the traumatic experience (Child Welfare Information Gateway, 2012). TF-CBT caregiver goals include helping nonoffending caregivers cope effectively with their own emotional distress while supporting their child's recovery (Child Welfare Information Gateway, 2012; Cohen et al., 2006).

TF-CBT Core Values

The TF-CBT authors outline six core values that are foundational to how the model works and can be easily remembered with the acronym C-R-A-F-T-S (Cohen et al., 2006). First, the model is *components based,* meaning that the model helps children learn new skills in a progressive manner. Like elementary school math lessons, each skill builds on the previously learned skill, which allows the counselor to tailor each component to the needs of the child and family they serve, rather than just following a session-by-session manual. Second, the TF-CBT model strives to be *respectful of cultural differences* and even encourages counselors to adapt the model to the unique needs of their clients, which may be one of the factors in TF-CBT's documented effectiveness with a variety of cultures, including Latino (De Arellano, Davidson, & Felton, 2012), Native American (BigFoot & Schmidt, 2010), and African (Murray et al., 2013; O'Callaghan, McMullen, Shannon, Rafferty, & Black, 2013) populations. As represented in the first two core values, the TF-CBT model endeavors to be *adaptable and flexible.* The authors encourage counselors to use their creativity and clinical judgment in implementing the various components to match the needs of the children and their caregivers. Because TF-CBT can be effective for traumatized children as young as 3 years and as old as 18 years, the activities used to meet the goals for each session, and the ways in which caregivers are involved in the treatment, vary dramatically, depending on the age of the child.

The TF-CBT developers cite the fourth core value, *family focused,* as being one of the most important in the model. Along with the child, nonoffending parents and other primary caregivers, such as adoptive parents, experience their own unique thoughts and feelings about the traumatic event(s) (Holt, Jensen, & Wentzel-Larsen, 2014). Several studies by TF-CBT authors (Cohen, Deblinger, Mannarino, & Steer, 2004; Deblinger, Lippmann, & Steer, 1996), as well as other clinical researchers (Holt et al., 2014), have shown that including caregivers in TF-CBT treatment is efficacious for both the child and the caregiver. Thus, the TF-CBT model expects that each intervention session will be tailored to the unique needs of the identified child and caregiver.

The fifth core value emphasizes the importance of the *therapeutic relationship* in the TF-CBT model. Researchers have found that key factors of the child–therapist relationship, such as empathy and therapeutic alliance, are important predictors for successful outcomes (Norcross & Wampold, 2011; Shirk, Karver, & Brown, 2011). Cohen et al. (2006) concur and suggest that the therapeutic relationship helps the child and the caregiver to reestablish "trust, optimism, and self-esteem" (p. 33) following traumatic events. Strictly following an evidence-based model's components is not sufficient to ensure positive outcomes for clients; sound clinical competency and a strong therapeutic relationship are necessary for optimal client outcomes.

In TF-CBT, the therapeutic alliance is consciously developed by engaging the client in interactive activities that build the client's sense of competence, while decreasing the client's symptoms. For example, TF-CBT counselors use positive reinforcement, including specific praise, throughout sessions when clients and caregivers are able to effectively use their new skills and talk openly about aspects of their trauma experiences. Another way a TF-CBT counselor facilitates the therapeutic alliance is when the counselor judiciously self-discloses in various sessions, such as mentioning a time he or she felt scared about something that happened to him or her or expressing surprise at a particular child sexual abuse fact, to help normalize the experience for the child or caregiver.

The sixth and final TF-CBT core value is *self-efficacy*. Cohen et al. (2006) want all children and caregivers in TF-CBT to leave treatment with the ability to regulate their emotions, thoughts, and feelings. These regulation skills will not only mitigate the deleterious effects of the traumatic event but will also help build resilience in the child and caregiver for the future. Although childhood traumatic incidents are sometimes perceived by caregivers, and even at times counselors, as difficult and grim topics, the developers of TF-CBT want counselors to understand and model that children can and *do* recover from these life events and that the therapy, though difficult at times, will be fun. In fact, TF-CBT trainers frequently inform trainees that if the child and counselor are not having fun, then they are not doing TF-CBT right! Although this concept may seem very strange in the context of trauma treatment, it is a hallmark of the success of the model in randomized-controlled trials (Cohen et al., 2006) and supports TF-CBT's core value of self-efficacy by increasing the client's new, positive associations of mastery with the trauma material.

Training in the TF-CBT Model

Counselors interested in becoming competent in this model have a range of training options from a free, 10-hour web-based introductory training (see https://tfcbt.musc.edu) to the national TF-CBT certification process (see https://TF-CBT.org). The developers of the TF-CBT model have written textbooks (Cohen et al., 2006; Cohen, Mannarino, & Debinger, 2012) and several clinical articles (see Cohen, Berliner, & Mannarino, 2010; Cohen, Mannarino, Kliethermes, & Murray, 2012; Cohen, Mannarino, & Murray, 2011) to help counselors apply the model to various subpopulations.

There are also developer-endorsed TF-CBT trainers located throughout the United States. These trainers employ several different training approaches. Some trainers adopt a 2-day, in-person training model that includes 12 TF-CBT-specific, group consultation calls. Other trainers use a "learning collaborative model" where a selected group of clinicians have several day-long trainings at the beginning of a year and then spend the rest of the year in face-to-face, monthly supervision sessions where the newly trained TF-CBT counselors share cases with seasoned TF-CBT clinicians. These endorsed training models are supported by research on implementation science, which looks not only at how to effectively train clinicians in the model but also how to support the organizational changes needed to implement evidence-based interventions with fidelity (Markiewicz, Ebert, Ling, Amaya-Jackson, & Kisiel, 2006).

RESEARCH SUPPORT

The TF-CBT model has more than 10 randomized, controlled, clinical trials indicating TF-CBT's effectiveness at reducing various trauma symptoms and mental health disorders, including anxiety, depression, and PTSD, and has several other studies in process. In their book, Cohen et al. (2006) cite five randomized, controlled trials with positive TF-CBT outcomes, as compared with a waitlist control or nondirective, client-centered therapy. In one of these studies, Cohen et al. (2004) randomly assigned 229 children, who had PTSD symptoms stemming from sexual abuse, and their primary caregivers to a manualized TF-CBT or supportive child-centered therapy (CCT) intervention. The TF-CBT intervention followed the description outlined in this chapter and the manualized CCT intervention followed a typical Rogerian (Rogers, 1995) theoretical framework and technique. For the children, CCT also included basic child-centered play and art techniques. At posttreatment, the children in the TF-CBT group demonstrated significantly greater improvement in PTSD symptoms, depression, behavior problems, abuse-related negative attributions, and shame. The caregivers in the study had greater improvements in self-reported depression, distress, support of the child, and parenting practices (Cohen, Deblinger, & Mannarino, 2004). Cohen, Mannarino, and Knudsen (2005) conducted a similar study and measured outcomes at 6 and 12 months posttreatment. They found that there were significantly greater improvements for the TF-CBT-treated children in depression, anxiety, sexual behavior problems, and dissociation at the 6-month follow-up and in PTSD and dissociation symptoms at the 12-month follow-up (Cohen et al., 2005).

Since then, these findings have been expanded and confirmed by other clinical researchers across a variety of traumatic events, symptoms, and cultural groups. For example, O'Callaghan et al. (2013) implemented a culturally adapted, group-based TF-CBT intervention led by supervised, nonclinical facilitators for girls exposed to trauma in the Democratic Republic of Congo and found significantly improved trauma, anxiety, depression, and conduct symptoms and improved prosocial behaviors at the end of 3 months posttreatment (O'Callaghan et al., 2013). Similar results were found in a study of TF-CBT provided to orphans and vulnerable children in low-resourced communities in Zambia (Murray et al., 2013).

Recent meta-analyses have confirmed the earlier findings. Cary and McMillen (2012) conducted three sets of meta-analyses that included 10 controlled studies. They reviewed studies that included the formal TF-CBT model, as well as several similar trauma models with corresponding components, and compared them with waitlist control, treatment-as-usual, child-only CBT, or CCT (Cary & McMillen, 2012). Cary and McMillen (2012) found that both the formal TF-CBT model and the informal models with similar components were effective at improving child symptoms of PTSD at the end of treatment and at 12 months posttreatment.

Given the plethora of quality empirical research, the TF-CBT model has attained the highest scientific rating as an evidence-based practice by multiple governmental and nonprofit organizations, such as the National Child Traumatic Stress Network (NCTSN, 2012, see www.nctsn.org/sites/default/files/assets/pdfs/TF-CBT_general.pdf), California

Evidence-Based Clearinghouse (www.cebc4cw.org/program/trauma-focused-cognitive-behavioral-therapy), Substance Abuse and Mental Health Services Administration (SAMHSA's) National Registry of Evidence-Based Programs and Practices (http://www.samhsa.gov/nrepp), U.S. Children's Bureau (Child Welfare Information Gateway, 2012), and U.S. Department of Justice (Saunders, Berliner, & Hanson, 2003).

In sum, TF-CBT is a well-established intervention that has shown efficacy in treating children with a wide variety of traumatic symptoms; however, there remain some questions about how well the TF-CBT model is being fully implemented in community settings. Allen and Johnson (2012) found that some counselors do not consistently implement all the TF-CBT components. The TF-CBT model developers have empirically demonstrated that it is critical to implement the model with fidelity to the core values described earlier, and the components described in the next section, to produce the best results for traumatized children and their families (Cohen et al., 2006).

Though the TF-CBT model has been used with children who have had a variety of different traumatic exposures, there are some child subpopulations that may initially require other therapeutic interventions to address problem behaviors before the traumatic symptoms can be addressed directly. For example, children with conduct disorders, acutely suicidal behaviors, self-injurious behaviors, and ongoing substance abuse may need to have the predominant safety and behavioral symptoms addressed first before moving in to the TF-CBT intervention (Child Welfare Information Gateway, 2012).

TF-CBT TECHNIQUES

TF-CBT is designed to specifically treat child and adolescent posttraumatic stress. Thus, the first step in any TF-CBT treatment begins with a comprehensive child evaluation, including a standardized assessment of symptoms of trauma (PTSD), and other common mental health disorders, such as depression and anxiety, child traumatic grief, and family dynamics (Cohen et al., 2006). Once a thorough assessment has been completed, the client, the caregiver, and the counselor can use the assessment results to set treatment goals and begin to work through the TF-CBT components. The developers of TF-CBT believe both a comprehensive assessment *and* fidelity to the components are necessary for efficacious TF-CBT treatment. These two foundational TF-CBT ingredients are reviewed as follows.

TF-CBT Assessment

Because trauma can impact child functioning across multiple domains, the TF-CBT developers recommend that counselors explicitly assess six potentially problematic domains: cognitive, relationship, affective, family, traumatic behavior, and somatic concerns (see Cohen et al., 2006, for more detailed information). There are a myriad of instruments that assess these domains in children aged 3 to 18 years. Some of the frequent assessments employed in clinical practices are reviewed in the following text.

For children older than 8 years and their caregivers, a trauma history screener and symptom measure such as the University of California at Los Angeles Posttraumatic Stress Disorder Reaction Index for *Diagnostic and Statistical Manual of Mental Disorders* (5th ed.; *DSM-5*; American Psychiatric Association, 2013; Pynoos & Steinberg, 2014) is useful. For the caregivers of young children, the Young Child PTSD Checklist (YCPC; Scheeringa, 2010) is generally recommended. Both of these instruments measure multiple trauma domains and are available in English and Spanish. There are a number of other excellent trauma assessments available for review at the NCTSN (2012, www.nctsn.org).

In addition to screening for traumatic experiences and trauma symptoms, the counselor should assess for general social and emotional problems with a standardized measure, such as the Strengths and Difficulties Questionnaire (SDQ; Goodman, 1997) or the Child Behavior Checklist (CBCL; Achenbach & Rescorla, 2001). These measures provide the counselor with a broad picture of client functioning, and they also help to determine if other clinical levels of mental health symptoms are present.

Given the high rate of sexualized behaviors seen in children impacted by child sexual abuse, counselors should include a standardized measure of child sexual behaviors in client cases with histories of sexual trauma. The Child Sexual Behavior Inventory (Friedrich, 1997), the Trauma Symptom Checklist for Children (Briere, 1996), and the Trauma Symptom Checklist for Young Children (Briere et al., 2001) are instruments we find useful. Results from these measures help the counselor address these issues directly and from the beginning of the treatment by incorporating them in treatment planning and goals.

If the complete assessment, including standardized tools, such as those mentioned earlier, indicate the trauma and its sequelae are indeed driving the need for treatment, and the child has a verbal memory of the trauma, then TF-CBT is likely an excellent option. The next step is to explain the assessment results to the caregiver and, if age appropriate, to the child as well. The counselor can use a metaphor to help explain to the child why symptoms develop following a traumatic event(s), such as in this commonly used metaphor:

> Imagine you walk through a park near your home every afternoon. You have been there hundreds of times and have always found it to be a peaceful and relaxing place. Then, one day on your walk, you almost step on a poisonous snake! You might run away from the scene, scream, freeze, and/or attack the snake, because you are scared that you might be hurt or even killed!
>
> Now, think about how you will feel the next day when you are walking in the same park. Your body is now on high alert. Your eyes look back and forth on the ground. Then, you see a stick! Your brain may think the stick is a snake, because you are worried about seeing one again. Your eyes might actually *see* the stick *as* a snake, which is actually your brain working to keep you safe from poisonous snakes!

Sharing the results of the assessment measures in graphs can also help caregivers and older clients see where they agree on the child's trauma symptoms, and where they see things differently. In partnership with the child and the caregiver, the counselor can develop a treatment plan with specific measureable goals and explain to the child and caregiver how the TF-CBT components will help the child feel better in a fairly short period of time.

The counselor can use the results of the assessment as the basis for the initial psychoeducation session for both the caregiver and the client about the child's symptoms (and possibly the caregiver's symptoms as well) and about how the TF-CBT model will address the symptoms. Using the previous metaphor, the counselor can explain that when people experience events that are so scary they think they might die or be seriously hurt, their brain reacts in some very specific ways. First, the brain engages the fight/flight/freeze response that ensures the person does not die in the moment. Next, the brain records everything occurring in that scary moment to help the person remember all the details to help prevent the person from getting into the same circumstance again. In that moment, the brain stops filtering information and instead records all the sensory information, both internal and external, in meticulous detail, similar to the effects seen on a *high definition* movie or television. This sensory information includes all the very specific details we remember when we are very scared, such as when a child can remember the song on the radio when the tornado came, the smell of the potatoes in the cellar where the child waited out the tornado, or the soft feel of the child's blanket held during the storm. After the traumatic event has passed, any sensory memories from the child's traumatic event may serve as a trauma reminder for a child, sending a *red alert* message to the brain that danger may be imminent. Automatically, the trauma symptoms are employed to ensure safety. The counselor explains how TF-CBT will gradually build the child's repertoire of skills to manage his or her *red alert* symptoms, as the child is able to tolerate more and more details of the trauma memories. This gradual exposure process is necessary, because these symptoms can worsen over time and become more entrenched if they, and the underlying trauma memories, are not directly addressed.

TF-CBT Components

After a counselor has had training in TF-CBT and has completed a thorough, developmentally appropriate assessment of the client, the counselor then moves into the specific techniques of TF-CBT. In general, TF-CBT treatment can be divided into thirds. The first third focuses on client stabilization by decreasing symptoms and increasing distress tolerance. The second third focuses on trauma narrative development and processing, and the final third focuses on consolidating the gains the client has made and promoting healthy development for the future.

TF-CBT treatment consists of a number of cognitive behavioral components. The developers summarize these components with the acronym, PRACTICE (Cohen et al., 2006): *P*sychoeducation, *R*elaxation, *A*ffective expression and modulation, *C*ognitive coping and processing, *T*rauma narrative, *I*n vivo mastery of trauma reminders, *C*onjoint child and parent sessions, and *E*nhancing future safety and development. The components are designed to be followed generally in order and build on one another. In each component, the client and caregiver work on similar goals and are assigned homework to practice the strategies learned. What follows is our adapted description of TF-CBT's components.

Psychoeducation for Client and Caregiver

Psychoeducation about the impact of trauma and common childhood reactions to trauma begins with the very first contact with the family. Beginning at assessment and continuing throughout TF-CBT treatment, the goal is to normalize both client and caregiver responses to trauma. The counselor explains that many children have had scary things happen in their lives, have gotten help, and gotten better. As mentioned earlier, the counselor is constantly and consistently conveying to both the child and caregiver an attitude of confidence in the child's ability to overcome this trauma. Counselors should be careful to monitor their nonverbal responses to the traumatic events being described. If the counselor asks about the child's trauma experiences with a pained expression, the family may believe their trauma story may be too much for the counselor to emotionally tolerate.

The counselor also gives caregivers psychoeducation on how to support their children behaviorally and emotionally throughout the treatment. Frequently called *parenting skills* in other versions of the PRACTICE acronym (Cohen et al., 2006), the counselor provides the caregiver with psychoeducation on the behavioral issues frequently present in children who have experienced trauma and on developmentally appropriate, positive discipline techniques to help the caregiver manage these behaviors. Two parenting techniques frequently taught by TF-CBT counselors are positive reinforcement and selective attention. Most counselors are familiar with the behavioral concept of praising behaviors that you would like to see increased. In TF-CBT, caregivers are taught to praise specific child behaviors that increase the child's verbalization and integration of the trauma, such as praising the child for going to therapy, talking about traumatic memories, and using their new coping skills.

Selective attention is the skill of ignoring or minimizing attention provided to undesired behaviors. Caregivers are taught to use this skill when the child exhibits unhelpful symptoms, and to positively reinforce the child's use of coping strategies learned in treatment. For example, a caregiver dealing with a child who has been triggered by a sensory reminder of a trauma and is having an anxious response (i.e., crying, screaming, and holding on to the caregiver's legs) may selectively notice a small moment when the child slows down to take a breath and then specifically praise the child for taking a deep breath and using a coping skill.

Caregivers are also given psychoeducation about how to optimally respond to their child's emotional needs as the child progresses through TF-CBT. Emotion coaching occurs when the caregiver supports the child's identification, expression, and regulation of emotions related to the traumatic event. TF-CBT counselors explicitly teach this skill to caregivers to help aid in the child's mastery over his or her traumatic experience.

Relaxation

Next, the counselor teaches the client strategies to specifically manage the physiological impact of trauma symptoms. This may involve some combination of progressive muscle relaxation, diaphragmatic (i.e., belly) breathing, grounding, and mindfulness. In separate caregiver sessions, the counselor coaches the caregiver on how to effectively support the child's use of the new relaxation skills. The child and caregiver practice these new techniques in sessions, at home with homework, and throughout the rest of the treatment.

Affective Expression and Modulation

Once the child and caregiver have some familiarity with relaxation, they can begin to work on affective expression and modulation. Here, the child and caregiver learn how to identify and verbally communicate their feelings, including trauma-related feelings, in order to decrease the intensity of the feelings. They also learn to identify the physiological impact and intensity of the feelings, so they can begin to use the newly learned relaxation strategies *before* the feelings become overwhelming.

Cognitive Coping and Processing

Once the child and caregiver have some ability to manage their trauma-related affect, they can then learn how their thoughts, feelings, and behaviors influence one another (i.e., the cognitive triangle). Learning that your thoughts can impact your behaviors is not something most clients initially understand, but it is an amazingly powerful concept that has been demonstrated to be effectively taught to even preschool age children (Quakley, Reynolds, & Coker, 2004). Children and caregivers can learn how to manage their unhelpful thoughts in daily life as well as their trauma symptoms with cognitive coping skills, such as thought stopping, visualization, positive self-statements, and thought replacement. These skills are then employed in the second third of the model, trauma processing, to help alter unhelpful trauma-related thoughts.

The counselor will also encourage the child and caregiver to use these skills while discussing and expanding their knowledge about how the child's specific trauma symptoms compare with other children's symptoms that have had similar trauma experiences. Frequently, TF-CBT counselors use Socratic questioning to expand the child's critical thinking about the trauma. In Socratic questioning, the counselor asks the client open-ended questions to assess and broaden the child's knowledge of the trauma. The counselor uses examples based on other children with similar traumatic experiences in order to provide the child with enough emotional distance to effectively explore his or her own cognitions and knowledge base. Negative cognitions about the traumatic event are not directly challenged at this point, but factual information that counters the cognition may be judiciously provided.

Trauma Narrative

Trauma narration, in which the child describes his or her personal trauma story, is an important component of TF-CBT treatment. The client works with the counselor to develop a narrative account of the trauma experiences. The narrative focuses on the moment-by-moment recollections of the child's cognitions, affect, and physiological responses during the trauma. In constructing the narrative, the counselor sensitively guides the client to add specific details about the trauma, particularly those details that the child may have been avoiding. The portions of the narrative that the child avoids are often clues to what needs to be further explored by the child and counselor to help the child continue to heal. The counselor helps the client identify and integrate the traumatic events in the larger context of the child's life. Meanwhile, the counselor meets separately with the caregiver, sharing the narrative and allowing the caregiver an opportunity to process his or her own feelings and reactions to the story privately, as well as develop a supportive response to share with the child after the narrative has been completed.

In Vivo Mastery of Trauma Reminders

At any point after a traumatic event, a child may begin to avoid an innocuous trauma reminder ("stimulus") to a degree that interferes with daily functioning. An often underutilized component of TF-CBT but a well-known fear-reduction technique (Pfefferbaum et al., 2014), in vivo desensitization pairs the child's learned relaxation and cognitive coping skills and the caregiver's parenting skills with exposure to gradually more anxiety-producing stimuli, leading up to the avoided innocuous stimulus. This helps the child gradually decrease the anxiety associated with the stimulus and return the child to pretrauma functioning.

For example, let us imagine the protagonist, in the "stick and snake" metaphor reviewed earlier, stops going to the park every day. Later, the protagonist actually becomes afraid of all sticks and avoids any place where there may be sticks on the ground. The TF-CBT counselor may want to help the protagonist first practice relaxation and coping skills while thinking about seeing a stick on the ground. After using relaxation strategies to decrease stress levels, the TF-CBT counselor may show the protagonist a picture of a stick and repeat the process. This would gradually lead up to the counselor and protagonist going outside and possibly collecting sticks while the protagonist continued to practice relaxation and coping skills. This can continue as long as necessary until the client is no longer experiencing fear on stimulus presentation.

Conjoint Child and Parent Sessions

As just reviewed, TF-CBT therapists meet individually with the client and the caregiver during the aforementioned components, and then bring them together to practice skills learned in choreographed conjoint sessions. These sessions are distributed throughout treatment. Ideally, the TF-CBT counselor will first meet with the caregiver individually, before the conjoint session, to ensure thorough support, coaching, and direct practice with role-plays. This prepares the caregiver to remain positive and supportive during the conjoint sessions. A conjoint session after the trauma narrative is a TF-CBT requirement.

Enhancing Future Safety and Development

In the final component of treatment, the counselor's focus is on decreasing the child's risk for future victimization, increasing the client's sense of self-efficacy, and ensuring the client is able to consolidate and transfer skills learned in TF-CBT. Meeting these goals often involves role-playing various situations in a *fire drill* fashion.

This is also the time when the counselor meets individually with the caregiver to predict together the areas of the child's future development that are likely to be impacted by the traumatic events. The counselor plans with the caregiver how the caregiver will address these issues in the future, role-playing future conversations, and sharing helpful resources.

Post-Assessment and Termination

Completing all components of TF-CBT does not automatically indicate the completion of a child's mental health treatment. Once all components have been completed, it is imperative that the counselor administer the same battery of standardized assessment tools administered at pretreatment in order to ensure that the client and family have symptom relief and improved functioning. In 80% of cases, we expect to see significant treatment improvements. When these results are shown to clients and caregivers, it reinforces their self-efficacy and is very empowering. The counselor can then celebrate the success of treatment with the client and the caregiver, and discuss what types of circumstances might arise in the future that would indicate that the client may need to come back for additional treatment.

CASE EXAMPLE: JOEY'S STORY

Meet 6-year-old Joey. Joey has a 3-year-old brother, James. Their mother, Shirley, and Shirley's boyfriend, Rick, are raising the two boys. Rick is the biological father of James but not Joey. Shirley and the boys have lived in Rick's trailer for the past 3.5 years, but lately, the couple has been arguing because Shirley works all the time and Rick has not had a job for 10 months. Joey was sexually abused by Rick when his mother was at work and he was home for the summer break.

One fall night while giving the boys their bath, Shirley caught Joey putting his mouth on his younger brother's penis in the bathtub. Shocked, Shirley yelled, "What are you doing?" Joey told his mom, "That's what Rick does to me when I take a nap." Incensed, Shirley immediately contacted the police and filed charges. She moved out of Rick's trailer and into a family member's home with the boys.

Since that time, Shirley reported that Joey has been extremely clingy to her. She complained, "He climbs in my bed every night, and he won't even let me go to the bathroom by myself!" She reported he has been getting in trouble for fighting at school, and she has seen him masturbating on several occasions. He also began fighting with his little brother more often.

Beth, Joey's TF-CBT trained counselor, begins a comprehensive assessment of Joey's trauma history, symptoms, and current functioning in his environment and relationships, considering both risk and resiliency factors. First, Beth meets alone with Shirley to gather as much information as she can about Joey's life and functioning thus far. She learns that he did well in kindergarten and that Shirley has a good working relationship with his new first grade teacher. She also learns that Shirley works full time and that Joey attends the afterschool program at the same day care center as his brother. Beth engages Shirley in a discussion about her previous experiences with mental health providers and other helping professionals and learns that the family has not had any previous interactions with such services. Shirley asks if Beth will be able to meet with Joey just before dinnertime to accommodate her work schedule, and Beth assures her she will.

(*continued*)

Beth verbally administers the YCPC (Scheeringa, 2010) to Shirley to learn more about Joey's trauma history and symptoms. After they go through the assessment tool, Beth asks Shirley to clarify her affirmative responses and provide examples, so Beth can determine if the endorsements are truly clinical issues. Beth also administers the SDQ (Goodman, 1997) and the Child Sexual Behavior Inventory (Friedrich, 1997). Results from the Child Sexual Behavior Inventory indicate that Shirley had not remembered to tell Beth about Joey's other sexualized behaviors, many of which had developed in the past 3 months.

Beth then asks Shirley about her initial response to Joey's disclosure. Shirley expresses regret, noting she was so shocked and angry by what she saw that she spanked Joey. Beth assures her that many parents respond similarly, and they will address this response in the course of treatment when Shirley will have the opportunity to have a better response. Beth informs Shirley that researchers have found that the more supportive caregivers can be to their child during the course of TF-CBT treatment, the more likely the child will have a positive treatment outcome (*psychoeducation*; Cohen & Mannarino, 1997).

Beth scores all of the measures and sees that, according to his mother's report, Joey is having clinically significant difficulty with separation anxiety, some recent toileting accidents, difficulty going to sleep alone, nightmares, sexual behavior problems, and irritability. Shirley agrees that these are the primary concerns she would like to be addressed in Joey's treatment and expresses some doubt that it will really get better. Beth explains to Shirley that TF-CBT was designed to get these very symptoms better, has helped children around the world, and that research on the model shows that 80% of children show significant improvement following TF-CBT treatment (*psychoeducation*). Beth explains to Shirley that she will meet individually with Joey and then bring Shirley and Joey together to discuss aspects of his trauma experience. She emphasizes the importance of Shirley talking positively about Joey in his presence and supporting his ability to talk about his trauma experiences.

In Beth's first *psychoeducation* session with Joey, she talks to him about the fact that his mommy brought him to see her because she

(*continued*)

(*continued*)

is someone who helps kids when they have had something really scary happen. Beth tells Joey that his mother told her Rick sexually abused Joey, and that Joey was really smart because he told his mommy. Beth reads Joey a book called *A Terrible Thing Happened* (Holmes, Mudlaff, & Pillo, 2000). The book is about a young raccoon that sees something terrible and begins to experience trauma symptoms, until he goes for counseling and talks about what he saw. Beth shows Joey pictures representing different trauma symptoms and also shows him a picture of a raccoon and a boy. Beth explains that as she reads the book, Joey's job is to find a picture that represents the trauma symptom described in the book and place it on the raccoon. Beth then asks Joey to look at all the symptom pictures and tell Beth which symptoms he struggles with the most. Beth praises Joey as he is able to talk about his trauma symptoms. As his mother did, Joey mentions feeling scared a lot, having bad dreams, and not wanting to sleep alone. Beth suggests that she will bring Joey's mother into the session, too, and he will be able to show her how he can describe the symptoms he is experiencing.

Beth meets individually with Shirley to explain what will happen in the *psychoeducation* conjoint session. Shirley is able to demonstrate a positive response, and so Beth engages Shirley in a role-play to practice how Shirley will specifically praise Joey for talking about his trauma symptoms, provide warmth and support, and indicate how they will phrase the treatment goals for Joey. Beth then brings Shirley into the conjoint session and encourages Joey to show his mother the book they read and explain the symptoms he is having. Beth quietly coaches Shirley to specifically praise Joey for sharing the information. Shirley and Joey decide that things will feel much better when Joey does not feel so angry all the time, when he can play alone for 5 to 10 minutes at a time, and when he can get to sleep by 8 p.m. and stay asleep until 7 a.m. (i.e., the treatment goals).

In the next session, Beth meets alone with Shirley first to focus on *psychoeducation* for the caregiver. She gives Shirley positive feedback on her support of Joey the previous week, and helps Shirley describe each of Joey's symptoms very specifically so they will be able to measure and track them throughout treatment. Beth explains

(continued)

that when children experience a trauma, such as sexual abuse, they often have symptoms very similar to Joey's. Beth points out that Joey feels safest when he is near his mother, so he is trying to stay close to her all the time. Beth suggests that as they figure out how to help him feel safe again, he will be able to get back to playing and sleeping independently.

Beth also explains that parents often feel guilty about their child's victimization. Shirley, while shedding a few tears, admits, "I do feel guilty. I should have known. I should have wondered what Rick was doing all day with the boys and why he wanted to do things with Joey not James. I thought Rick was just annoyed with 3-year-olds and wanted to bond with Joey. I just want to let Joey do whatever he wants. I mean who cares if he hits sometimes? I feel so bad, so guilty, I want to make it up to him."

Beth notes that while these feelings are understandable, even trained professionals are often fooled by perpetrators. Beth empathizes with Shirley's impulse to let Joey "do whatever he wants," but she explains that becoming permissive when a child had experienced trauma may actually exacerbate trauma symptoms in children. Beth encourages Shirley to keep to her normal rules and routines, which will make Joey feel safe.

Beth explains the efficacy and structure of TF-CBT, including how she will meet individually with both Joey and Shirley and then bring them together for conjoint sessions where they will practice skills and engage in fun activities with trauma content. Beth explains that the goal is to change how Joey feels when he thinks about the sexual abuse. Beth and Shirley then discuss Joey's symptoms, and Beth helps Shirley figure out the positive opposite of each of those. She engages Shirley in role-play scenarios to practice, specifically praising the positive opposites of his symptoms. Beth then explains that she will meet alone with Joey and explain about the function of trauma symptoms and how TF-CBT works and will then bring them back together to play a game about the new information. Beth and Shirley practice how and what Shirley will praise of Joey's behavior in the next conjoint session.

(continued)

(*continued*)

Beth then meets individually with Joey to provide more *psychoeducation*. She shows him a large poster board with velcro strips that she uses to help structure weekly sessions for clients. Beth explains to Joey how he will get to choose certain activities during the session and attach them to the poster board when they have finished with the activity.

Beth explains to Joey that when kids get really scared, like when they are sexually abused, the memory can start to *bully* them. Their brain tries to protect them by keeping them ready for danger and by keeping them away from things that remind them of the sexual abuse (*psychoeducation*). As she talks, Beth asks Joey to draw a picture of his trauma memory bully. Joey draws a scary monster. Beth explains that she and Joey will learn new tricks together that will shrink the scary monster (trauma memory bully). Soon the bully will not be so scary anymore, and his brain will not have to work so hard to fight the bully. Beth also shows Joey certificates of completion. She explains that he will earn them as he completes different parts of the treatment, and that in another few months he will be done with treatment and will feel comfortable playing and sleeping alone again. Beth then brings Shirley back into the session and has Joey show her his picture and explain how his brain is working to protect him from the bully. Shirley praises Joey's ability to talk openly about the sexual abuse and his symptoms and to stay calm.

The sessions progress in a similar pattern, with Beth meeting individually with Joey and with Shirley and then bringing them together for *conjoint sessions*. In these sessions, Shirley and Joey practice the skills Joey is learning. At home, Shirley uses praise to help Joey master the skills. Shirley also learns how to decrease the amount of attention Joey receives when he cannot sleep at night.

In a subsequent *relaxation* session, Beth engages Joey in an egg hunt. She hands him a magnifying glass and tells him he is a detective. Although he is hunting for eggs, they will also detect why his trauma memory bully is coming out to bother him at certain times. When he finds an egg, Joey opens it and eats the candy inside. Then, he hands the egg to Beth, who reads him the question inside the egg. One question asks what time of the day Joey feels the most worried.

(*continued*)

Another question asks if there is ever a time Joey feels comfortable when he is not with his mother; another asks what happens before he goes to sleep on the nights he has nightmares. Joey recalls that Rick came in and touched his penis when he was playing alone in the living room. Beth repeats this and writes it down, noting Joey is *shrinking his bully* when he shares details about the sexual abuse. Beth asks Joey what he does now when he finds himself alone in the living room. He says, "I run and find mommy!" Beth suggests that is really smart but also wonders if this means he does not have as much time to play? Beth teaches Joey a technique called *bubble breathing* (diaphragmatic breathing) and asks him to imagine being alone in the living room while he practices it. Beth then invites Shirley into the session. As Beth had prepared her to do, Shirley praises Joey's demonstration, and the two role-play how they will practice the strategy at home (*conjoint child and parent sessions*).

In a later *affective expression, and modulation session* with Joey, Beth gives Joey a large drawing of a human body outline and explains to him that feelings live in different places in people's bodies. Beth gives Joey crayons and asks him to pick a color representing happy. Joey chooses yellow, and Beth asks him to tell her a time he felt happy. Joey describes, "I went to the store with mommy, and we got ice cream with sprinkles!" Beth asks him to think about where he felt happy in his body during the outing and to then use the yellow crayon to color on the drawing where he felt the happy feeling in his body. Beth then asks Joey what feelings he had the first time he came to see her for therapy. Joey says he felt nervous, scared, and embarrassed. Beth has him choose colors to represent each of those feelings and then color on the drawing where he felt them. Without changing the tone of the session, Beth praises Joey for his good work in describing his feelings and asks him which feelings he had when Rick touched his penis. Joey says he felt gross and scared. Beth notes Joey had said he felt scared coming to see Beth for the first time and asks if he felt scared in the same parts of his body. Joey examines his picture and notes that it was in the same places (stomach, legs, and shoulders) but it was much bigger with Rick. Beth praises Joey's ability to talk about the sexual abuse and his feelings. She reminds

(*continued*)

(*continued*)

Joey that he is continuing to shrink the power the memory bully has over him.

As they continue this activity, Beth asks Joey if he knows what grown-ups call what Rick did to him. Joey appears confused. Beth says, "Grown-ups call that sexual abuse." Joey nods and says he knows what that is. Beth asks Joey to tell her what he knows about sexual abuse. Joey says, "Sexual abuse is when a grown-up touches a kid's privates" (*psychoeducation*).

Beth praises Joey's answer and asks if there is ever a time a grown-up touches a "kid's privates," but it is not sexual abuse. Joey initially says no. Beth asks about a doctor examination or a parent helping a young child take a bath. Joey considers these ideas and agrees they are not sexual abuse. Beth asks Joey what he thinks the difference might be. Joey considers and says he is not sure. Beth wonders, "Hmm, Joey, maybe it is about grown-ups that help kids?" Joey shares that Rick told him he was helping him to feel good when he touched Joey's penis. Beth praises Joey for thinking with her about this! Beth says, "Boy! This can be really confusing, Joey! I'm so glad you told me that Rick said that. I think Rick was trying to confuse you." Beth asks Joey if she, Joey's mother, and he can play a game together to help figure this confusion out.

In another session with Joey, Beth brings out the body drawing and several different colored balloons. Beth engages Joey in drawing a feelings face on each of the different colored balloons to match the colors he had previously identified for each feeling. Beth tells Joey that sometimes a feeling can be small, and sometimes it can be big. She demonstrates by blowing up the balloons with Joey's feelings faces on them. Beth shares that sometimes when feelings get really big, they move in your body. She brings the body drawing back out and blows up the excited balloon really big. Beth asks Joey what happens in his body if he is really, really excited. Joey tells Beth that his heart beats really fast, and he cannot stay still. Beth agrees and then blows the scared balloon up similarly. She asks Joey what happens in his body if he is really, really scared. Joey says, "Hey! It's the same thing!" Beth tells Joey that this can confuse your brain. Beth explains that when a person has been really scared about

(*continued*)

something because he or she was in danger, like during the sexual abuse, the person's brain pays really close attention to how the body felt at that time. When the body feels that in other situations, the brain thinks the person may be in danger again. Beth then shows Joey how to use his different relaxation skills when his feelings get really big. She also practices with him how he can use his bubble breathing to shrink his big feelings (*relaxation*).

Beth has a similar session with Shirley, where she explains the concept of internal trauma reminders. She and Shirley discuss how to talk with Joey about what sexual abuse is. Beth shows Shirley a game they can play with Joey about sexual abuse. They role-play Shirley's potential responses. Beth explains and demonstrates emotion coaching for Shirley (*affective expression and modulation*). Beth also shows Shirley how she can help Joey notice his body's response and label his feelings when he is having them. They practice this with several different situations in role-plays. Shirley learns how to use selective attention when Joey is experiencing separation anxiety at home and how she can specifically praise Joey's increasing affect regulation before holding a conjoint session. They also discuss the use of selective attention and time-out in managing Joey's sexualized behaviors.

In a *cognitive coping* session, Beth shows Joey two small mailboxes. On one is a picture of a heart (feelings) and on the other is a picture of a thought bubble (thoughts). Beth explains that thoughts and feelings are connected but they are not the same. She notes that how you think about something affects how you feel about it and vice versa. Beth brings the body drawing back out and notes that thoughts live in your head while feelings live in your body. Beth ties the body drawing to the pictures on the mailboxes. Beth reads several sentences to Joey. Some sentences indicate thoughts; others indicate feelings. She has Joey sort the sentences into the appropriate mailboxes. Joey does this easily, and Beth praises his effort. She then changes the pictures on the outside of the mailboxes to one representing helpful thoughts and one representing unhelpful thoughts. Beth then reads several sentences to Joey, such as "No one likes me"; "I am ugly"; "I will always feel scared all the time"; "I will have a nightmare tonight"; "I have two really good friends";

(*continued*)

(*continued*)

"I am good at making people laugh"; "I can be the boss of my sleep"; and "My mom and my teachers keep me safe." Once these sentences are sorted, Beth shows Joey a magic wand toy which she says can change "cold prickly thoughts" into "warm fuzzy thoughts." Beth encourages Joey to use the magic wand to change the "cold prickly thoughts." Joey tries it and says, "Maybe now instead of saying, 'I will have a nightmare tonight,' I can say, 'I can be the boss of my sleep.'" Beth praises Joey's warm fuzzy thought (*cognitive coping and processing*).

Beth asks Joey about his thoughts related to the sexual abuse. She asks him if he thinks others have experienced sexual abuse. Joey says he thinks he is probably the only one. Beth employs Socratic questioning to help Joey think about the fact that other children are also sexually abused, explore his thoughts about perpetrators, and determine how perpetrators might trick kids. Beth brings up Joey's earlier comment about Rick telling Joey he was helping, when he was really hurting, Joey. Joey says, "He was trying to trick me" (*cognitive coping and processing*).

In a separate session with Shirley, Beth explains the concept of the cognitive triangle and how changing your thoughts can actually change the outcome in situations. Beth shows Shirley how this works, using several different examples, including one which she states is very common among parents whose children have been sexually abused. Beth notes that parents often have thoughts, such as, "My child will never be the same again." Shirley agrees she has had these thoughts. Beth explains that believing those thoughts can impact how Shirley parents Joey in ways that are not healthy for her or Joey. After a fruitful discussion about this, Beth shows Shirley how she simplified the cognitive triangle to explain it to Joey. Beth and Shirley role-play several examples of how Shirley can recognize when Joey is having unhelpful thoughts at home and, instead, help Joey focus on more positive thoughts. Beth explains how this can be used to help Joey manage some of his symptoms.

After preparing both separately, Beth brings Joey and Shirley together to play a game about what they have learned so far in treatment. Beth explains that she will ask a series of questions and

(*continued*)

the two can each earn points in one of three ways: (a) they can answer the question Beth asks; (b) they can add to the other's response; or (c) they can specifically praise each other's responses. The two laugh together throughout the game, responding to questions about tricky perpetrators, sexual abuse, relaxation skills, feelings, and warm fuzzy/cold prickly thoughts (*conjoint child and parent sessions*).

In the next session, Beth reads Joey another book, called *Please Tell!: A Child's Story About Sexual Abuse* (Jessie, 1991), a story about a young girl who was sexually abused by her uncle. Beth asks Joey what he thinks is the same and different between what happened to the girl in the story and what happened to him. Joey responds, "The girl was sexually abused by her uncle, and I was sexually abused by my mom's boyfriend. Plus, I'm a boy and the person in the story is a girl, so she didn't have her penis touched."

Beth agrees and praises Joey for thinking about that so carefully. Beth points out to Joey that in the book *Please Tell!: A Child's Story About Sexual Abuse* (Jessie, 1991), the girl writes a little about herself, tells what happened to her, talks about how she is doing now, and finally, offers advice to other kids who have been sexually abused. Beth suggests that Joey can write a book like that about his own experience of sexual abuse.

Joey appears doubtful, but Beth is already pulling out paper and asking Joey to consider what he will put in his book. Beth asks Joey to draw a picture of himself, and while he is drawing, he can dictate to her what he wants his book to say about him (*trauma narrative*). At the end of this activity, Beth praises Joey for all of his hard work and points out how much he did. She demonstrates enthusiasm as she tells him she is excited to tell his mom what great work he is doing.

Over the course of the next several *trauma narrative* sessions, Beth meets first with Joey and then with Shirley. In each session with Joey, she checks in on his level of distress, engages him in a relaxation activity, checks on his distress again, then reads what he has written in his narrative thus far, again asks about his level of distress, offers a very brief relaxation activity, and asks about his level of distress again. She then has him draw and dictate his trauma narrative to her to write in his book. At the end of each session, Beth

(*continued*)

(*continued*)

reminds Joey of his homework for the week of practicing his relaxation strategies.

Using the previous structure, Beth guides Joey through talking about a specific incident of sexual abuse by Rick. As he recalls the day of the sexual abuse in as much detail as he can, Beth asks him to describe everything he can remember about what he was thinking, feeling, and what his body felt like. Beth explains that as Joey is telling her about this, she will write it down. Beth says she wants Joey's words to create a movie in her head of exactly what happened. In this way, Joey provides as much detail as he can about a specific time when he was sexually abused. Beth also asks Joey to draw a map of the room in the house where Rick sexually abused him. She then has him draw a separate picture of himself and of Rick, which they cut out so Joey can move the figures around the map to demonstrate what happened where (*trauma narrative*).

Beth does not have him talk about every single incident of abuse, as that is not necessary nor helpful, but she does have him talk about the incident he thought was the scariest. Over the next several sessions, Beth reviews this chapter of the trauma narrative with Joey by asking questions to clarify the distorted cognitions and feelings he describes.

Beth's sessions with Shirley mirror Joey's during this phase of treatment. She reads Shirley all the material Joey has dictated and helps Shirley separately process her thoughts and feelings about the material. Beth helps Shirley understand how some of the information Joey provides may not feel accurate to Shirley but was his perception at the time of the traumatic incident. Beth also helps Shirley use relaxation and cognitive coping strategies to manage her thoughts and feelings when hearing the story. Finally, Beth helps Shirley consider the places in which Joey is making helpful meaning of his experiences and where he is struggling with unhelpful thoughts. Beth practices with Shirley how she will talk with Joey about these thoughts in the conjoint session after the trauma narrative is completely processed, so she can give him her best response, not her initial response.

After several weeks, the trauma narrative is completed. Beth then engages Joey in a game to find the *bully* in his trauma narrative.

(*continued*)

She has Joey find the places in the narrative where he had unhelpful thoughts (cold prickly thoughts), even if they are accurate; Beth then helps him replace these with more helpful, accurate (warm, fuzzy) thoughts. She also helps him identify places in the narrative where he was brave or smart, either in what he was thinking or what he was doing. Finally, Beth helps Joey consider how his experience can be used to help other kids who have been sexually abused and what he learned about himself and his mother by having this experience. Joey notes he learned that he is a really strong kid and that his mom will always work to keep him safe when he is brave enough to tell her. He exclaims, "I learned that sometimes grown-ups are jerks and will hurt kids and that is not the kid's fault."

When Beth meets with Shirley, Shirley tells Beth she does not want Joey thinking all grown-ups are jerks. Beth role-plays with Shirley how she will help Joey understand that some grown-ups break rules, and that when they do and kids are brave enough to tell other grown-ups, the grown-up who is "being a jerk" (or breaking important safety rules) will be stopped.

After much individual planning with Joey and Shirley, Beth facilitates a *conjoint session* where Joey reads his trauma narrative, including all of his more helpful cognitions, the new helpful ways he feels about his experience, the places he was masterful both then and now, and how he understands his experience in the context of the rest of his life. Shirley praises Joey throughout this process. She tells Joey she is sorry she spanked him when she saw Joey put his mouth on his brother's penis, but she did not understand then what Rick had done to Joey. She tells him that she understands now that Joey was confused about what had happened to him. Shirley says, "It's my job to make sure everyone stays safe and that means no one touches or looks at anyone else's private body parts in our house!" She tells Joey that is why he gets a time-out if he tries to touch his brother's penis. She also praises him, because he has been following all of the touching rules in the house.

In the next session, Beth meets first with Shirley to begin discussing any safety concerns Shirley has about Joey's sexualized behaviors. Beth explains that she will engage Joey in role-play using puppets

(*continued*)

(*continued*)

to provide him with an opportunity to consider safe responses that focus on his newly developing competence (*enhancing future safety and development*). They discuss various situations, such as an adult family member patting his buttocks at a party, an older teen family member or neighbor asking him to do something sexual, accidentally being left alone with his younger brother or another younger child, and several other potential future situations. Beth and Shirley discuss how Shirley would like Joey to respond and also come up with several positive responses Shirley can provide if these situations arise. They practice these responses in preparation for a conjoint session.

Beth then meets individually with Joey and tells him, "Most kids don't know about sexual abuse until it happens to them, so they don't know what to do when it is happening." Beth explains that kids often feel uncomfortable with the perpetrator, even before he or she touches the child. Beth explains this is the child's *uh-oh* feeling at work. Beth tells Joey that perpetrators sometimes do things to trick kids into not listening to their *uh-oh* feelings (*enhancing future safety and development*). She has Joey provide some examples of this. Beth then takes out puppets and engages Joey in role-plays to consider how he can use all of his new expertise to help him when he feels uncomfortable with someone.

During a *conjoint session,* Beth facilitates Joey demonstrating his safety and assertiveness skills in a number of different situations. Beth gives Shirley a "mommy" puppet and Shirley uses her puppet to praise Joey and to act protectively within the role-plays.

Beth then meets individually again with Joey. She asks him to think about any questions he has about his body, other people's bodies, and how relationships work. Joey says he wonders when he will get hair on his penis like Rick had. He also expresses interest in how girls urinate without a penis and why they have blood coming out of their vaginas. Beth praises Joey for thinking of such good questions. She tells him he and his mom will play a game to answer some of those questions in his next session.

Beth then meets individually again with Shirley and explains the questions Joey has about the differences between boys and girls and puberty. Shirley expresses shock and embarrassment that Joey

(*continued*)

seems to know about menstruation. Beth processes with Shirley how she can cultivate an open atmosphere in the home where Joey can ask these types of questions, so he gets accurate, age-appropriate information from her, instead of from his peers.

In this session, Beth also asks Shirley to consider places in Joey's development where his sexual abuse history might resurface in unhelpful ways. Shirley worries adolescence may be difficult. Beth helps Shirley consider the ways in which adolescence may trigger new thoughts and feelings about the sexual abuse and how Shirley can be prepared to helpfully respond. Beth and Shirley review various online and print resources. Like in previous sessions, Beth then facilitates a fun conjoint session where Shirley and Joey compete in a "body talk" quiz game together following the same structure as their earlier games.

As treatment nears completion, Beth gives Shirley the same battery of measures that she completed during the pretreatment assessment. After scoring the measures, Beth shows Shirley all the posttreatment improvement Joey has made, and they look together at the treatment progress. Shirley agrees that Joey has clearly met his treatment goals.

In a conjoint session, Beth suggests the two consider how they would like to celebrate their successful completion of TF-CBT. Joey says, "I want to have a party with cupcakes, balloons, and mommy." Beth agrees to bring the cupcakes and tells Joey he will also be asked to put his hand in paint and put his handprint on a special wall mural in the waiting area for all the kids who have been really scared but learned to *tame their bully*.

In the final conjoint session, Beth, Joey, and Shirley eat cupcakes and celebrate Joey's success. Beth brings the trauma symptom pictures back out and shows Joey how he has worked on shrinking all of his symptoms throughout treatment. She also gives him a *toolkit* from therapy that contains reminders of all of his coping strategies, directions on how to change cold prickly thoughts into warm fuzzy ones, and some of the helpful thoughts he came up with in writing his trauma narrative. The *toolkit* also contains a superhero cape, which Beth explains will remind Joey of how brave, strong, and smart he is. Before he leaves, Joey places his handprint on the mural in the waiting room and leaves wearing his superhero cape.

REFERENCES

Achenbach, T. M., & Rescorla, L. A. (2001). *Manual for the ASEBA school-age forms & profiles*. Burlington, VT: University of Vermont, Research Center for Children, Youth, & Families.

Allen, B., & Johnson, J. C. (2012). Utilization and implementation of trauma-focused cognitive-behavioral therapy for the treatment of maltreated children. *Child Maltreatment, 17*(1), 80–85. http://dx.doi.org/10.1177/1077559511418220

American Psychiatric Association. (2013). *Diagnostic and statistical manual of mental disorders* (5th ed.). Arlington, VA: American Psychiatric Publishing.

BigFoot, D. S., & Schmidt, S. R. (2010). Honoring children, mending the circle: Cultural adaptation of trauma-focused cognitive-behavioral therapy for American Indian and Alaska native children. *Journal of Clinical Psychology, 66*(8), 847–856. http://dx.doi.org/10.1002/jclp.20707

Briere, J. (1996). *Trauma symptom checklist for children*. Lutz, FL: Psychological Assessment Resources.

Briere, J., Johnson, K., Bissada, A., Damon, L., Crouch, J., Gil, E., . . . Ernst, V. (2001). The Trauma Symptom Checklist for Young Children (TSCYC): Reliability and association with abuse exposure in a multi-site study. *Child Abuse & Neglect, 25*(8), 1001–1014. http://www.sciencedirect.com/science/article/pii/S0145213401002538

Cary, C. E., & McMillen, J. C. (2012). The data behind the dissemination: A systematic review of trauma-focused cognitive behavioral therapy for use with children and youth. *Children and Youth Services Review, 34*(4), 748–757. http://dx.doi.org/10.1016/j.childyouth.2012.01.003

Child Welfare Information Gateway. (2012). Trauma-focused cognitive behavioral therapy for children affected by sexual abuse or trauma. Retrieved from https://www.childwelfare.gov/pubs/trauma/

Cohen, J. A., Berliner, L., & Mannarino, A. (2010). Trauma focused CBT for children with co-occurring trauma and behavior problems. *Child Abuse & Neglect, 34*(4), 215–224. http://dx.doi.org/10.1016/j.chiabu.2009.12.003

Cohen, J. A., Deblinger, E., & Mannarino, A. (2004). Trauma-focused cognitive-behavioral therapy for sexually abused children. *Psychiatric Times, 21*(10), 109–121.

Cohen, J. A., Deblinger, E., Mannarino, A. P., & Steer, R. (2004). A multi-site, randomized controlled trial for children with abuse-related PTSD symptoms. *Journal of the American Academy of Child & Adolescent Psychiatry, 43*(4), 393–402.

Cohen, J. A., & Mannarino, A. P. (1993). A treatment model for sexually abused preschoolers. *Journal of Interpersonal Violence, 8*(1), 115–131. http://dx.doi.org/10.1177/088626093008001009

Cohen, J. A., & Mannarino, A. P. (1997). A treatment study for sexually abused preschool children: Outcome during a one-year follow-up. *Journal of the American Academy of Child and Adolescent Psychiatry, 36*(9), 1228–1235. http://www.jaacap.com/article/S0890-8567(09)62648-4/abstract

Cohen, J. A., Mannarino, A. P., & Deblinger, E. (2006). *Treating trauma and traumatic grief in children and adolescents.* New York, NY: Guilford Press.

Cohen, J. A., Mannarino, A. P., & Debinger, E. (Eds.). (2012). *Trauma-focused CBT for children and adolescents: Treatment applications.* New York, NY: Guilford Press.

Cohen, J. A., Mannarino, A. P., & Knudsen, K. (2005). Treating sexually abused children: 1 year follow-up of a randomized controlled trial. *Child Abuse & Neglect, 29*(2), 135–145. http://dx.doi.org/10.1016/j.chiabu.2004.12.005

Cohen, J. A., Mannarino, A. P., Kliethermes, M., & Murray, L. A. (2012). Trauma-focused CBT for youth with complex trauma. *Child Abuse & Neglect, 36*(6), 528–541. http://dx.doi.org/10.1016/j.chiabu.2012.03.007

Cohen, J. A., Mannarino, A. P., & Murray, L. K. (2011). Trauma-focused CBT for youth with ongoing traumas. *Child Abuse & Neglect, 35*, 637–646.

De Arellano, M. A., Davidson, C. K., & Felton, J. W. (2012). Children of Latino descent: Culturally modified TF-CBT. In J. A. Cohen, A. P. Mannarino, & E. Deblinger (Eds.), *Trauma-focused CBT for children and adolescents: Treatment applications* (pp. 253–279). New York, NY: Guilford Press.

Deblinger, E., & Heflin, A. H. (1996). *Treating sexually abused children and their nonoffending parents: A cognitive behavioral approach. Interpersonal violence.* Thousand Oaks, CA: Sage Publications.

Deblinger, E., Lippmann, J., & Steer, R. (1996). Sexually abused children suffering posttraumatic stress symptoms: Initial treatment outcome findings. *Child Maltreatment, 1*(4), 310–321. http://dx.doi.org/10.1177/1077559596001004003

Friedrich, W. N. (1997). *Child sexual behavior inventory: Professional manual.* Lutz, FL: Psychological Assessment Resources.

Goodman, R. (1997). The strengths and difficulties questionnaire: A research note. *Journal of Child Psychology and Psychiatry, 38*(5), 581–586. http://onlinelibrary.wiley.com/doi/10.1111/j.1469-7610.1997.tb01545.x/full

Holmes, M. M., Mudlaff, S. J., & Pillo, C. (2000). *A terrible thing happened.* Washington, DC: Magination Press.

Holt, T., Jensen, T. K., & Wentzel-Larsen, T. (2014). The change and the mediating role of parental emotional reactions and depression in the treatment of traumatized youth: Results from a randomized controlled study. *Child and Adolescent Psychiatry and Mental Health, 8*(1), 11. https://capmh.biomedcentral.com/articles/10.1186/1753-2000-8-11

Jessie, S. (1991). *Please tell!: A child's story about sexual abuse.* Center City, MN: Hazelden.

Markiewicz, J., Ebert, L., Ling, D., Amaya-Jackson, L., & Kisiel, C. (2006). *The learning collaborative toolkit*. Los Angeles, CA, and Durham, NC: National Center for Child Traumatic Stress.

Murray, L. K., Familiar, I., Skavenski, S., Jere, E., Cohen, J., Imasiku, M.,... Bolton, P. (2013). An evaluation of trauma focused cognitive behavioral therapy for children in Zambia. *Child Abuse & Neglect, 37*(12), 1175–1185. http://dx.doi.org/10.1016/j.chiabu.2013.04.017

National Child Traumatic Stress Network. (2012). Empirically supported treatments and promising practices. Retrieved from http://www.nctsn.org/resources/topics/treatments-that-work/promising-practices

Norcross, J. C., & Wampold, B. E. (2011). Evidence-based therapy relationships: Research conclusions and clinical practices. *Psychotherapy, 48*(1), 98–102. http://dx.doi.org/10.1037/a0022161

O'Callaghan, P., McMullen, J., Shannon, C., Rafferty, H., & Black, A. (2013). A randomized controlled trial of trauma-focused cognitive behavioral therapy for sexually exploited, war-affected Congolese girls. *Journal of the American Academy of Child and Adolescent Psychiatry, 52*(4), 359–369. http://dx.doi.org/10.1016/j.jaac.2013.01.013

Pfefferbaum, B., Sweeton, J. L., Nitiéma, P., Noffsinger, M. A., Varma, V., Nelson, S. D., & Newman, E. (2014). Child disaster mental health interventions: Therapy components. *Prehospital and Disaster Medicine, 29*(5), 494–502. http://dx.doi.org/10.1017/S1049023X14000910

Pynoos, R. S., & Steinberg, A. M. (2014). *The UCLA PTSD reaction index for* DSM-5. Los Angeles, CA, and Durham, NC: National Center for Child Traumatic Stress.

Quakley, S., Reynolds, S., & Coker, S. (2004). The effect of cues on young children's abilities to discriminate among thoughts, feelings and behaviours. *Behaviour Research and Therapy, 42*(3), 343–356. http://www.sciencedirect.com/science/article/pii/S0005796703001451

Rogers, C. (1995). *On becoming a person: A therapist's view of psychotherapy*. Boston, MA: Houghton Mifflin.

Saunders, B. E., Berliner, L., & Hanson, R. F. (2003). *Child physical and sexual abuse: Guidelines for treatment. Final report*. Retrieved from http://eric.ed.gov/?id=ED472572

Scheeringa, M. S. (2010). *Young child PTSD checklist*. New Orleans, LA: Tulane University Institute of Infant & Early Childhood Mental Health. http://www.infantinstitute.org/wp-content/uploads/2014/05/YCPC_v5_23_14.pdf

Shirk, S. R., Karver, M. S., & Brown, R. (2011). The alliance in child and adolescent psychotherapy. *Psychotherapy, 48*(1), 17–24. http://dx.doi.org/10.1037/a0022181

CHAPTER 6

Child Parent Relationship Theory

JODIE ELDER

Concerns over the increasing prevalence and severity of children's mental health issues have led to calls for interventions that focus on the family. In a report of the Surgeon General's Conference on Children's Mental Health, the United States' national action agenda included the development of cost-effective, empirically validated prevention and intervention strategies that engage families (U.S. Department of Health and Human Services, 2000). Similarly, during a Surgeon General's workshop on the prevention of child abuse, speakers declared a need for age-appropriate, family-centered, and culturally competent services and reached a consensus that educating parents early is essential in the prevention of child maltreatment (Office of the Surgeon General, 2005). Preliminary evidence already supports the position that the involvement of caregivers in children's mental health treatment amplifies positive outcomes for caregivers and children (Richards, Bowers, Lazicki, Krall, & Jacobs, 2008), and child parent relationship training (CPRT) represents a unique and promising approach helping both.

A form of filial therapy, CPRT teaches parents to use child-centered play therapy (CCPT) skills with their children. Based on attachment theory, CPRT espouses that a secure bond between parent and child is mandatory for children's healthy development. Through a structured, 10-session format that integrates didactic instruction, group processing, and experiential exercises, parents are taught to interact with their children in ways that strengthen the parent–child relationship.

CPRT HISTORY

The roots of CPRT can be traced back to Carl Rogers (1951), whose client-centered approach asserted that a formative tendency exists in all living beings. In the context of genuineness, acceptance, and accurate empathy, this inherent predisposition toward growth and maturity helps individuals to harness their own potential and essentially heal themselves. Rather than applying techniques to induce client change, Rogers believed that "being with" clients in a specific way provided a safe holding environment in which they could overcome obstacles and achieve optimal development.

Virginia Axline (1969), a student of Rogers, applied this client-centered approach to play sessions with children to develop CCPT. Illustrated in her seminal work, *Dibs in Search of Self*, Axline's (1964) methods relied on this specific type of therapeutic relationship as the primary agent of change. Child-centered play therapists communicate acceptance of children, allow children to lead, reflect their feelings, and strive to understand their experiences from their perspective so that children can develop self-trust and self-regulation. Axline (1969) fervently believed in children's capacities to find their own resolutions in their own time, as "the therapist only helps to release what already exists in the child" (Landreth, 2002, p. 86).

These therapeutic conditions between counselor and child began to be tentatively explored between parent and child in the early 1950s. Clark Moustakas (1953) regularly consulted with parents as part of the individual play therapy process, but he also reported actually having a parent in the room while conducting several play therapy sessions due to a child's extreme separation anxiety. Much to his surprise, he discovered that this new presence "seemed to speed up free emotional expression from both mother and child" (p. 103). In 1959, Moustakas described positive results using regular in-home play sessions between parent and child, during which the parent provided a presence similar to the child-centered play therapists. These and other early explorations laid the groundwork for the filial therapy revolution of the mid-1960s.

Influenced by Rogers (1951) and Axline (1947), Bernard Guerney (1964) fully integrated parent–child relationships with CCPT and founded filial therapy. His belief in using parents as primary therapeutic agents in children's healing represented a startling shift from the major assumption in the field at the time, which suggested that parents were the root cause of children's problems (Guerney, 2000). Two paradigm shifts occurring at the time contributed to Guerney's new perspective (Guerney, 2000). First, there were not enough doctoral level clinicians to meet demands for mental health services, so the community mental health movement began and enlisted paraprofessionals to provide services under the supervision of professionals. In this way, more clients could be served, and professionals could spend their valuable time providing more specialized services. Filial therapy applied this paradigm shift to effecting change in the lives of children, as parents were recruited into the treatment of their children in the hopes that more powerful and long-lasting outcomes could be achieved. In addition, working with many parents in a group setting allowed therapists to treat more children in a more time-efficient manner (Guerney, 2000).

A second modification in the dominant discourse revolved around the evolution of family therapy (Guerney, 2000). The prevailing philosophy in mental health treatment during the 1940s was heavily influenced by Freud and rested on the assumption that dysfunction resulted from intrapersonal processes. Therefore, it was believed that treatment should focus on the individual (Gil, 1994; Goldenberg & Goldenberg, 2013; Guerney, 2000). In fact, the inclusion of family members in treatment was considered detrimental to the client. Therefore, treatment in the 1950s entailed a clinician meeting with only the problematic family member and maintaining strict confidentiality. Parents and children were typically treated by separate therapists who collaborated but did not integrate the parent and child together (Guerney, 2000). However, innovators in the family therapy movement, such as Nathan Ackerman, considered the "grandfather of family therapy," and John Bell began meeting with entire families to treat behavior problems in children (Goldenberg & Goldenberg, 2013). This new approach appealed to Guerney and his wife Louise, as they too believed that parents and children could be treated together (Guerney, 2000).

The Guerneys named their approach *filial therapy* because filial means "of or pertaining to a son or a daughter in relation to the parent" (Guerney, 2000, p. 4), but the name later shifted to *group filial therapy* (GFT), *filial family therapy* (FFT), and *child–parent relationship enhancement family therapy* (CREFT; Cornett & Bratton, 2015). They also applied the same therapeutic approach to couples and families with adolescent and adult children, called Relationship Enhancement® Couple/Family Therapy (Guerney, 2000). Louise Guerney (2000) argues that the original name, *filial therapy*, is now the preferred name for this approach.

Guerney (1964) hoped that their innovative approach would accomplish several goals. In theory, training parents to apply CCPT techniques with their children would help children experience parents in new ways, assist children with communicating their needs and desires to the parent through play, and enhance children's self-esteem and confidence. The original model echoes how filial therapy is practiced today. During stage 1 of the intervention, therapists offer an explanation of the approach and didactic instruction about play therapy skills. Parents observe a play session between a therapist and child and then attempt to conduct a play session under therapist supervision. In stage 2, parents implement play sessions with children at home and discuss their experiences in a group using recordings of the sessions when possible. During this phase, the focus shifts from didactic to more emotional processing of parents' reactions to the sessions and skill practice. Last, stage 3 allows for continued practice with collaborative determination of completion and readiness for termination (Guerney, 1964). Filial groups initially met once a week for 2 hours for the course of 1 year (Guerney, 1964). A shorter model is now being used, which produces the same research outcomes, where groups meet once a week for 2 hours for 5 to 6 months (Guerney, 2000; Landreth & Bratton, 2006). Guerney and Ryan (2012) recently published *Group Filial Therapy: The Complete Guide to Teaching Parents to Play Therapeutically With Their Children*, which outlines their method. The Guerneys' approach has also been widely spread through the work of two of their students, VanFleet (2013) and Ginsberg (2004).

In the late 1970s and early 1980s, Garry Landreth introduced the 10-session filial therapy format (Landreth & Bratton, 2006). Landreth was attracted to filial therapy because of its integration of play therapy, group therapy, and teaching, all of which he enjoyed. However, he recognized the difficulty parents experienced with maintaining a long-term commitment to treatment and experimented with different treatment periods. His goal was to reduce the required period of parental commitment and subsequently increase treatment adherence, and he eventually found that parents responded best to a 10-session format (Landreth & Bratton, 2006). Because parents were not familiar with the term *filial therapy*, Landreth changed the name of his approach to Child-Parent-Relationship-Training (C-P-R) in the late 1980s. He later adopted the name Child Parent Relationship Therapy (CPRT), which is the focus of this chapter. In 2006, Landreth and Bratton published *Child Parent Relationship Therapy (CPRT): A 10-Session Filial Therapy Model*, a textbook that provides a rationale for filial therapy, an in-depth explanation of the 10-session model, case studies, and a review of the supporting literature. Bratton, Landreth, Kellam, and Blackard (2006) developed a corresponding treatment manual, which is designed to support practitioners' implementation of the model and to assist researchers with ensuring standardization of treatment protocols (Bratton, Landreth, & Lin, 2010; Bratton, Opiola, & Dafoe, 2015). The manual includes the 10-session training protocol, therapist's guide, parent notebook with handouts, supplemental resources, and a CD with parent training materials.

Although nondirective play therapy approaches certainly permeate the history of CPRT, filial therapy is classified as a directive approach (Gil, 1994). Directive therapies are more short-term, symptom-oriented approaches that invite therapists to be more leading in the therapeutic process. Gil (1994) asserts that both directive and nondirective approaches "are equally useful and can be used in an integrative framework" (p. 14). Filial therapy and, by extension, CPRT represent a particularly ingenious blend of directive and nondirective techniques. Therapists use didactic instruction to educate parents and supervision to develop parents' CCPT skills, while simultaneously harnessing the power of nondirective play therapy to heal the relationship between parent and child. Incorporating both directive and nondirective techniques allows therapists to capitalize on the strengths of both approaches and empower parents to "become the primary change agents" with their own children (Landreth & Bratton, 2006, p. 7).

Rationale for Integrating Family Therapy With Child Therapy

Pioneers in the field of play therapy have long recognized the value of a systemic approach and advocated for the integration of play and family therapy. Family therapists Napier and Whitaker (1978) asserted that "working directly with the totality of the forces that influence the individual is such a logical idea that it is hard to deny its validity" (p. 59). Although they appreciated the positive outcomes created from working with individuals, they found it almost heretical to ignore the powerful impact of addressing individuals in the context of their relationships. Similarly, Landreth stated, "The skills of those in the mental health professions must be given away through training to parents, who are in the best position to profoundly impact the lives of future adults" (Landreth & Bratton, 2006, p. 1). One of the major tenets of filial therapy rests on the assumption that the parent–child relationship is central to a child's effective functioning and therefore should be the focus of treatment, which is itself a systemic concept.

In fact, Guerney and Guerney (1987) cautioned against working solely with individual children and outlined the potential damage of this approach. In play therapy, a strong therapeutic relationship with the child is essential in order to effect change. Ironically, this very bond can engender jealousy on the part of the parent, who often already feels as if his or her personal failure has contributed to the child's problems. Given that parents solely hold the power to discontinue the child's therapy at any time, filial therapy harnesses this parental power and elicits parent involvement as a vital component of the restorative process in an effort to increase the likelihood of continued treatment (Guerney, 1964; Guerney & Guerney, 1987). In addition, while the therapist and child work diligently to build new skills and create behavioral changes, parents who are not involved can consciously or unconsciously use their formidable influence to cause regression in children's behavior (Guerney & Guerney, 1987).

Guerney and Guerney (1987) offered four characteristics of interventions that successfully integrate child and family therapy and provided evidence to support the assertion that filial therapy meets all of these criteria. First, the child is empowered as a full participant. Traditional family therapy focuses on discussing interpersonal dynamics, and, in doing so, inherently excludes the equal participation of young children who are not developmentally able to contribute to these discussions. Gil (1994) asserted the importance of integrating young children into family therapy, instead of giving them something to "keep them busy" while working with older children and parents:

> My basic contention is that adults must stop inflicting adult interactions on children and making demands that children participate in ways they cannot successfully negotiate. Instead, I encourage clinicians to enter, and direct parents to enter, the world of children, thereby offering them opportunities for rich and reciprocal emotional contact with the adult world. (pp. 37–38)

Filial therapy uses the child's natural language of play and consequently allows full engagement of the child in the healing process (Guerney & Guerney, 1987).

Second, Guerney and Guerney (1987) suggest that effective approaches must simultaneously address personal factors affecting the functioning of both the child and the parent. Interestingly, parents' struggles with the facilitation of play sessions often mirror their parenting struggles in everyday life (Bratton et al., 2015; Guerney & Guerney, 1987). Processing these struggles in the context of a didactic environment with the focus on acquiring new skills allows them to tackle these issues in a much less defensive manner than in the corrective atmosphere sometimes present in traditional family therapy. Insights can lead to permanent shifts in parents internally as well as in the parent–child relationship (Guerney, 1964). Filial therapy not only allows the child to work through internal struggles during play sessions, but also provides space for parents to express their struggles during the supervision process.

A third criterion requires that interventions integrating child and family therapy must also promote change in the family system (Guerney & Guerney, 1987). In the terminology of the family systems approach, effective family therapy does not settle for first-order change, or superficial behavioral changes, but instead seeks to create second-order change, a reorganization of the family structure and interaction patterns that result in more effective levels of functioning (Goldenberg & Goldenberg, 2013). Ample evidence exists to support filial therapy's profound impact on parent–child relationships, such as improved parental acceptance of children, increased empathic responses to children, and decreased parent–child relationship stress (Bratton et al., 2010).

Finally, the approach should pursue both intrapsychic and systemic changes concurrently (Guerney & Guerney, 1987). Changes in individuals and the family work together to enhance, rather than counteract, one another. Through filial therapy, parents become more responsive to their children's needs, which allows children to experience their parents in new and exciting ways. Once children learn to trust this new way of being, they often begin to experiment with new, more adaptive behaviors, thereby resulting in a reduction of parent–child relationship stress (Bratton et al., 2010, 2015). Reciprocal individual changes, therefore, amplify each other, as well as changes in the entire system.

In summary, filial therapy represents a powerful integration of child and family therapy. Not only does the use of CCPT allow children to participate in meaningful and developmentally appropriate ways, but the critical element of parental involvement results in synergistic changes in the intrapersonal, interpersonal, and systemic facets of families.

FILIAL THERAPY DEFINITION AND GOALS

In the CPRT model, filial therapy is defined as:

> A unique approach used by professionals trained in play therapy to train parents to be therapeutic agents with their own children through a format of didactic instruction, demonstration

> play sessions, required at-home laboratory play sessions, and supervision in a supportive atmosphere. Parents are taught basic child-centered play therapy principles and skills including reflective listening, recognizing and responding to children's feelings, therapeutic limit setting, building children's self-esteem, and structuring required weekly play sessions with their children using a special kit of selected toys. (Landreth & Bratton, 2006, p. 11)

The primary objective of CPRT is to increase the security of the parent–child bond by teaching parents to relate to children in ways that engage their innate capacity for self-healing (Bratton et al., 2015; Landreth & Bratton, 2006).

Expectations for children's healing in CPRT exceeds the typical emphasis on the reduction of symptoms and includes outcomes, such as increased problem-solving skills, more self-directed behavior, and improved self-esteem. CPRT strives to help children express their needs and feelings, regulate their emotions, and develop more adaptive ways to ensure that their needs are met (Bratton et al., 2015; Landreth & Bratton, 2006).

Coveted changes in parents who participate in CPRT focus on increased parenting skills and self-efficacy, increased understanding of and affection for their child, the development of insight into themselves as they relate to their child, and reconnection with the joys of parenting (Bratton et al., 2015; Landreth & Bratton, 2006). Parents whose children need therapy often blame themselves, and this sense of inadequacy strongly influences their ability to interact in positive ways with their children. CPRT strives to encourage and support parents in the acquisition of new skills so that they can feel more capable in their relationships with their children, experience increased self-acceptance, and consequently be more accepting of their children (Landreth & Bratton, 2006).

Moreover, CPRT aims to promote changes in the parent–child relationship and the entire family system. This intervention not only allows parents to change negative perceptions of their children by understanding and seeing the world through their children's eyes (Landreth & Bratton, 2006), but also permits children to experience parents in new ways through the safe holding environment of the play sessions (Bratton et al., 2015). In this way, CPRT yields enhanced parent–child bonds that serve a preventive function, as both parents and children are better able to manage stressors in the future using their newly developed perceptions and skills (Bratton, Ray, Rhine, & Jones, 2005; Bratton et al., 2015; Cornett & Bratton, 2014).

Principles and Theories Underlying CPRT

The foundation of filial therapy rests on attachment theory (Bratton et al., 2015). Described as empathic, calm, and consistent, the presence of an emotionally responsive caregiver significantly impacts not only children's social and emotional development (Sunderland, 2006), but also their executive functioning (Bernier, Beauchamp, Carlson, & Lalonde, 2015). Because of their primary attachment role, parents are a more powerful influence on children's development than therapists (Guerney, 1964; VanFleet, 2013). Filial therapy is based on the assumption that a secure parent–child relationship is vital for children's optimal health, so it focuses on bolstering this relationship through the transfer of CCPT skills from therapist to parent.

Although it is understood that parental stress can inhibit their ability to provide an environment supportive of children's growth, the founders of filial therapy adopted the position that child problems result from lack of parental skill and knowledge (Guerney, 2000). CPRT also believes that parents have the capacity to learn the skills needed to build a secure parent–child relationship and that once they have done so, children's maladaptive behaviors will self-correct (Bratton et al., 2015). This positive attribution to parents beckons them to become involved in the healing process and empowers them to grow and change.

Philosophies originating from Rogers' (1951) person-centered and Axline's (1969) CCPT approaches permeate filial therapy. Rooted in Rogers' (1951) formative tendency, both CCPT (Axline, 1969) and CPRT (Landreth & Bratton, 2006) espouse that children's behavior is always growth directed and will self-correct in the context of a secure relationship. Similarly, Rogers' phenomenological approach is reflected in CPRT's emphasis on understanding the child's world from his or her perspective. CPRT implores parents to "look through the child's eyes" (Landreth & Bratton, 2006, p. 4) to enhance understanding of and connection with the child. As filial therapy essentially teaches parents CCPT skills, the influence of CCPT is readily apparent. More important than the technical skills associated with CCPT is the parents' fundamental presence. The "Be-With" attitudes (I am here, I hear you, I understand, and I care) communicate respect and treasuring of children (Landreth, 2002), and this rare and coveted engagement forms the foundation for the healing process. During the playtimes, parents focus only on the child and his or her experiences, not on their problems or fixing them.

Finally, CPRT acknowledges the significance of play in children's development. Landreth's (2002, p. 27) oft-quoted phrase, "Birds fly. Fish swim.

Children play" illustrates the essential nature of play in children's lives. In fact, Landreth (2002) asserts that "the natural medium of communication for children is play and activity," (p. 9) and CPRT enables parents to connect with children in developmentally appropriate ways through play. Because children are not able to use abstract reasoning until around age 11 years (Piaget, 1962), efforts to bond with them through verbal expression before this age prove ineffective. Instead, adults must crawl into the concrete world of children's play (Landreth, 2002; Piaget, 1962). Although parents are taught to honor the symbolic significance of their children's play, the interpretation and understanding of the symbolic meanings are not emphasized or required (Landreth & Bratton, 2006).

Contraindications

CPRT is more effective than CCPT in a shorter period of time and is applicable to a wide range of parents and presenting problems (Landreth & Bratton, 2006). However, in certain circumstances, treating the child individually in CCPT may be a more appropriate intervention. For instance, CPRT is contraindicated if parents lack the motivation or resources to commit to the process. In total, CPRT requires parents to attend an intake session, participate in filial group for a minimum of 20 hours over 10 weeks, and conduct 3½ hours of at-home play sessions. Common factors inhibiting parents' ability to adhere to this significant commitment include guilt, resentment, time, money, and effort (Bratton et al., 2005). In addition, parents' own stress and emotional condition may at times be too consuming to allow them to focus on the needs of the child, and they may need their own individual therapy. Finally, when a child's emotional disturbance is too extreme for the parent to provide the structure and safe holding environment essential to the play sessions, CCPT is warranted (Bratton et al., 2005; Landreth & Bratton, 2006).

ROLE OF THERAPIST

The facilitation of CPRT groups requires extensive preparation (Landreth & Bratton, 2006). To begin, therapists must be a master's level licensed mental health professional with both specialized training and clinical experience in CCPT. In addition, training in group therapy as well as the facilitation of the CPRT model are required (Bratton et al., 2015; Landreth & Bratton, 2006). Landreth and Bratton argue that all of these elements are critical to adequately prepare a clinician to teach parents in a group setting to use play therapy skills. For instance, to become a filial therapist through the University of North Texas, graduate students must take an Introduction to Play Therapy course with a supervised practicum component, a Group Play Therapy course with a supervised practicum component, and finally a Filial Therapy course with a 10-session filial therapy supervised practicum (Landreth & Bratton, 2006).

Filial therapists play many roles, including play therapy trainer, supervisor, group facilitator, and mentor (Bratton et al., 2015). Supervision assists new filial therapists with managing these roles and the tasks associated with each. In addition, Landreth and Bratton (2006) emphasized that supervision of new filial therapists should focus on personal awareness and insight, because "parents are impacted much more by the person of the therapist than by the knowledge of the therapist" (p. 37). Just as filial therapy trains parents to work through their own internal struggles to promote acceptance of the child, filial therapists should wrestle in supervision with their own feelings and beliefs that interfere with their ability to provide an accepting and supportive environment for parents.

In some ways, CPRT relieves pressure from therapists because in this model therapists are not the central person responsible for creating family change (Bratton et al., 2015). However, therapists are held accountable for both teaching new concepts and facilitating parental insight, and they often find it challenging to balance the didactic and process components of the group (Bratton et al., 2015; Landreth & Bratton, 2006). To help balance these tasks, Landreth and Bratton suggest using coleaders. Although this structure requires frequent and honest communication between coleaders to be effective, it offers the advantages of having another set of "clinical eyes" on the parents and the group process, helps to ensure that the didactic parts of the material are covered, and allows more time for therapist self-reflection.

CPRT MODEL

Materials

Materials needed for the facilitation of CPRT include the CPRT textbook by Landreth and Bratton (2006) and the CPRT treatment manual by Bratton et al. (2006). The manual includes a 10-session training protocol, therapist's notebook and study guide, parent notebook, supplemental resources, and a CD-ROM with all parent training materials. The

University of North Texas Center for Play Therapy also offers a demonstration video titled *Child Parent Relationship Therapy (CPRT) in Action*, in which Landreth and Bratton facilitate a CPRT group. Finally, CPRT facilitators will need the required toys and play therapy materials with which to demonstrate CCPT skills during group sessions.

Overview and Structure

CPRT groups typically include six to eight parents who meet once a week for 2 hours over the course of 10 weeks (Bratton et al., 2015; Landreth & Bratton, 2006). Because essential material is covered each week, groups are closed, and new parents are not allowed to join once groups begin (Landreth & Bratton, 2006). Ideally, groups are held in a setting with a two-way mirror for live demonstrations, and child care is provided.

Although CPRT is most effective for children aged 2 to 10 years, it can be adapted for older children. Applying the same CCPT skills during developmentally appropriate activities, such as baking cookies and building projects, can improve parent–child relationships as well (Landreth & Bratton, 2006).

Heterogeneous groups, where parents are together with other parents whose children are struggling with different issues, are preferred (Landreth & Bratton, 2006). Parents often benefit from hearing different perspectives on their children, and this advantage may not occur if parents in the group all feel stuck in the same challenges.

Although the traditional CPRT format involves one 2-hour session per week for 10 weeks, the schedule can be amended as needed to meet the needs of families (Bratton et al., 2015; Guerney, 2000; Landreth & Bratton, 2006). In fact, Landreth and Bratton described several possible variations of the 10-session CPRT model, including meeting twice-a-week for 5 weeks, twice weekly for 45 minutes over 10 weeks, every day (12 sessions in 14 days), four consecutive Saturdays, and 1 hour per week over 10 weeks with individual parents and couples. Initial investigations support the efficacy of these variations. For instance, Ferrell (2004) found similar significant improvements in parental self-acceptance, empathic responses to children, and child behavioral problems when comparing an intensive 4-week CPRT format to the traditional 10-week format. Although the timing and logistics may change, Landreth and Bratton emphasized that therapists should preserve the content of the curriculum in order to achieve results similar to those found using the traditional CPRT model.

CPRT represents a combination of educational, interactive, and experiential processes, and group processing for parents is a vital component of this model. Guerney (2000) reported discovering during the founding of filial therapy that "through play with their child and the processing of it with the therapist, parents seemed to open up relationship issues in a way that typical parent therapies did not elicit" (p. 8). Landreth and Bratton (2006) concur, as they noted that during group processing, parents often identify personal issues, perhaps wounds from their own experiences as children, which are currently interfering with their ability to effectively relate to their children. Not only do therapists provide valuable feedback, but hearing other parents' struggles normalizes their own and helps parents feel less defensive and isolated (Landreth & Bratton, 2006). Parents' ability to process their own emotional reactions and beliefs during the group enables them to more fully grasp the material and implement new skills with their children (Landreth & Bratton, 2006). Eardley's (1978) research supports the critical nature of the processing component, as he found that a strictly didactic approach with only therapist feedback about play sessions was not as effective when compared with a filial approach that integrated both skill building and group processing for parents.

Notwithstanding the power of the group process, therapists must also ensure that specific skills are taught and practiced during group time. Teaching strategies suggested by Landreth and Bratton include repetition of important material, using stories and analogies to illustrate points, providing concrete examples, modeling skills for parents, focusing on strengths when reviewing videotapes, affirming parents' efforts to try new skills, and identifying shifts in parent and child behavior. The CPRT model and treatment manual provide concise handouts and simple homework assignments to enhance the likelihood of parent success, therefore resulting in increased parent self-efficacy and continued engagement with the training process (Bratton et al., 2006; Landreth & Bratton, 2006). To this end, the model also uses simple "Rules of Thumb" that illustrate important concepts in ways that are easy to understand and retain (Bratton et al., 2006).

The experiential component of CPRT relies on demonstration, role-play, and at-home play sessions (Bratton et al., 2015). CCPT skills are initially shown to parents through either video of a CCPT play session or live demonstration by the therapist, and parents then role-play the new skills with each other. For the at-home playtimes, parents set up a specific group of toys in a designated area and conduct 30-minute play sessions once per week, during which they apply CCPT attitudes and skills.

Videos of play sessions are shown in the group, and parents receive supervision from the therapist and feedback from other group members (Bratton et al., 2015). Seeing themselves and other parents is an invaluable tool to promote learning and change because parents are often not cognizant of the negative nature in which they communicate with their children, and parental self-report of play sessions is often biased (Landreth & Bratton, 2006). Not only does the process of reviewing videos promote parent accountability, but it also enhances personal and vicarious learning (Bratton et al., 2015).

Landreth and Bratton (2006) encourage meeting with individual parents to ensure their appropriateness for the group. During these screening sessions, therapists explain CPRT and address parent questions, gather background information, and assist parents with selecting the child with whom they will conduct special playtimes. In addition, administrative issues, such as fees and informed consent, are managed at this time, so they do not infringe on the first group meeting (Landreth & Bratton, 2006).

Sessions 1 to 3

The first three sessions focus on building a safe container and connecting parents. The ultimate goal is for parents to internalize the acceptance they experience in the group, resulting in increased acceptance of themselves and thus increased acceptance of their children (Bratton et al., 2015). Techniques used to enhance group cohesiveness include normalizing parent struggles, linking parents' struggles and experiences, inviting parents to respond to each other's questions, and encouraging parents to express their feelings more thoroughly (Landreth & Bratton, 2006).

Therapists must also be mindful of the strong didactic component in these introductory sessions (Bratton et al., 2015). This part of the curriculum covers basic CCPT principles and skills, such as the CCPT "Be-With" attitudes (I am here, I hear you, I understand, and I care), structuring, following the child's lead, reflection of feelings, and reflection of verbal and nonverbal content of children's play (Bratton et al., 2015; Landreth & Bratton, 2006). Therapists also provide a list of toys for the special playtimes and explain the reasoning for reach (Landreth & Bratton, 2006). To help parents grasp the concepts, therapists demonstrate or show video of a typical play session and lead parents in role-playing with each other. After session 3, parents are expected to conduct their first at-home play session (Landreth & Bratton, 2006).

Sessions 4 to 8

Sessions 4 through 8 emphasize the continual development of CCPT skills and the processing of at-home play sessions (Landreth & Bratton, 2006). As at-home play sessions begin after session 3, each parent conducts a total of seven 30-minute playtimes with his or her child over the course of the 10-week treatment program. Each week, two parents review their tapes with the group (Bratton et al., 2015), and the therapist's role is to identify at least one positive aspect of the at-home play session for each parent. In doing so, therapists model for parents the strengths-based approach they are encouraged to use in their perceptions of themselves and their children (Landreth & Bratton, 2006). During this supervision process, therapists role-play with parents to help them work through times when they struggled with responses during their 30-minute play sessions (Bratton et al., 2015).

Further skill development in these sessions includes limit setting, choice giving, encouragement, and self-esteem-building responses (Bratton et al., 2015; Landreth & Bratton, 2006). Initially, parents are instructed to restrict their skill practice to the 30-minute play sessions, as gradual implementation of the skills helps improve their chances of success (Bratton et al., 2015; Landreth & Bratton, 2006).

Sessions 9 to 10

Sessions 9 and 10 continue the reviews of at-home play session videos and begin discussing with parents how to generalize the CCPT skills to everyday interactions with their children (Bratton et al., 2015; Landreth & Bratton, 2006). Session 10 includes a review and reflection on progress in both parents and children, and therapists bolster parent self-efficacy by encouraging them to take credit for their child's improvements (Bratton et al., 2015). Certificates of completion are provided, and parents are encouraged to continue play sessions after termination and even sign a contract indicating their commitment to do so (Landreth & Bratton, 2006). Therapists may reinforce learning by conducting 1-month and 3-month follow-up group sessions (Bratton et al., 2015).

RESEARCH SUPPORT

Filial therapy outcomes were initially investigated in the late 1960s by the Guerneys under a grant from the National Institute for Mental Health (NIMH; Guerney, 2000). Using their filial therapy model over 1 year of treatment with 71 mothers of children with behavioral and emotional problems, the Guerneys and their team found that children showed a reduction in symptoms and mothers increased their ability to respond empathically to and offer acceptance of their children (Guerney, 2000). This preliminary investigation provided exciting results for this promising new approach.

As interest in play therapy increased in the mid-1980s, so too did professionals' interest in filial therapy. The formation of the Association for Play Therapy, the increased general acceptance of working with families rather than individuals, and Landreth's development of the 10-session CPRT model all contributed to the upswing in filial therapy's popularity (Guerney, 2000). Empirical studies of CPRT began in the early 1990s, and since that time, its efficacy has been thoroughly investigated and documented.

In a meta-analysis of 93 studies covering almost five decades, Bratton et al. (2005) found that filial therapy in general produced stronger positive effects on children's behavior, social adjustment, and personality than traditional CCPT facilitated by a trained therapist and did so in a shorter time frame. Additional analysis revealed that adhering to the Guerney and Landreth models of filial therapy with parents generated even larger effect sizes (Bratton et al., 2005). Bratton et al. (2010) further analyzed the data from Bratton et al. (2005) to reveal that the largest effect sizes were produced when researchers specifically implemented the 10-session CPRT model with parents. These results fit well with managed care expectations for short-term interventions that have been empirically validated (Landreth & Bratton, 2006).

In an effort to introduce even more robust empirical support for CPRT, Bratton et al. (2010) conducted an extensive review of CPRT literature limited only to studies using a control or comparison group. In total, 32 studies with 916 participants were included. Published between 1995 and 2010, 13 of the studies employed an experimental design, and the remainder used a quasi-experimental design due to lack of random assignment. Most investigated the effects of teaching CCPT techniques to parents, but one third of the studies examined the effects of training teachers and student mentors. Of the 23 studies focusing on parents, 12 gathered outcome data using independent raters, which allowed them to circumvent the complications of self-report data and lend further reliability to their findings. The children in the studies ranged in age from 3 to 10 years, with a mean age of 5.5 years. The superiority of CPRT interventions over control groups was evident in the moderate to large effect sizes produced in these studies (Bratton et al., 2010). Improvements in children included decreases in both internalizing and externalizing behavior problems and increased self-esteem. Parent changes involved improved ability to accept children's need for autonomy and self-direction, and progress in parent–child relationships focused on increases in parents' empathic interactions with their children, reduced parent–child relationship stress, and increased parental acceptance of children. Similar results were found in a more recent meta-analysis, in which Lin and Bratton (2015) confirmed the amplification of treatment outcomes with caregiver involvement. Of the 52 studies of CCPT included in the review, 24 studies that used partial or no caregiver involvement, defined as only periodic consultation or complete exclusion from the treatment process, resulted in statistically significantly lower effect sizes than the 24 studies that used full caregiver involvement, defined as filial therapy. These results illustrate that the CPRT model clearly and significantly enhances the lives of children and parents.

Reviews of filial therapy literature not only reinforce the ability of CPRT to produce positive outcomes for children, parents, and parent–child relationships, but also support its use in multiple settings to address a variety of treatment issues (Bratton et al., 2010; Cornett & Bratton, 2015; Landreth & Bratton, 2006). Bratton et al. (2010) found CPRT produced significant results when implemented in mental health treatment centers, schools, hospitals, churches, shelters, prisons, and Head Start programs. They also provided evidence for its efficacy with diverse presenting issues, including children deemed "at-risk" due to behavioral problems, children whose parents were incarcerated, and children struggling with developmental disorders, learning disabilities, attachment problems, witnessing domestic violence, chronic illnesses, and sexual abuse. In their review of 50 years of filial therapy research, Cornett and Bratton (2015) extended this list to include children diagnosed with selective mutism and intellectual disabilities, as well as children whose parents were mandated to therapy for child maltreatment.

CPRT also yields promising results for persons from many different ethnicities, backgrounds, and family structures. Combining the results of Landreth and Bratton's (2006) review of 33 studies involving more than 800 participants with Cornett and Bratton's review of 50 years of research, filial therapy has consistently shown positive outcomes for diverse parents, including: Native American, Hispanic, Israeli, Jamaican, Korean, African American, German, Iranian, and Sudanese parents, as well as immigrant parents of Hispanic, Chinese, and Korean descent. Significant results have also been found with parents in various family structures, such as single parents (Bratton & Landreth, 1995), married parents, adolescent parents, adoptive and foster parents, blended families, custodial grandparents, and divorcing parents. Finally, CPRT's effectiveness has also been demonstrated with nonoffending parents of sexually abused children, incarcerated mothers and fathers, and parents referred by Child Protective Services (Cornett & Bratton, 2015).

As has been intimated in the literature, preliminary studies indicate that CPRT positively impacts not only the parent–child relationship, but also family functioning as a whole. Using a single case study design, Cornett and Bratton (2014) investigated the impact of CPRT on eight families, consisting of 15 parents and 17 children ages 2 to 13 years. Families rated not only their perceptions of changes in overall family functioning, but also observed behavior changes in target areas, such as emotional responsiveness, discipline, and encouragement. Statistically significant improvement was observed in the target areas, and practically significant changes occurred in cohesion, flexibility, communication, and satisfaction. Due to its small sample size, lack of random sampling, and lack of reliability and validity of the rating scales, the results of this study merit only cautious generalization. However, the results provide encouraging preliminary support for the supposition that CPRT transforms entire families.

CONCLUSION

More than 50 years of empirical evidence provides support for the efficacy of filial therapy in changing the lives of parents, children, and families. With its directive, structured, 10-session format integrating education, processing, and supervision, CPRT offers parents and children the opportunity to experience each other in new and exciting ways that result in strengthened parent–child bonds and decreased maladaptive symptoms in children. CPRT's emphasis on play engages children and their caregivers in age-appropriate, family-centered ways, and it provides a resounding response to the call for cost-effective, empirically validated strategies that engage families to address the mental health needs of children (U.S. Department of Health and Human Services, 2000).

RECOMMENDED RESOURCES

For further investigation consider these resources: *Child Parent Relationship Therapy (CPRT) Treatment Manual: A 10-Session Filial Therapy Model for Training Parents* by Bratton, Landreth, Kellam, and Blackard (2006) and *Child Parent Relationship Therapy (CPRT): A 10-Session Filial Therapy Model* by Landreth and Bratton (2006).

CASE EXAMPLE: SARAH'S STORY

Sarah was a 6-year-old, Hispanic female in the first grade when she was referred to the clinic by her school counselor. Her teacher described Sarah as defiant and reported that she would often talk back and break class rules. As a result, Sarah was frequently sent home with "yellow" or "red" ratings in her daily behavior chart. Both the Child Behavior Checklist (CBCL; Achenbach & Rescorla, 2001) completed by her mother and the CBCL-Teacher Report Form (CBCL-TRF; Achenbach & Rescorla, 2001) completed by her teacher were high for externalizing behaviors, such as arguing a lot, breaking rules, refusing to comply, and temper tantrums. Sarah's academic performance was average or below average for most subjects, but the teacher commented that this was mostly due to noncompliance, because Sarah was intellectually capable of doing the work when she chose to do it. Her teacher and mother reported that she did not have many friends, and they both attributed this to her lack of social skills, in that her interpersonal bossiness and insistence on having her own way prevented her from forming lasting relationships.

The counselor, Joan, conducted an initial assessment with Sarah's mother, Mary, who was a 23-year-old Hispanic woman with one child. Mary became pregnant with Sarah at age 16 years, at which time she dropped out of high school and began living with Sarah's father and his family. Their relationship was conflictual, and Mary and Sarah's father split when Sarah was 3 years old. Sarah still had contact with her father through an every other weekend visitation schedule, with which Mary reported he was consistent. Mary later completed her high school equivalency degree and was working full time as a medical receptionist. At the time of the intake, Mary and Sarah were living with Mary's partner of 2 years, but Mary reported that he was not very involved with the discipline of Sarah, leaving the management of the child mostly to Mary. Throughout this time, Mary had continued close contact with her family who lived only 10 minutes from her. Sarah's maternal grandmother often kept Sarah until Mary got home from work, and Mary reported that Sarah was challenging and often tried to usurp adult power with her grandmother as well. Mary reported that she had tried giving rewards for green days at school and good behavior at home with no success. Mary reported

(*continued*)

(*continued*)

significant anger and frustration with Sarah and reported feeling hopeless that there would be any improvement. She attributed the problems to Sarah's character, in that Mary perceived Sarah as being "determined to be the center of attention at all times" and "not happy unless she's making someone mad." When asked if this behavior represented a change from previous behavior, Mary reported that Sarah had been "demanding from birth." When Joan asked how Mary and Sarah spent time together, Mary reported being busy with her full-time job and explained that most of her time with Sarah was spent in power struggles, such as trying to get Sarah to come to the dinner table, eat her food, take a bath, and clean her room. Mary reported that even when she did try to play with Sarah, the play typically ended in a conflict between the two of them because Sarah "always tries to order me around."

In order to assess the parent–child dynamics, Joan introduced a family puppet interview during the intake session (Gil, 1994). Mary and Sarah were provided a group of puppets and were given instructions to create an original story with a beginning, middle, and end and then act out the story using their chosen puppets. Sarah immediately began exploring the various puppets, while Mary seemed a bit hesitant to get involved, only half-heartedly sorting through the puppets. Sarah developed an idea and with excitement began instructing her mother about the characters and actions. Mary accepted the character assigned to her by Sarah but suggested a different idea for how her character would respond in the story. Their conflict soon escalated from a simple disagreement to an all-out battle, with Mary first trying to persuade Sarah with an explanation and then pleading with Sarah to let her character do what she wanted. Finally, Sarah began crying and screaming at her mother, while Mary looked at Joan with defeat in her eyes and stated, "This is what I'm talking about. She always has to have her way."

CPRT was chosen as the most appropriate intervention for Sarah and Mary. Although the referral originated from school, the assessment indicated that Sarah's misbehaviors originated at home before Sarah entered a school setting. In addition, the teacher's report that

(*continued*)

Sarah was intellectually capable of performing at her academic grade level ruled out the possibility that Sarah's behavior was an expression of frustration or an attempt to mask her inability to do the work. Finally, Mary's persistent negative perceptions of Sarah and the therapist's observations of the family puppet interview suggested significant deficits in the parent–child relationship were the likely cause of Sarah's oppositional behavior.

Once Joan had explained the recommendation of CPRT and the model to Mary, she expressed reservations about the process. Mary did not understand how something as simple as playing with Sarah would change her misbehaviors, and she was frustrated about the time and energy it would require of her. First Joan normalized her confusion by admitting that it sounded deceptively simple. However, Joan then reframed the play as an opportunity to be with Sarah in a very different way than either of them was accustomed to and emphasized that this different way of "being with" Sarah was the key to change (Landreth & Bratton, 2006). In response to Mary's concerns about the time commitment, Joan accepted her feeling somewhat resentful of what the CPRT process would require of her, given that she felt that Sarah was the one who needed to change. Joan also reflected Mary's feelings of hopelessness about her own ability to effect any change in Sarah. At the same time, Joan emphasized that, as her mother, Mary was the most important figure in Sarah's life and therefore had the capacity to impact her more than anyone, even a trained therapist. She reiterated that in the group sessions, Mary would be learning skills for improving her relationship with Sarah that she could apply for the rest of her life, and that empowering her in this way was the best way to make sure that changes in Sarah were maintained over time. Despite her reservations, Mary agreed to begin the sessions the following week.

Session 1

During session 1, Mary was initially somewhat reserved and nonverbal. However, when another mother reported feeling very out

(*continued*)

(*continued*)

of control with her child, Mary quickly chimed in and complained that she felt Sarah had too much control. Her wish was for Sarah to learn to obey her and other adults. Joan used this moment as an opportunity to explain one of the CPRT Rules of Thumb, "Be a thermostat, not a thermometer" (Landreth & Bratton, 2006, p. 134). This rule emphasizes the importance of parents responding, rather than reacting, to their children. By maintaining a calm but firm presence, parents actually maintain control of the situation and model self-control for their children. Mary admitted that she often got so frustrated with Sarah that "I get sucked into fighting with her," and many of the other parents disclosed similar experiences. First, to create a safe environment and to model acceptance, Joan normalized parents' frustrations with child misbehaviors and reflected their feelings that children seem to know just the right buttons to push to anger parents. Then Joan also reframed the concept of control from regulating kids to maintaining self-control, and this new approach helped Mary to understand the impact of her choices and to have some sense of power and hope of success. Although she may not be able to control Sarah's behavior, changing her own behavior was definitely possible. Joan also explained that altering her responses to Sarah would change Sarah's responses to her. Although Mary remained somewhat skeptical of Sarah's behavior change, she was willing to focus on her own responses. Being in a group setting also helped Mary, as she benefitted from hearing that she was not alone and that other parents also felt extreme frustration with their children.

Session 3

Another turning point for Mary came in session 3, when Joan was teaching the concept of letting the child lead the play session. In CPRT, as in traditional CCPT, parents are taught to follow the child's lead and allow the child to direct the play (Landreth, 2002; Landreth & Bratton, 2006). Mary challenged Joan about this point and expressed concern that letting Sarah lead during the play sessions might reinforce Sarah's belief that she is in charge and only

(continued)

strengthen her demand for control outside of the play sessions. After reflecting and validating Mary's concerns, Joan explained that from a child's perspective, grownups are always in charge, telling them what to do and how to do it. Most children feel they have very little power in their lives, and Mary agreed that Sarah was constantly being redirected by some adult in her life due to her bad behavior. Joan explained that letting Sarah lead during the special playtimes allows her to experiment with making her own decisions and taking responsibility, rather than having a parent impose control on her, which will eventually change her perception of herself from being inadequate and incapable to a belief that she is capable of leading, being responsible, and using self-control (Landreth & Bratton, 2006). Joan further clarified that while the child does take the lead, the parent does not relinquish all control during the sessions. First, parents start each session by saying, "You can play with the toys in lots of ways that you want," not "any way that you want," because there are limits on children's behaviors. Using the ACT limit-setting formula (acknowledge the feeling, communicate the limit, target acceptable alternatives), parents set limits on behavior during the playtime if it is harmful to the environment, the toys, the child, or the parent (Landreth & Bratton, 2006). Lastly, the parent handles ending play sessions on time and, in doing so, returns control and responsibility back to the adult (Landreth & Bratton, 2006). Mary seemed to understand the contradictory concept that she could gain control by giving control during the play session, and she expressed that she certainly wanted Sarah to develop more self-control. In fact, she did fairly well in allowing the "child" to lead during the role-play with another parent during this group session.

Session 5

The most significant turning point for Mary occurred in session 5. In this session, Mary shared her videotape of a play session with Sarah. Joan pointed out the strengths of her interaction, in that Mary consistently attended to and oriented her body toward Sarah,

(continued)

(*continued*)

she allowed Sarah to lead the play, and she even tried out a few reflections of Sarah's feelings. Joan then observed that Mary's voice tone and facial expressions did not quite match Sarah's affect and inquired about how Mary was feeling during the play session. Mary immediately began to cry and disclosed that even though she was doing what she had been taught to do, the whole time she was feeling resentful of having to do the play session with Sarah. She admitted feeling ashamed that she did not want to spend time with her own child, especially when she could see how much Sarah enjoyed having time with her in this way. Mary shared that because she had gotten pregnant at 16 years old, she had never really wanted Sarah. She had often let her cry in her crib as a baby instead of responding to her, as she felt robbed of her own childhood and resentful of how much having a child took from her. She reported that while she had always cared for Sarah's physical needs, she had not cared for her emotional needs, just as she was physically but not emotionally present during the play sessions. Once she had come to an end of her disclosure, Joan thanked Mary for her honesty and then asked if any of the other parents in the group ever felt resentful of how their lives had changed after becoming a parent. Several mothers empathized with Mary and shared that they too had not felt prepared for all of the ways their lives would change after having children, even in their early to mid-20s when they had their first child. Another mother revealed feeling bored during playtimes and feeling very inconvenienced by having to fit the playtimes into her busy family schedule. Receiving acceptance and support from the other parents in the group helped Mary accept herself and her own feelings, so that she could begin to be more emotionally present for and accepting of Sarah as well.

Follow-Up Sessions

From that point forward, Mary reported experiencing Sarah differently. She began to enjoy the playtimes, and she found it felt more natural to offer encouragement and esteem-building comments,

(*continued*)

because now she really felt affection for Sarah and meant what she was saying. Her perceptions of Sarah changed outside of the play sessions as well. Rather than sensing demands and ultimatums from Sarah, Mary perceived Sarah as seeking to be more connected with her. She responded in kind by spending time playing with Sarah even when it was not required. By the end of the 10 sessions, Mary reported that Sarah's bossy and defiant behavior had decreased and her compliance had increased both at home and school. Although Sarah continued to challenge the rules at times, Mary felt more capable of managing the situation without reacting and escalating her own behavior. Although there were still challenges to overcome for both Mary and Sarah, the relationship between them was much more connected and emotionally responsive than it had ever been before.

REFERENCES

Achenbach, T. M., & Rescorla, L. A. (2001). *Manual for the ASEBA school-age forms & profiles*. Burlington, VT: University of Vermont, Research Center for Children, Youth, & Families.

Axline, V. M. (1947). *Play therapy*. New York, NY: Ballantine.

Axline, V. M. (1964). *Dibs in search of self.* New York, NY: Random House.

Bernier, A., Beauchamp, M. H., Carlson, S. M., & Lalonde, G. (2015). A secure base from which to regulate: Attachment security in toddlerhood as a predictor of executive functioning at school entry. *Developmental Psychology, 51*(9), 1177–1189.

Bratton, S. C., & Landreth, G. L. (1995). Filial therapy with single parents: Effects on parental acceptance, empathy, and stress. *International Journal of Play Therapy, 4*(1), 61–80.

Bratton, S. C., Landreth, G. L., Kellam, T., & Blackard, S. R. (2006). *Child parent relationship therapy (CPRT) treatment manual: A 10-session filial therapy model for training parents*. New York, NY: Routledge.

Bratton, S. C., Landreth, G. L., & Lin, Y. D. (2010). Child parent relationship therapy: A review of controlled-outcome research. In J. N. Baggerly, D. C. Ray, & S. C. Bratton (Eds.), *Child-centered play therapy research: The evidence base for effective practice* (pp. 267–293). Hoboken, NJ: John Wiley & Sons.

Bratton, S. C., Opiola, K., & Dafoe, E. (2015). Child-parent relationship therapy: A 10-session filial therapy model. In D. A. Crenhaw & A. L. Stewart (Eds.), *Play therapy: A comprehensive guide to theory and practice* (pp. 129–140). New York, NY: Guilford Press.

Bratton, S. C., Ray, D., Rhine, T., & Jones, L. (2005). The efficacy of play therapy with children: A meta-analytic review of treatment outcomes. *Professional Psychology: Research and Practice, 36*, 376–390.

Cornett, N., & Bratton, S. C. (2014). Examining the impact of child parent relationship therapy (CPRT) on family functioning. *Journal of Marital and Family Therapy, 40*(3), 302–318.

Cornett, N., & Bratton, S. C. (2015). A golden intervention: 50 years of research in filial therapy. *International Journal of Play Therapy, 24*(3), 119–133.

Eardley, D. (1978). *An initial investigation of a didactic version of filial therapy dealing with self-concept increase and problematic behavior decrease.* Unpublished doctoral dissertation, The Pennsylvania State University, University Park, PA.

Ferrell, L. G. (2004). A comparison of an intensive 4-week format of the Landreth 10-week filial therapy training model with the traditional Landreth 10-week model of filial therapy (Doctoral dissertation, University of North Texas, Denton, 2003). *Dissertation Abstract International, A, 64*(12), 4369.

Gil, E. (1994). *Play in family therapy*. New York, NY: Guilford Press.

Ginsberg, B. G. (2004). *Relationship enhancement family therapy*. Doylestown, PA: Relationship Enhancement Press.

Goldenberg, H., & Goldenberg, I. (2013). *Family therapy: An overview* (8th ed.). Belmont, CA: Brooks/Cole.

Guerney, B. (1964). Filial therapy: Description and rationale. *Journal of Consulting Psychology, 28*, 304–310.

Guerney, L. (2000). Filial therapy into the 21st century. *International Journal of Play Therapy, 9*(2), 1–17.

Guerney, L., & Guerney, B., Jr. (1987). Integrating child and family therapy. *Psychotherapy, 24*(35), 609–614.

Guerney, L. F., & Ryan, V. (2012). *Group filial therapy: The complete guide to teaching parents to play therapeutically with their children*. London, UK: Jessica Kingsley Publishers.

Landreth, G. L. (2002). *Play therapy: The art of the relationship* (2nd ed.). New York, NY: Taylor & Francis.

Landreth, G. L., & Bratton, S. C. (2006). *Child parent relationship therapy (CPRT): A 10-session filial therapy model*. New York, NY: Routledge.

Lin, Y., & Bratton, S. C. (2015). A meta-analytic review of child-centered play therapy approaches. *Journal of Counseling and Development, 93*, 45–58.

Moustakas, C. (1953). *Children in play therapy: A key to understanding normal and disturbed emotions.* New York, NY: McGraw-Hill.

Moustakas, C. (1959). *Psychotherapy with children: The living relationship.* New York, NY: Harper & Row.

Napier, A. Y., & Whitaker, C. (1978). *The family crucible.* New York, NY: Harper Collins.

Office of the Surgeon General. (2005). *Surgeon general's workshop on making prevention of child maltreatment a national priority: Implementing innovations of a public health approach.* Proceedings of the National Institutes of Health, Bethesda, MD, March 30–31, 2005. Retrieved from http://www.ncbi.nlm.nih.gov/books/NBK47482/#precis.Public_Health_Approach

Piaget, J. (1962). *Play, dreams, and imitation in childhood.* New York, NY: Routledge.

Richards, M. M., Bowers, M. J., Lazicki, T., Krall, D., & Jacobs, A. K. (2008). Caregiver involvement in the intensive mental health program: Influence on changes in child functioning. *Journal of Child and Family Studies, 17*(2), 241–252.

Rogers, C. (1951). *Client-centered therapy.* Boston, MA: Houghton Mifflin.

Sunderland, M. (2006). *The science of parenting.* New York, NY: DK Publishing.

U.S. Department of Health and Human Services. (2000). *Report of the surgeon general's conference on children's mental health: A national action agenda.* Washington DC: U.S. Department of Health and Human Services. Retrieved from http://www.ncbi.nlm.nih.gov/books/NBK44233

VanFleet, R. (2013). *Filial therapy: Strengthening parent-child relationships through play* (3rd ed.). Sarasota, FL: Professional Resource Press.

CHAPTER 7

Creativity in Play Therapy Using Technology

LINDA L. AUTRY

Creativity is a subject that has been explored for eons. This exploration has sought to define and identify creativity and answer questions such as: What is creativity? What does it mean to be creative? Who is creative? How does an individual know if he or she is creative? How are intelligence and creativity related? What is the link between creativity and psychological disorders? An additional question that will be explored in this chapter is: What does it mean to integrate or incorporate creativity into counseling through the use of technology and how does one do that?

Creativity gives us space for fun in our lives (Bodine, 1999). In the realm of artistic expression, creativity allows us to escape the stressful issues in our lives and spend a few moments immersing ourselves in something we enjoy. It allows us to express a deeper side of ourselves, which we may choose to share with others. It can be a very positive force in our lives and that of our clients. It can reduce stress, improve health, give us joy and happiness, comfort and nurture us. Not only can creativity positively affect clients, but it is appropriate for clients with a variety of presenting issues: victims of domestic violence (Binkley, 2013), children with chronic illnesses (Frels, Leggett, & Larocca, 2009), victims of sexual abuse (Pifalo, 2006), self-esteem issues (Hartz & Thick, 2005), autism spectrum (Epp, 2008), selective mutism (Fernandez, Serrano, & Tongson, 2014), acute and chronic sleep disorders (Wang, Sun, & Zang, 2014), and grief (Slyter, 2012).

According to Kaufman and Beghetto (2009), not only is the question of what constitutes creativity ignored, but the other side of the matter is that there are too many different answers. According to Gladding (2011), there are more than 200 definitions for creativity. Plucker, Beghetto, and Dow (2004) have suggested that a lack of research in the area of creativity may be due to the many definitions of creativity. Although many definitions point to an individual's novel approach to problem solving, Plucker et al. (2004) suggest the following definition: "Creativity is the interaction among *aptitude, process, and environment* by which an individual or group produces a *perceptible product* that is both *novel and useful* as defined within a *social context*" (p. 90). Such a definition allows for a broader interpretation of the construct of creativity than some of the more narrowly focused definitions.

Perhaps identifying the concept of creativity is as ambiguous as attempting to define it. Rather than attempt to define creativity, some researchers have suggested models of creativity—*Big-C* and *little-c*. *Big-C* creativity encompasses the work of high-profile creators. On the other hand, *little-c* is defined as everyday creativity, typically found in average individuals who engage in creative endeavors, such as problem solving or participating in hobbies (Richards, 1990, as cited in Kaufman & Beghetto, 2009). Beghetto and Kaufman (2007) advocate for a third model that would account for creativity in the process of learning, which they have identified as *mini-c*. The *mini-c* model accounts for the discoveries and the expressions of creativity found in children as they explore and learn.

The importance of creativity in childhood development cannot be overemphasized. "Arts education can be beneficial to individuals of every age and is extremely important to children" (Woodruff, Bolen, & Thomas, 2014, p. 107). The creative arts can assist children in several areas of development—cognitive, social, and physical. According to Smith (2009), children demonstrate gains in critical thinking skills as well as academic subjects, such as math and reading. Social development is expanded as children engage with other students in play and other creative endeavors. Physical development is enhanced by manipulating art materials or participating in playing musical instruments as well as activities, such as dance (Fox & Schirrmacher, 2012). As some children begin formal education as early as 4 years of age, it is important for schools to nurture creativity in children and provide opportunities for them to express their creativity.

According to Wengrower (2001), creative approaches used in classrooms reach many more students than those who go to a counselor. Collard and Looney (2014) emphasized the role that teachers and parents have in supporting and nurturing creativity in children. I would extend that role to counselors as well. Many of the applications of creativity to teaching might well be carried out or extended in the counselor's office, especially in light of the barriers to creativity and expressive arts in education. Cachia et al. (as cited in Collard & Looney, 2014) identified several barriers to creativity, one of which is paramount in the United States and that is the curriculum. Typically, curricula are prescribed by assessment or high stakes testing, leaving little latitude in education for teachers to be creative or nurture the creativity in their students.

Some authors have sought to establish a link between creativity and intelligence, generally suggesting that individuals with higher intellect are more prone to creativity (Nakano, Wechsler, Campos, & Milian, 2015; Nusbaum, Silvia, & Beaty, 2014). A second model proposes that intelligence is not related to creativity so that one may possess intelligence without creativity and vice versa. A third model suggests that a relationship exists if the intelligence quotient (IQ) is 120. Nakano et al. (2015) lamented the lack of assessments that can evaluate both constructs. Furthermore, Nakano et al. (2015) expressed concerns regarding the small number of assessments that measure creativity.

A starting point or foundation for the consideration of adding creativity to the counselor's repertoire is Howard Gardner's multiple intelligences. Gardner went far beyond what many people think of as intelligence, which is typically an intelligence quotient. The intelligences that he identified are: (a) musical, (b) bodily-kinesthetic, (c) logical–mathematical, (d) linguistic, (e) spatial, (f) naturalistic, (g) interpersonal, and (h) intrapersonal (Gardner, 2006).

There is also the long-standing debate regarding the connection between psychological disorders (Acar & Runco, 2012; Fink, Slamar-Halbedl, Unterrainer, & Weiss, 2012; Johnson, Tharp, & Holmes, 2015; Richards, 1993) and creativity. There are annual conferences, such as the Creativity and Madness Conference held in Santa Fe, New Mexico, with a variety of sessions addressing this connection. Attendance at this conference exposes one to an eclectic group of counselors, physicians, and other health care professionals who discuss the relationship of psychological disorders and creativity in the lives of such legendary individuals as Beethoven, Mozart, Picasso, and Pollock, to name a few. In addition, the Association for Creativity in Counseling (ACC), a division of the American Counseling Association (ACA), holds an annual conference.

There are a number of challenges to integrating creativity into counseling, but perhaps the greatest is the challenge we harbor within ourselves. Carson and Becker (2004) suggested that, "creativity is not an inborn trait but a process we engage in every day that can be nurtured, both within ourselves and our clients" (p. 112). As a professor in higher education for a number of years, I have had the opportunity to challenge students to explore their creativity in many of the subjects I have taught. However, it has been my experience that when I assign a project that allows students (undergraduate and graduate) to be creative, many of them express dismay. "I'm not creative," they moan and whine. This often affords the opportunity for them to talk about early expressions or lack of expressions of creativity. Many of them say they have not been encouraged to think outside the box or have not been given the opportunity to participate in ambiguous assignments that encourage creativity since elementary school in many cases. Even in elementary school, some students say their opportunities to be creative were limited due to specific guidelines for creative endeavors that did not allow them to express themselves fully. By middle school, students say that unless there were art or music classes, there was little opportunity for creativity in school due to the prescribed curriculum that focused on state testing.

Although counselors may not have given much thought to creativity, Carson and Becker (2004) believed that it is incumbent on them to develop and foster their own creativity. I believe that every individual is creative in some way, but often that creativity has been blocked by challenges experienced by the individual or, perhaps, by the definition or myths surrounding the topic of creativity. In our society, it often seems that creativity is synonymous with art. While I believe that creativity does involve the arts, this definition is limiting. People are creative in myriad ways on a daily basis—how they meet the tasks and duties of their employment, how they interact with people, how they get to and from work, how they make lists and shop, even how they spend their free time (Kaufman & Beghetto, 2009). Whether or not we believe we are creative, the fact remains that we are constantly creating "thoughts, feelings, and ideas that construct our view of the world and our experience of reality" (Allen, 1999, p. 168).

Another challenge may be the perception of people outside the field. Counselors know that so-called *talk* therapy is generally ineffective because children "tend to lack the introspective and interactional skills required" (Kottman, 2011, p. 4) for this kind of approach. In addition, using creativity is another way to establish a relationship with resistant clients or clients who have been so traumatized that they are unable to talk about the traumatic event (Gil, 1991; Gladding, 2005; van der Kolk, 2014). However, I believe that individuals of all ages can benefit from the integration of creativity into counseling. If nothing else, affording the client a safe place to explore his or her creativity can be a way of connecting to that client and his or her experiences for the counselor. Allowing clients to explore their feelings and experiences through creative avenues can be powerful for them, and it can help build and maintain the counselor–client relationship.

There are a variety of ways in which creativity can manifest in the counseling process and relationship. Creativity can develop as the counselor and client interact on a personal level, each bringing his or her uniqueness to the relationship in combination with the process of therapy. Creativity lends itself well to a client-centered approach as the client leads the way with his or her creative endeavors. One of the many appeals to creativity is much like one of the basic tenets of counseling: "Building on strengths rather than remediating weaknesses" (Plucker et al., 2004, p. 83). Collard and Looney (2014) suggested that it is important to support learning autonomy. Again, autonomy is one of the basic tenets of counseling. Finding the client's creative outlet may present challenges, as many individuals' first response to the idea of creativity is that they are not creative. Typically, younger children are more in touch with their own creativity because they have not yet subscribed to society's limiting definition. Children and teenagers may already be engaged in creative pursuits; by meeting clients where they are, you can easily incorporate what they are already doing to build the therapeutic alliance and help clients explore the difficulties they are encountering.

No matter what the theoretical foundation of a counselor is, it is possible to find ways to integrate elements of that theory with creativity. For example, elements of solution-focused counseling integrate well with creativity. The miracle question allows children to use their imaginations and think about the future, giving them the opportunity to act out or draw or paint how their world would look after a miracle. Scaling questions can be adapted for children in more concrete ways using stepping-stones or the rungs of a ladder (Lethem, 2002). Helping clients identify times that they have been successful in dealing with an issue is a crucial aspect of solution-focused therapy. This can be done creatively through the use of role-play, or some other type of artistic endeavor.

What does it mean to integrate or incorporate creativity into counseling? That is open to the interpretation of the counselor and the client. There are those who believe creativity is synonymous with the arts. Although in most cases the arts are a very important aspect in creativity, this is somewhat limiting. Incorporating creativity into counseling can mean the creative way with which you approach building the relationship with your client; your creative approach in helping your client implement goals; or your method for allowing the client to be creative in his approach to his problems. To some, it would mean encouraging the client to use some type of art form as a method of expression in counseling. To others, it might mean incorporating more than one form of artistic expression, such as acting out or role-playing a scene from artwork that the client has done (Levy, 2014). For others, it may be techniques and skills you already use that are inherent in the practice of counseling. There may be a creative aspect to your ability to build a relationship with a resistant client. It may be in the ways you work with the family and/or teachers of a client.

RESEARCH SUPPORT

Effectiveness is an important consideration with any type of counseling, whether it is a particular theory or technique. For reimbursement purposes, insurance companies require the use of methods and techniques that have proven to be effective. Although there is a plethora of research in various creative arts with specific populations, there is little research that specifically addresses creativity in counseling. There is a large body of research that encompasses the expressive arts and combinations of expressive arts and other therapies, such as cognitive behavioral therapy (CBT) and solution-focused brief therapy (SFBT), but according to Gladding (2011), "less than one half of 1% of all research in counseling and psychology is conducted on creativity" (p. 2). Plucker et al. (2004) believe that the myths held by scholars, lack of direction, and misunderstanding of the subject create a climate that contributes to difficulty in researching creativity.

Research has been conducted with a variety of populations, such as children and adolescents diagnosed with autism spectrum disorder, sexual abuse, posttraumatic stress disorder (PTSD), domestic violence, and low self-esteem. There have been several meta-analytic reviews done for child-centered play therapy (CCPT; Lin & Bratton, 2015), CCPT in schools (Ray, Armstrong, Balkin, & Jayne, 2015), and dance therapy (Koch, Kunz, Lykou, & Cruz, 2014). In an empirical study done by Pifalo (2006), results indicated that a combination of art therapy, CBT, and group counseling resulted in a reduction of symptoms in 41 children who had suffered sexual abuse. The children were administered the Trauma Symptom Checklist for Children (TSCC) before and after 8 weeks of group therapy. Of the 12 subscales of the TSCC, nine showed a significant statistical reduction of symptoms over the 8-week group experience (Pifalo, 2006). Using a framework of expressive therapies continuum (ETC), Fernandez et al. (2014) conducted a case study of a 10-year-old boy with selective mutism symptoms. Over a period of several sessions, the client was able to move from "yes/no" answers to extended verbal responses with the therapist and later with individuals in his home.

In a 10-week study done with 31 adolescent female offenders, Hartz and Thick (2005) compared art psychotherapy (cognitive group) and art as therapy (process group) as a method for increasing self-esteem. The authors used the Self-Perception Profile for Adolescents (SPPA) to measure self-esteem. They designed their own 20-question posttreatment questionnaire in order to determine how art therapy affected self-esteem. The authors concluded that art psychotherapy and art therapy addressed different components of self-esteem, with art therapy being an effective treatment for increasing self-esteem in this population.

Epp (2008) studied the use of art therapy in social skills groups for autism spectrum children. Sixty-six children of similar age and communication were assigned to small groups of six and met once a week for an hour. As part of an ongoing group experience, participants had been exposed to social skills through the use of comic strips and had been encouraged to draw their own comic strips. Progress was measured using the Social Skills Rating System (SSRS). Due to variance in social skills exhibited in school and home, teachers and parents were asked to fill out SSRS questionnaires that examined social skills and problem behaviors. Although improvement was not statistically significant in all areas of social skills and specific behaviors, there was some improvement overall.

Merry et al. (2012) used a computer program called Smart, Positive, Active, Realistic, X-factor thoughts (SPARX) as an intervention with depressed adolescents. SPARX is an interactive fantasy computer game based on CBT. Participants, aged 12 to 19 years, were divided into two groups—94 participants were assigned to the SPARX treatment, and 93 received the usual treatment of face-to-face counseling. Using a variety of assessments, such as the Kazdin hopelessness scale for children, the Spence children's anxiety scale, and the Reynolds adolescent depression scale (2nd ed.), results showed that SPARX was an effective intervention for depressed adolescents.

A meta-analysis of the efficacy of play therapy conducted by Bratton, Ray, Rhine, and Jones (2005) demonstrated the effectiveness of play therapy, but discussed the need for more quantitative research that would address such limitations as research designs where the effectiveness of play therapy is compared with the absence of intervention rather than to other psychotherapies. According to VanFleet, Sywulak, and Sniscak (2010), case studies and surveys do little to promote CCPT as an evidence-based approach. These authors suggest that qualitative research is valuable for providing explanations or understanding data gathered from quantitative research, but quantitative research is a more objective approach to establishing CCPT as an effective therapy for children. They encourage the use of research designs, such as quasi-experimental research designs and time series designs, that seek to control some of the variables associated with counseling research (VanFleet et al., 2010). Ray et al. (2015) suggest the need for research that examines the long-term effects of CCPT as little research has been done to see if effects of CCPT hold over.

TECHNIQUES

There are an infinite number of ways to integrate creativity into counseling. First, the counselor needs to decide whether integrating creativity into his or her counseling is something that he or she can do and how it will benefit clients. As the counselor, you must be willing to explore your own creativity and do some self-reflection. To assist with self-reflection, you might consider answering questions, such as: How comfortable am I with integrating a variety of creative endeavors into my counseling? How comfortable am I with using technology in my counseling? How will I respond when the client asks me to evaluate his or her creative endeavors? Am I able to deal with deep emotions that creative activities may evoke from my client? How will I respond if the client's creative efforts offend me or my beliefs in some way?

Technology is one area that is gaining greater acceptance in the field of counseling. As more and more children and adolescents have access to smartphones and tablets such as iPads, counselors can help clients use technology in a variety of ways. Counselors may be hesitant to use technology as a creative endeavor in counseling, but children and adolescents have embraced it for the most part. Many of them have devices or smartphones they use throughout the day. Asking them to go without these devices even during a counseling session may do little to advance the therapeutic relationship. Embracing technology through a variety of counseling-related activities is one way to build the therapeutic relationship as well as assist the child or adolescent in overcoming challenges that he or she faces on a daily basis. Counselors can employ different programs and apps that may be beneficial for children with a variety of issues. The use of apps and programs can enhance counseling and may serve as a motivator for students to engage in counseling activities.

Although not every child has a personal smartphone or iPad, schools often have iPads that can be checked out by students. If you are in private practice, consider factoring into your budget a notebook or iPad of some kind that students may use while in your office. Along with that, you might research apps that you think would be beneficial to your clients and budget for those also. Many useful apps are free, but some have a minimal cost. Some of the free apps add features if you pay a slight fee for a full version of the app. If the child or adolescent has his own iPad, obtain permission from parents before having the client download an app, even if it is free. Read reviews about the apps you plan to use to ensure quality.

It is important to have a conversation with parents or guardians regarding the use of technology in counseling with children and adolescents. Parents with complaints about the amount of time their children spend on devices may hesitate to give them an additional reason to spend more time on their phones or tablets. If this is the case, the counselor should discuss the benefits of the child using a particular app with parents. If parents are still reluctant, see if they will allow the child to use the device in counseling sessions. Before a child or adolescent loads an app onto a device, ensure that the parent gives permission to do this. It is a good idea to get parental permission in writing.

Much of the artistic expression that was done with paper and markers or crayons in the past can be adapted to technology. Counselors can use books of activities they already have and find ways to incorporate technology into different activities. One example is Drawing a Solution (Leggett & Ybañez, 2011). Using a solution-focused approach, the client is asked to draw a picture of an issue that he is struggling with. Next, the client is given the miracle question and asked to draw a picture of the miracle. Clients could easily complete the activities using an art program on a computer or tablet. Another example is doodle art (Helms, 2015), an activity to help children cope during stressful situations. In its original form, the child is given paper and colored markers to draw a doodle. There are a number of apps, such as Kids Doodle, Doodle for Messenger, Doodle Buddy, and You Doodle Plus, that would enable a child to use an iPad or iPhone to draw on.

Incorporate the media that the client enjoys into your counseling, but keep in mind that there must be a purpose for the creative endeavor rather than entertainment. Carson and Becker (2004) advise that attempting to be creative may, in fact, "detract from the natural flow of interactions and process" (p. 111) in counseling. It is also important to think developmentally as you plan a strategy to incorporate technology into your counseling. As a counselor, you must also be aware that the client may express some deep emotions related to his or her use of creativity, and you must be able to manage those feelings and experiences in order not to harm or retraumatize the client. You must be comfortable with the expression of emotions that may surface from different techniques or activities that you ask the client to do. Ensure that the technique or activity you are using does not retraumatize the client. For older children, process the experience with them by asking process questions that focus on the here and now in order to avoid traumatization (Binkley, 2013). You must consider the way in which the technique or activity will benefit the client. To help the client process, you might ask him or her what this experience or using a certain app or computer program was like for him or her. Ask the client what his or her thoughts and feelings were as he or she worked on the activity (Paylo, Darby, Kinch, & Kress, 2014).

There are a number of different technologies that can be integrated into counseling. The counselor can assist children in telling their story through the use of Apple iBooks. This might be especially beneficial for children who are suffering a loss, whether through death or divorce. This program requires the use of Apple computers, which are available in many schools. Pictures, movie clips, and games can easily be incorporated into iBooks. Once the iBook has been created on the computer, it can be sent to an iPad so that the child can share the book with parents, guardians, or siblings if appropriate.

Bibliotherapy is another technique that can easily be adapted to technology. Books can be loaded to the child or adolescent's iPhone or iPad. As the typical adolescent already carries his phone everywhere, he might be more inclined to read a book on his smartphone rather than carrying a book around. As with traditional print books, the counselor and client can decide what book might be beneficial for the issue at hand as well as whether the book will be read and discussed in counseling sessions or read between sessions.

If the client would like to keep a journal, this can be done with a computer, iPad, or smartphone. Blogging is another way for a client to keep a journal. The client can share her blog with specific individuals or leave it open for anybody who finds it on the web. Having people respond to her blog might be a way of normalizing the client's situation. The counselor and client can discuss how the blog will be used in counseling. The client will need to decide whether the counselor can read the blog or if the client will bring journal entries into the session and process them there.

CREATIVE ACTIVITIES

Digital Photography and Video

Many of the expressive arts can be adapted to technology and can easily be integrated with each other and into counseling. Although there is much to be said for art that is done free hand, more and more children and adolescents are using technology to express themselves. Most smartphones and tablets come with basic video and digital photography editing programs already installed. If not, there are free photography apps available that allow basic editing. There are many apps that allow students to take, edit, and create pictures and videos. Children can write stories and plays and create their own movies. They can draw their own illustrations for the stories they create using art programs. Photo collages featuring topics that interest the child can easily be created with an app rather than cutting pictures out of magazines. For those nonverbal or withdrawn clients, writing their stories and music or producing their own movie affords the opportunity to express themselves in ways that might not otherwise be available.

Exploring the Client's World
To get a sense of the child's perception of his home environment and community, have him take pictures of his world either with an iPad or iPhone. He can take pictures of his neighborhood, home, family, room, pets, or any other important aspects of his environment. Have him show you the pictures and talk about his world. What does he like about his world? From an SFBT perspective, the counselor can talk about what the child might want to change about his world. With a basic editing app, you could have the child change his picture by editing out people or changing the color in his pictures until he has his *perfect* world. Or, the child might wish to create a collage using the pictures he has taken.

Creating a Memorial Book
For children dealing with grief issues, whether through death, divorce, or some other type of loss, an Apple iBook is one way for the child to memorialize the person or object of his loss. There are iBook tutorials available on YouTube so that the counselor can learn ahead of time how to use this program in order to assist the client in writing her book and helping the student add photographs, movie clips, and games. Young children will need assistance, but adolescents should be able to watch the YouTube videos and learn how to do most of the work without assistance.

The iBook must be developed, written, and produced on a desktop Mac; it can then be transferred to an iPad using a Quick Response (QR) code. There are several templates for the client to choose from to start writing his or her book. Pictures and movies can easily be integrated into the book. There are also many widgets that can be added to the book so that the author can add games such as a word search. When the book is finished, the child can share it with family members who have iPads. Apple iBooks Author software is available as a free download from the Mac app store.

Digital Music

Use of iTunes and Music Programs
Children and adolescents can share their favorite music. In addition to asking them how they relate to the music, you might also ask how they relate to the artist. On iTunes there is information about artists and albums, which can be useful for discussions of what the adolescent has in common with the artist. You might ask the client how he or she is similar to or different from the artist. For older adolescents, you can discuss themes of songs or explore the theme you see in the adolescent's music in general (positive, negative, and dark).

There are music programs that allow children and adolescents to write their own music complete with different instruments. Music composition programs, such as GarageBand, installed on Apple computers, offer some basic guitar and piano lessons as well as allowing the individual to compose music incorporating a wide variety of instruments and sounds. Depending on the emotion the client is feeling, he or she might compose a song that reflects that emotion. Other ways to use music might be to set a poem the client has written to downloaded music or music the client composes. Clients can add music they have composed or downloaded to movies they have produced. The counselor can discuss with the client the choice of music and the emotions it evokes from the client. The counselor can ask the client to share a story about a favorite song. With the use of iTunes, the client can listen to music while painting, drawing, or playing therapeutic games in the session.

Games

A Jeopardy game can easily be set up for computers. Using a Jeopardy game template available online, the counselor might consider using pictures to help young children identify feelings. The counselor might initially use emoticons for the feeling pictures. Next, the child could be exposed to pictures of real people rather than emoticons. The counselor could also take pictures of the child's face expressing different emotions and use those in the Jeopardy game.

Word search templates are also available online. The word search can be tailored to the issue the client is facing. If the client is struggling with emotions, a word search using feeling words might be appropriate. The client can complete the word search on a computer or tablet, or the counselor can print it for the child to work on at home.

Apps

Relaxation

For children with anxiety, stress, or sleep issues, there are free apps that can help them learn to relax. Smiling Mind, iCan: Anxiety Free, Sleep Meditations for Kids, and My First Yoga are all free apps. Smiling Mind and iCan: Anxiety Free apps are designed to help children as young as 6 years of age cope with stress and anxiety-producing situations. In order to determine the appropriateness of a particular app for a client, the counselor should familiarize herself with apps before demonstrating them to children. Some apps, such as iCan, may require up to 30 minutes of time to complete, so the counselor may need to help the child determine an appropriate time to use the app.

Emotions

The ABA Flash Cards & Games—Emotions is a free app that can help children learn to identify feelings. It is customizable by allowing users to add their own cards. The timing, fonts, colors, and play modes can be adjusted to the child's needs. Another way to use a flash card app is to make flash cards with positive messages for the child. Using the voice memo app installed on most phones, you or the child can record positive messages to listen to when he or she needs encouragement.

CONCLUSION

There are as many ways to integrate creativity into counseling as there are individuals. However, the counselor should always be mindful of practicing ethically (Rosen & Atkins, 2014), so be sure you know what the guidelines are for the state in which you practice. According to the *ACA Code of Ethics* (2014): "Counselors who engage in the use of distance counseling, technology and/or social media develop knowledge and skills regarding related technical, ethical, and legal considerations (e.g., special certifications, additional course work)" (p. 17). Counselors who wish to obtain certifications or licenses in specialized therapies, such as art, dance, or music, must seek information from their particular state licensure boards as many states are different. There are also national organizations, such as the American Art Therapy Association and American Music Therapy Association, that can give some direction regarding additional coursework and practicums for more specialized certifications. Whatever the activity, remember that it is about the client and what the client is comfortable with in terms of creativity. If you do not feel you have the expertise to integrate certain creative endeavors into your counseling, then you should not use them. If you have questions, seek supervision or consultation. To ensure networking and current research and relevant information, join organizations that promote professional identity, such as the ACA and the ACC. In addition, read articles and books by authors who are prominent in the field of creativity in counseling, such as Samuel Gladding, Thelma Duffey, and Lynne Shallcross. To learn about creativity in general, read the works of Amabile, Runco, and Sternberg.

I would caution the counselor who is interested in integrating creativity into counseling to consider carefully four things. First, explore your own creativity. If you are hesitant to do this or feel that you are not creative, this may not be an area for you to consider. Second, as with any kind of counseling, it is important to consider the developmental level of your client—physical, cognitive, social, and psychological development. Third, always consider the cultural context of your client. Some cultures are more open to certain kinds of expression (i.e., dance) than others may be. Finally, be sure your creative endeavors with the client are ethical in terms of your professional competence and scope of practice.

CASE EXAMPLE: DORI'S STORY

It was easily the hottest day of the year. It was the day before school started in August, and at the elementary school where I worked as a school counselor, we were frantically trying to get ready.

(*continued*)

The elementary school had every label imaginable—Title 1, lower socioeconomic status (SES), Chapter 1, 504, to name a few. Approximately 95% of our students were on free or reduced lunches, and at least 80% scored 1 or more years below reading level.

We were an elementary school, third through fifth grade. Our students came to us as third graders with very low or no reading levels, and we had to prepare them to pass Texas Examiners of Educator Standards (TExES). We had a high number of minority students. However, worst of all, our students fought at any time over anything. They fought before, after, and during school; they fought all the time. In fact, our challenges were so great for a campus of 200 students that we had a principal, vice principal, social worker, and counselor. We all came on board at the same time.

For all practical purposes, regardless of how we were promoted in the district, we were the dumping ground for other elementary schools. It was a challenging environment. Teachers who had been comfortable teaching on other campuses in the districts were reassigned to our school. Several of them were on antidepressants and antianxiety medicines.

In the midst of preparations that frantic day, I got a call from a counselor at another one of the four elementary schools in the district. She cheerfully told me that a student from her school would be starting the year in our school. Dori was an 11-year-old White female with multiple issues. She lived with her grandmother because her mother was unable to raise her. She was borderline mentally retarded, autistic, and was on seizure medications. She would be entering our school as a fifth grader mainstreamed for a few classes, but spending most of her time in the special education classroom. Because of her autism diagnosis, the counselor assured me that she would probably "freak out" on the chaotic first day of school in a new environment with a new and different schedule, not to mention staff and students. The counselor assured me that she would probably stand in the hallway, cover her ears, and make loud yelling noises. I groaned inwardly. I had never worked with a student with autism and had no clue what to do other than to meet her at the door on the first day of school and escort her either to my office or the special education classroom.

(*continued*)

(*continued*)

Shortly after the phone call from the counselor, I was summoned to the principal's office. She was equally concerned about Dori's presence on our campus, and her answer was for me to see this student three times a week. Even though we only had 200 students on our campus, devoting time to seeing a student three times per week was a little over-the-top, I thought. I agreed to see Dori (did I really have a choice?) three times a week, but only for 30-minute sessions. With our student population, I generally kept my counseling sessions short. I really did not have much confidence in my ability to work effectively with Dori given her circumstances and issues. I had even more misgivings than normal about the opening day of school. What could we possibly do with this student?

The next day, I met Dori and her grandmother on the front steps of the school. Dori was a tall fifth grader, slightly overweight with blond hair and blue eyes. Other than her hair being slightly uncombed, she was well groomed. It was obvious that she was well cared for, physically and emotionally. Her grandmother was unable to stay and help me introduce Dori to our school because she had to get to work. We had already determined that we needed to find a quiet place for Dori until school settled down on that first day. I would not be able to stay with her as I needed to move about the school and help new students, especially those who were crying as they entered the door.

Midmorning, I was able to spend some time with Dori. For the most part, Dori was wide-eyed with a "deer-in-the headlights" expression. She looked like she might bolt at any second. However, to my knowledge, she had not put her hands over her ears and screamed at all. I was relieved about that, but still did not quite know what to do with Dori.

The first session, we just "talked." Dori was able to talk more than I initially thought and was fairly willing to do so. We talked about some of her favorite things. Then I took her on a tour of the school and walked her over to the cafeteria that we shared with the sixth-grade campus.

I had taken a play therapy graduate-level course postgraduation because I wanted to learn more about incorporating play therapy

(continued)

into my counseling, especially as I had spent most of my time working in elementary schools. I had also been to a one-day Violet Oaklander workshop. I had graduated from a person-centered program, an approach that lends itself well to play therapy as it is client centered with the client directing the play sessions, but this was the extent of my "training" as far as play therapy.

Up to this point, I had not had much experience with play therapy other than allowing students to use the sandtray, draw, paint, or use puppets. Initially, I used the sandtray and puppets with Dori. I attempted to explore her feelings about being in our school. It did not seem like Dori was making much progress in our school, but she did not appear to be regressing, which I took as a positive sign as I was grasping at straws. For the most part, she still appeared wide-eyed, but no screaming meltdowns took place. Weeks of sandtray went by. I felt like I was trekking through a wilderness with no direction. I kept telling myself that, in Dori's case, stability was a positive.

One day after several weeks, Dori told me she wanted to "perform" for me. Frankly, I was a little stunned that she knew the word "perform." Not having spent a great deal of time exploring creativity or the expressive arts in counseling, I was a little hesitant. Truthfully, I was taken aback. But as a client-centered counselor, I acquiesced. She proceeded to sing a song for me. She was not that great of a singer in terms of staying on key, but seemed to enjoy demonstrating her singing ability. From then on, at every session, she "performed" a song. More time passed. It seemed like Dori was beginning to fit into our school, and she did not seem so wide-eyed anymore. She was fairly compliant. About that time, I approached the principal and suggested that I cut her sessions down to twice a week. Because there had been no outbursts, the principal agreed. One day, Dori came to our session and said she wanted to act something out for me. I quickly gave her permission. She proceeded to act out a seizure complete with dropping to the floor of my office and writhing around. Although I tried my best not to show it, I was aghast! She quickly jumped up and asked if I knew what she was acting out. I told her a seizure. She began to jump up and down and said, "You know. You know." (Honestly, if I had not known she was

(continued)

(*continued*)

on seizure medication, I'm not sure I would have recognized her acting.) For some strange reason, it seemed to be extremely validating to her that I knew what she was acting out. I can only surmise that having a seizure in school may have been a huge fear for her. It seemed like this particular session was a turning point for her. I do not take any credit for her continued development, but it seemed that she began to gain confidence in herself and in our school.

I worried about her transition to sixth grade because she was in our school only for that year. I began months ahead of time working with the sixth-grade counselor to ensure that Dori would have a smooth transition. We visited the sixth-grade classrooms and the counselor on several occasions. I told her that I would check on her frequently when she moved to sixth grade, which I did. As our school shared a cafeteria with the sixth grade, I did see her occasionally during her year at that school. She always looked happy and confident. I do not know what happened to her after that, but I was always thankful that I was able to let her express herself in a way that fit for her in our counseling sessions. It was a huge lesson for me in working with students with multiple issues and allowing them to express themselves creatively in a way that was meaningful for them.

REFERENCES

Acar, S., & Runco, M. A. (2012). Psychoticism and creativity: A meta-analytic review. *Psychology of Aesthetics, Creativity, and the Arts, 6*(4), 341–350. http://dx.doi.org/10.1037/a0027497

Allen, P. B. (1999). Intention and creativity: Art as spiritual practice. In T. P. Myers & A. Arrien (Eds.), *The soul of creativity: Insights into the creative process* (pp. 168–183). Novato, CA: New World Library.

American Counseling Association (ACA) Code of Ethics. (2014). Section H, distance counseling, technology, and social media. Retrieved from counseling.org

Beghetto, R. A., & Kaufman, J. C. (2007). Toward a broader conception of creativity: A case for "mini-c" creativity. *Psychology of Aesthetics, Creativity and the Arts, 1*(2), 73–79. http://dx.doi.org/10.1037/1931–3896.1.2.73

Binkley, E. (2013). Creative strategies for treating victims of domestic violence. *Journal of Creativity in Mental Health, 8*, 306–313. http://dx.doi.org/10.1080/15401383.2013.821932

Bodine, E. (1999). The healing power of creativity. In T. P. Myers & A. Arrien (Eds.), *The soul of creativity: Insights into the creative process* (pp. 120–125). Novato, CA: New World Library.

Bratton, S. C., Ray, D., Rhine, T., & Jones, L. (2005). The efficacy of play therapy with children: A meta-analytic review of treatment outcomes. *Professional Psychology: Research and Practice, 36*(4), 376–390. http://dx.doi.org/10.1037/0735-7028.36.4.376

Carson, D. K., & Becker, K. W. (2004). When lightning strikes: Reexamining creativity in psychotherapy. *Journal of Counseling & Development, 82*, 111–115.

Collard, P., & Looney, J. (2014). Nurturing creativity in education. *European Journal of Education, 49*(3), 348–364. http://dx.doi.org/10.1111/ejed.12090

Epp, K. M. (2008). Outcome-based evaluation of a social skills program using art therapy and group therapy for children on the autism spectrum. *Children & Schools, 30*(1), 27–36.

Fernandez, K. T. G., Serrano, K. C. M., & Tongson, M. C. C. (2014). An intervention in treating selective mutism using the expressive therapies continuum framework. *Journal of Creativity in Mental Health, 9*, 19–32. http://dx.doi.org/10.1080/15401383.2013.873706

Fink, A., Slamar-Halbedl, M., Unterrainer, H. F., & Weiss, E. M. (2012). Creativity: Genius, madness, or a combination of both? *Psychology of Aesthetics, Creativity, and the Arts, 6*(1), 11–18. http://dx.doi.org/10.1037/a0024874

Fox, J. E., & Schirrmacher, R. (2012). *Art & creative development for young children* (7th ed.). Belmont, CA: Wadsworth.

Frels, R. K., Leggett, E. S., & Larocca, P. S. (2009). Creativity and solution-focused counseling for a child with chronic illness. *Journal of Creativity in Mental Health, 4*, 308–319. http://dx.doi.org/10.1080/15401380903372646

Gardner, H. (2006). *Multiple intelligences. New horizons.* New York, NY: Basic Books.

Gil, E. (1991). *The healing power of play: Working with abused children.* New York, NY: Guilford Press.

Gladding, S. T. (2005). *Counseling as an art: The creative arts in counseling* (3rd ed.). Alexandria, VA: American Counseling Association.

Gladding, S. T. (2011). Using creativity and the creative arts in counseling: An international approach. *Turkish Psychological Counseling and Guidance Journal, 4*(35), 1–7.

Hartz, L., & Thick, L. (2005). Art therapy strategies to raise self-esteem in female juvenile offenders: A comparison of art psychotherapy and art as therapy approaches. *Art Therapy: Journal of the American Art Therapy Association, 22*(2), 70–80.

Helms, B. T. (2015). Doodle art—just for fun? In S. Degges-White & B. R. Colon (Eds.), *Expressive arts interventions for school counselors* (pp. 65–70). New York, NY: Springer Publishing.

Johnson, S. L., Tharp, J. A., & Holmes, M. K. (2015). Understanding creativity in bipolar I disorder. *Psychology of Aesthetics, Creativity, and the Arts, 9*(3), 319–327. http://dx.doi.org/10.1037/a0038852

Kaufman, J. C., & Beghetto, R. A. (2009). Beyond big and little: The four c model of creativity. *Review of General Psychology, 13*(1), 1–12. http://dx.doi.org/10.1037/a0013688

Koch, S., Kunz, T., Lykou, S., & Cruz, R. (2014). Effects of dance movement therapy and dance on health-related psychological outcomes: A meta-analysis. *The Arts in Psychotherapy, 41*, 46–64. http://dx.doi.org/10.1016/j.aip.2013.10.004

Kottman, T. (2011). *Play therapy basics and beyond* (2nd ed.). Alexandria, VA: American Counseling Association.

Leggett, E. S., & Ybañez, K. (2011). Drawing a solution. In S. Degges-White & N. L. Davis (Eds.), *Integrating the expressive arts into counseling practice: Theory-based interventions* (pp. 34–36). New York, NY: Springer Publishing.

Lethem, J. (2002). Brief solution-focused therapy. *Children and Adolescent Mental Health, 7*, 189–192.

Levy, F. J. (2014). Integrating the arts in psychotherapy: Opening the doors of shared creativity. *American Journal of Dance Therapy, 36*, 6–27. http://dx.doi.org/10.1007/s10465–014-9171–8

Lin, Y., & Bratton, S. C. (2015). A meta-analytic review of child-centered play therapy approaches. *Journal of Counseling & Development, 93*, 45–58. http://dx.doi.org/10.1002/j.1556–6676.2015.00180.x

Merry, S. N., Stasiak, K., Shepherd, M., Frampton, C., Fleming, T., & Lucassen, M. F. (2012). The effectiveness of SPARX, a computerised self help intervention for adolescents seeking help for depression: Randomised controlled non-inferiority trial. *BMJ (Clinical Research Ed.), 344*, e2598.

Nakano, T., Wechsler, S. M., Campos, C. R., & Milian, Q. G. (2015). Intelligence and creativity: Relationships and their implications for positive psychology. *Bragança Paulista, 20*(2), 195–206. http://dx.doi.org/10.1590/1413–82712015200201

Nusbaum, E. C., Silvia, P. J., & Beaty, R. E. (2014). Ready, set, create: What instructing people to "be creative" reveals about the meaning and mechanisms of divergent thinking. *Psychology of Aesthetics, Creativity, and the Arts, 8*(4), 423–432. http://dx.doi.org/10.1037/a0036549

Paylo, M. J., Darby, A., Kinch, S., & Kress, V. E. (2014). Creative rituals for use with traumatized adolescents. *Journal of Creativity in Mental Health, 9*, 111–121. http://dx.doi.org/10.1080/15401383.2013.859992

Pifalo, T. (2006). Art therapy with sexually abused children and adolescents: Extended research study. *Art Therapy: Journal of the American Art Therapy Association, 23*(4), 181–185.

Plucker, J. A., Beghetto, R. A., & Dow, G. T. (2004). Why isn't creativity more important to educational psychologists? Potentials, pitfalls, and future directions in creativity research. *Educational Psychologist, 39*(2), 83–96.

Ray, D. C., Armstrong, S. A., Balkin, R. S., & Jayne, K. M. (2015). Child-centered play therapy in the schools: Review and meta-analysis. *Psychology in the Schools, 52*(2), 107–123. http://dx.doi.org/10.1002/pits.21798

Reynolds, W. M. (2002). *Reynolds adolescent depression scale* (2nd ed.; RADS-2). Lutz, FL Psychological Assessment Resources.

Richards, R. (1993). Everyday creativity, eminent creativity, and psychopathology. *Psychological Inquiry, 4*(3), 212–217.

Rosen, C. M., & Atkins, S. S. (2014). Am I doing expressive arts therapy or creativity in counseling? *Journal of Creativity in Mental Health, 9*, 292–303. http://dx.doi.org/10.1080/15401383.2014.906874

Slyter, M. (2012). Creative counseling interventions for grieving adolescents. *Journal of Creativity in Mental Health, 7*, 17–34. http://dx.doi.org/10.1080/15401383.2012.657593

Smith, F. (2009). Why arts education is crucial, and who's doing it best. Edutopia. Retrieved from www.edutopia.org/arts-music-curriculum-child-development

van der Kolk, B. (2014). *The body keeps the score: Brain, mind, and body in the healing of trauma.* New York, NY: Viking.

VanFleet, R., Sywulak, A. E., & Sniscak, C. C. (2010). *Child-centered play therapy.* New York, NY: Guilford Press.

Wang, C. F., Sun, Y. L., & Zang, H. X. (2014). Music therapy improves sleep quality in acute and chronic sleep disorders: A meta-analysis of 10 randomized studies. *International Journal of Nursing Studies, 51*(1), 51–62.

Wengrower, H. (2001). Arts therapies in educational settings: An intercultural encounter. *The Arts in Psychotherapy, 28*, 109–115. http://dx.doi.org/10.1016/S0197-4556(00)00091-5

Woodruff, C., Bolen, Y., & Thomas, B. (2014). A rationale for art education in the formative years: Early childhood and elementary preservice teacher perspectives. *Review of Higher Education and Self-Learning, 7*(25), 106–110.

CHAPTER 8

Directive Filial Therapy Models With Very Young Children

EVETTE HORTON, DONNA POTTER, AND KELLY SULLIVAN

DIRECTIVE FILIAL WITH YOUNG CHILDREN

The research on how a young child socially and emotionally develops has grown immensely in the past 20 years. Child development researchers have converged on the findings that children, particularly young children, are developing emotionally, socially, and cognitively in the context of their relationships with their caregivers and that these relationships have an impact on the child's future development (Shonkoff, 2010). Therefore, counselors who are doing therapy with very young children *and* want to have the broadest impact on the young child's long-term development should involve the child's caregiver(s) (Zeanah & Zeanah, 2009). Filial therapy models aim to employ the power of the caregiver relationship to improve a child's social and emotional development.

The term *filial* was first used in the 14th century and designated various aspects of a relationship between a parent and child, such as in the display of *filial* affection that a son gives his mother or a father's *filial* duty to care for his son (Oxford University Press, 2015). However, the term was not used in conjunction with a child mental health intervention until Bernard Guerney's seminal article. Guerney (1964) first described *filial therapy* as a technique that engaged the parents/caregivers as the therapeutic agents with their own children. Guerney (1964) originally conceived *filial therapy* as a group parenting training program which taught a group of parents specific, child-directed play skills to use with their own children; recently, other researchers have developed filial models that train individual caregivers to use child-directed play interactions with their child (Dozier et al., 2009; Lieberman & Van Horn, 2011; Nixon, Sweeney, Erickson, & Touyz, 2003).

Guerney (1964) believed filial therapy had "potential as a preventative measure and as a method of building a foundation in childhood for better mental health and self-realization in adulthood" (p. 304), and researchers have confirmed Guerney's belief. For example, Bratton, Ray, Rhine, and Jones (2005) found in their meta-analyses that research studies that used filial therapy models had the largest effect sizes (ES = 1.15; $p < .01$), as compared with traditional play therapy models (i.e., therapist/child only). Similarly, attachment researchers have repeatedly found that nurturing and sensitive caregiver relationships, like those modeled in Guerney's child-directed filial model, have lasting positive impacts on a child's future social and emotional development (Thompson, 2008).

For this chapter, a *directive filial therapy intervention for young children* is defined as a therapeutic model for young children (ages 0–6 years) that includes: (a) the infant/child's caregiver in the therapeutic process (i.e., dyadic); (b) goals of improving various aspects of the caregiver–child relationship, child outcomes, and caregiver functioning; and (c) elements of direct instruction and/or coaching from the counselor. There are three evidence-based models that fit this definition of filial therapy and are used regularly in clinical practices: Attachment and Biobehavioral Catch-up (ABC; M Dozier et al., 2006), Child–Parent Psychotherapy (CPP; Lieberman & Van Horn, 2005), and Parent–Child Interaction Therapy (PCIT; Hood & Eyberg, 2003). There are other filial intervention models that fit this definition that are reviewed elsewhere in this text (e.g., see Chapter 6 of this text for Child–Parent Relationship Therapy [CPRT]; Landreth & Bratton, 2005) or in other texts (i.e., Theraplay, Booth & Jernberg, 2009).

These three evidence-based models differ widely. They each vary in number of sessions, ages of children targeted, therapeutic techniques, equipment needed, and goals. For clarity, Table 8.1 organizes and summarizes these differences. In the following sections, each directive filial model is reviewed in alphabetical order.

TABLE 8.1 COMPARING THREE EVIDENCE-BASED, FILIAL INTERVENTIONS FOR YOUNG CHILDREN

Aspects of Filial Models	Attachment and Biobehavioral Catch-Up (ABC)	Child–Parent Psychotherapy (CPP)	Parent–Child Interaction Therapy (PCIT)
Theoretical foundation(s)	Attachment Stress neurobiology	Attachment Psychoanalytic, child development, social learning, and trauma	Attachment Social learning Child development—parenting styles
Number of hour-long sessions	10 sessions	Approximately 52 sessions	Typically, 14–20 sessions, though length based on caregiver mastery and child symptom reduction
Child ages served	6 months–24 months	Birth–6 years	2.5–6.5 years
Target population	A child that has experienced any disruptions in attachments and the child's primary attachment figure; no clinical symptoms required	An infant/child with clinically significant trauma symptoms and the child's primary attachment figure	A child with clinically significant oppositional behaviors
Broad goals	Improving the parent–child attachment relationship by increasing caregiver nurturance, sensitivity, and delight and decreasing caregiver frightening behaviors	Improve parent–child relationship posttraumatic event(s)	Improving the parent–child attachment relationship

(*continued*)

TABLE 8.1 COMPARING THREE EVIDENCE-BASED, FILIAL INTERVENTIONS FOR YOUNG CHILDREN *(continued)*

Aspects of Filial Models	Attachment and Biobehavioral Catch-Up (ABC)	Child–Parent Psychotherapy (CPP)	Parent–Child Interaction Therapy (PCIT)
	Increase child attachment security and decrease disorganized attachment Increase child behavioral and biological regulation	Returning dyad to normal development, adaptive coping, and engagement, increase child attachment security and decrease posttraumatic stress and depressive symptoms in child and caregiver	Decreasing externalizing child behavior problems (e.g., defiance, aggression) Increasing child social skills, cooperation, and self-esteem
Types of techniques	Delivered in-home Counselor in room Video recording Counselor review video Gives video and in-the-moment feedback	Counselor in room providing: reflective unstructured developmental guidance, emotional safety and support, concrete assistance, protective behavior modeling, facilitation of a joint trauma narrative, facilitation of play-based interactions between	Counselor behind one-way mirror when coaching parent Live/in vivo coaching Specific behavioral goals for parents CDI—“PRIDE” skills PDI—effective commands

		caregiver and child, interpretation of current behavior in light of past trauma experiences, and recognition of benign influences in the past	
Technology needed	Laptop computer Video camera Webcam for supervision	None	Typically, two rooms with a one-way mirror, wireless communication system
Counselor training requirements	2- to 3-day training and a year of supervision	3-day initial workshop followed by two 2-day workshops at 6-month intervals	40 hours of intensive skills training followed by completion of two supervised cases before independent practice

CDI, child-directed interaction; PDI, parent-directed interaction.

Attachment and Biobehavioral Catch-Up

ABC (Dozier et al., 2006) was developed by Mary Dozier and her colleagues. After noticing the immense bond between her and her newborn son, Dozier wondered what it was like for infants and young children who had experienced separation from their primary caregivers. She and her colleagues studied infants and young children who were placed into the foster care system, and found that these children had higher levels of biological dysregulation and, despite being dysregulated, acted as if they did not need nurturing (Dozier, Higley, Albus, & Nutter, 2002; Dozier, Manni, et al., 2006). Dozier noticed that this had a negative impact on the foster caregivers caring for these maltreated children and that even nurturing foster caregivers began to provide non-nurturing care (Dozier et al., 2002). Based on neuroscience and attachment research, Dozier developed a manualized, 10-session filial therapy model for infants/children ages 6 to 24 months in foster care and their foster caregivers. In this filial model, the counselor video records play interactions with the dyad and coaches the caregiver to increase the nurturing, sensitive, and delightful interactions with the child, and to decrease caregiver behaviors that are frightening to the child (Bernard et al., 2012). The ABC model's long-term goal is to increase the child's attachment security, which has been linked to long-term, positive, developmental outcomes for the infant/child (Dozier, Peloso, Lewis, Laurenceau, & Levine, 2008). The early studies on the ABC model were examining children in foster families; however, the model has also been examined with children at risk for child maltreatment and their biological parents (Bernard, Hostinar, & Dozier, 2015).

Child–Parent Psychotherapy

CPP (Lieberman & Van Horn, 2005) was developed by Alicia Lieberman and Patricia Van Horn to support children ages birth to 6 years old who had been exposed to family violence and were experiencing trauma symptoms (Lieberman & Van Horn, 2005). Family violence and other traumatic family events often cause young children to feel unsafe, experience posttraumatic stress disorder (PTSD) symptoms, and, if not addressed, could have a negative impact on the child's future social, emotional, and physical development (Anda, 2007). Pulling primarily from attachment and psychodynamic theories, Lieberman and Van Horn (2011) developed a filial model in which the counselor meets weekly for up to a year with the young child and caregiver to focus on improving the dyad's relationship, normalizing the trauma-related responses, and returning the child to normal developmental functioning.

Parent–Child Interaction Therapy

PCIT (Hood & Eyberg, 2003) is a manualized, dyadic filial intervention, which was originally designed to help decrease child oppositional behaviors, such as defiance and aggression, in children aged 2.5 to 6.5 years. PCIT has two sections: child-directed interaction (CDI) and parent-directed interaction (PDI). The CDI section focuses on improving the caregiver–child relationship to let the child lead the play interactions, reflect and describe the child's play behaviors, and praise the child. Once a caregiver has mastered the CDI section skills, he or she then moves to the PDI section, which helps parents to learn specific discipline techniques to help decrease child problem behaviors. In both sections, the PCIT counselor coaches the caregiver, often through wireless communication and a one-way mirror, until the caregiver has reached mastery. Once both sections have been mastered by the caregiver and the child's symptoms have returned to within normal limits (typically taking between 14 and 20 sessions), the PCIT therapy is complete.

TRAINING IN ABC, CPP, AND PCIT

A counselor who wishes to work with young children should seek filial training in one or more of the aforementioned models. Initially, these models require a substantial commitment to training and supervision; however, the investment is worthwhile. Researchers have found that counselors who have effective training in evidence-based interventions may have a stronger impact on client positive outcomes (Weisz, Jensen-Doss, & Hawley, 2006). In the following sections, we list each model's endorsed training requirements.

ABC Training

ABC is the only one of the three models described here in which a counselor who is not licensed can be trained; however, counselors must attend a prerequisite, 30-minute screening interview that can be conducted in person or remotely. The screening has been very useful to the ABC training teams in predicting which parent coaches will be a good fit for the model. The model is taught by developer-endorsed trainers over the course of approximately 1 year. Trainees attend 3 days of face-to-face learning sessions; must subsequently submit three full, 10-session, video-recorded ABC intervention cases; and must attend two types of weekly supervision to review their recorded sessions. The first weekly 30 minutes of supervision is required to learn how to code the video-recorded material; the other weekly hour of supervision is required to ensure model fidelity. The model requires the use of a laptop computer, a video recorder, and access to video conferencing for supervision. At the end of the training period, counselors can be nationally rostered when they have demonstrated fidelity and adherence on their three completed ABC cases.

CPP Training

Unlike ABC, only licensed mental health clinicians can be trained in CPP. There are three developer endorsed ways to garner training in CPP: learning collaboratives, learning communities, and single agency trainings. Learning collaborative (Markiewicz, Ebert, Ling, Amaya-Jackson, & Kisiel, 2006) trainings require a competitive application process for counselors and administrative leaders in mental health agencies. When accepted into the learning collaborative, counselors obtain 18 months of training and support, including face-to-face training days and supervision on cases. The administrative leaders in the agency also receive training and consultation on how to make the organizational changes needed to fully support the CPP model. To ensure the model is being effectively delivered to children and their families, agencies involved in learning collaboratives must agree to collect monthly outcome data related to their CPP cases.

Learning communities are similar to learning collaboratives in that they involve several agencies training together and learning from one another; however, they do not involve training the administrative leaders at the agency or providing the implementation consultation used in the learning collaborative models that ensure the most efficient start-up and lasting fidelity to the evidence-based CPP model.

The third type of CPP training is available for single agencies with multiple licensed counselors. This training would include the face-to-face training days and supervision on cases. Because of the ongoing fidelity requirements for weekly supervision, individual private practitioners are typically not trained in the CPP model.

For any of the three CPP training modalities, agencies must meet certain prerequisite criteria to be approved for CPP training. Agencies must demonstrate that their staff has, or has the ability to, obtain expertise in the core competencies of CPP, including early childhood development, and that the staff will be given the time and ongoing ability to attend weekly reflective supervision. Agencies must also be able to serve children in the 0- to 5-year age range who have experienced trauma, and staff must have read the two manuals in advance of the initial face-to-face training. The face-to-face trainings involve an initial 3-day training, followed by two additional 2-day trainings, over an 18-month period. During that time, counselors are required to provide CPP on approximately four cases and receive case consultation from the developer-endorsed supervisors twice monthly in 1-hour group consultation calls. Counselors are also required to complete a series of fidelity tools to ensure they are delivering the model effectively. If all requirements are met, at the end of the 18-months, counselors can be nationally rostered.

PCIT Training

PCIT International is the developer-endorsed source for training in PCIT (www.pcit.org). It maintains the training guidelines and a list of master trainers and certified therapists. A master's degree or higher and a relevant professional mental health license is required for training. PCIT International requires 40 hours of face-to-face training and completion of two cases under consultation with video review of specific sessions. Counselors who complete their training can apply to be a certified PCIT therapist and need to be recertified every 2 years with completion of 3 hours of continuing education authorized by PCIT International.

RESEARCH SUPPORT

As mentioned earlier, ABC, CPP, and PCIT have strong evidence-based support for their effectiveness at improving child social and emotional outcomes and the caregiver–child relationship. It is beyond the scope of this chapter overview to examine all the peer-reviewed studies associated with these three models. Instead, a brief overview of the most rigorous studies and their outcomes is provided (Table 8.2).

TABLE 8.2 COMPARING RESEARCH FINDINGS OF ABC, CPP, AND PCIT FILIAL MODELS

Filial Model Aspects	ABC	CPP	PCIT
Evidence-based research studies	Multiple RCT with foster children/parents, child protective services children/parents	Multiple RCT dyads with exposure to domestic violence, child maltreatment	Multiple RCT with preschoolers, mentally handicapped preschoolers, maltreating parents/caregivers
Sample research outcomes • Infant/child • Adult	*Infant/child*—improved on attachment security, cortisol levels, emotion regulation, cognitive flexibility and theory-of-mind skills, and avoidance behaviors *Adult*—lowered total child abuse potential and parenting stress	*Infant/child*—decreased behavioral problems, PTSD symptoms; improved attachment security, maternal representations *Adult*—fewer avoidance behaviors, distress, and PTSD symptoms; increased empathic responses	*Child*—increased behavioral compliance *Adult*—increased positive interactions; lower parental stress and child abuse potential
Are there longitudinal follow-up studies?	Yes, from 1 month to 27 months follow-up	Yes, 6 months follow-up	Yes, 4 months–6 years follow-up
Cultural applications of models	Also been implemented in Spanish and Norwegian cultures	Also been implemented in Spanish/Latino cultures and a perinatal population	Spanish manual available. Also been implemented in Hong Kong, England, Russia, Canada, the Netherlands, and Australia

ABC, attachment and biobehavioral catch-up; CPP, child–parent psychotherapy; PCIT, parent–child interaction therapy; PTSD, posttraumatic stress disorder; RCT, randomized controlled trials.

ABC Research Summary

ABC is rated *1, Well-Supported by Research Evidence,* on the Scientific Rating Scale, which indicates that it has had at least two rigorous randomized controlled trials, with at least one study documenting a sustained treatment effect of at least 1 year (California Evidence-Based Clearinghouse for Child Welfare, 2015a). ABC has been studied with young children who have experienced child maltreatment who were currently in foster care placement or with parents who were involved with child protective services. In these studies, the infants/children improved their attachment security, emotion regulation, cognitive flexibility, and avoidance behaviors (Bick & Dozier, 2013; Dozier, Peloso, et al., 2006; Lewis-Morrarty, Dozier, Bernard, Terracciano, & Moore, 2012; Lind, Bernard, Ross, & Dozier, 2014; Sprang, 2009). ABC has also been shown to improve a biological marker of stress, cortisol levels, in these maltreated infants/children (Bernard et al., 2015; Dozier et al., 2008). This is important because infants/children who have experienced child maltreatment, and other forms of adversity, can have irregular patterns of cortisol levels throughout the day (Dozier et al., 2008) and long-term cortisol irregularities have been shown to be detrimental to brain development (Carrion & Wong, 2012). Researchers also found that caregivers who had the ABC intervention had lower child abuse potential and parenting stress (Dozier, Peloso, et al., 2006; Sprang, 2009).

CPP Research Summary

CPP is rated a *2, Supported by Research Evidence,* on the Scientific Rating Scale, which means it has had at least one rigorous randomized controlled trial with a sustained effect of at least 6 months (California Evidence-Based Clearinghouse for Child Welfare, 2015b). Infants/children improved on their problem behaviors, PTSD symptoms, attachment security, and maternal representations (Cicchetti, Rogosch, & Toth, 2006; Lieberman, Van Horn, & Ippen, 2005). Caregivers improved their avoidant behaviors, distress, PTSD symptoms, and empathy (Cicchetti et al., 2006; Lieberman, Van Horn, et al., 2005).

PCIT Research Summary

As was ABC, PCIT is also rated *1, Well-Supported by Research Evidence,* on the Scientific Rating Scale (California Evidence-Based Clearinghouse for Child Welfare, 2015c). Children who experienced the PCIT intervention had decreased parent-reported behavior problems, and caregivers had lower parental stress, fewer child abuse reports, and more positive interactions with their child (Bagner & Eyberg, 2007; Chaffin et al., 2004; Nixon et al., 2003; Schuhmann, Foote, Eyberg, Boggs, & Algina, 1998).

FILIAL MODEL TECHNIQUES

Though ABC, CPP, and PCIT are similar in that they are grounded in attachment theory and support work with young children, they each have quite distinct clinical techniques. What would be clinically acceptable in one filial model would not be clinically appropriate in another. The technology needed in each intervention also varies widely. In this section, the summary of techniques for each of these models can be seen in Table 8.1. It may be useful in providing clarity on the similarities and differences between the models.

ABC Techniques

ABC is a structured, video-recorded, 10-session, home-visiting filial model for infants and young children who have experienced early adversity (Dozier et al., 2009). According to the ABC developer, Mary Dozier, early childhood adversity may include exposure to domestic violence, parental substance abuse, homelessness, parental neglect, and/or parental separation. Researchers have clearly documented that these types of adversities in early childhood can have a negative impact on the future development of the child (Anda et al., 2002; Shonkoff, 2010; Thompson, 2008).

The ABC model is based on four primary assertions about infants and young children with early adversity. First, all children, but especially children who have experienced adversity, require nurturance even though they do not always outwardly demonstrate the need for nurturance. Second, caregivers, for a variety of reasons, are not always comfortable meeting a child's need for nurturance. Sometimes caregivers do not see the infant's bid for nurturance, and sometimes, the caregivers simply respond the same way the child responds to them. For example, a young child who is not used to having his needs for nurturance met might not cry when hurt, because he or she has learned not to expect comfort from anyone. While still distressed, the child does not outwardly appear to be. A foster mother might see that the child is not crying or coming to her and respond in-kind, by not going to the child and offering nurturance. The foster mother likely believes she is actually following the child's lead because he or she does not appear to need her in that moment. What's more, if she were to attempt to nurture, the child might resist. This would strengthen her belief that the child does not "want" her to nurture him or her, when, in reality, the child is simply responding based on his or her previous maltreated experiences. Third, the ABC intervention posits that early adversity has the capacity to cause infants and toddlers to become biologically and behaviorally dysregulated, and the final ABC assumption asserts that early adversity has the capacity to cause infants and toddlers to be particularly susceptible to a caregiver's frightening behavior.

Based on the earlier assumptions, the ABC intervention's parent coach helps caregivers: (a) nurture a distressed baby even if the infant does not elicit nurturing, (b) follow the baby's lead with delight, and (c) recognize and avoid being scary to the infant. ABC parent coaches use a combination of interactive activities including video recordings of the dyad, previously recorded videos of other dyads that serve as examples of caregiver behaviors, and in-the-moment commenting from the counselor coach. The parent coach provides feedback to the caregiver by specifically describing and praising the caregiver's behavior in one of the three target areas and linking the caregiver's behavior to both the immediate and long-term benefits to the child.

Before beginning ABC treatment, the counselor does an assessment of the dyad. The counselor coach video records a 5-minute play interaction and codes the caregiver on specific behaviors targeted in the intervention, such as sensitivity and intrusiveness. The counselor lets the caregiver know that each of the 10 ABC sessions will be video recorded in order to show the caregiver examples of the behaviors he or she is demonstrating and the impact of those behaviors on the child. Then, the counselor begins the first two ABC sessions that focus on psychoeducation about the attachment relationship and the importance of nurturing the child, even when it is difficult for the caregiver or when the child does not look like he or she needs the caregiver. While providing this information, the counselor is careful to take every possible opportunity to specifically praise the caregiver when he or she provides nurturance to the child during the session.

In the third and fourth session, the counselor uses a number of specific toys to facilitate play between the caregiver and child, so the counselor can facilitate the caregiver's ability to allow the child to set the course of the play and follow the child's lead with delight. In the fifth session, the counselor continues to support these new skills while helping the caregiver focus on the additional skill of reading the child's cues for disengagement or nurturance. In the remaining five sessions, the counselor/coach continues to consolidate these new skills while helping the caregiver examine his or her own history and overcome any tendencies the caregiver may have to be frightening or avoid nurturing. In the 10th session, the counselor coach may show the caregiver a video of a number of clips of the caregiver and child engaged in nurturing and playful interactions from the previous sessions. This video can be left with the caregiver as a memento, whereas the other session recordings are generally destroyed. The brief postassessment play interaction is then completed.

CPP Techniques

CPP is an infant mental health model designed to treat the trauma of interpersonal violence in young children (ages 0–6 years) and their primary attachment figures. The model considers the child–caregiver relationship, including the child and caregiver's system of jointly constructed meanings about their relationship, to be the *client*, rather than either the child or the caregiver as individual clients. Unlike other child treatment modalities where there is an emphasis on the counselor building a relationship with the child, CPP counselors emphasize building the relationship *between* the child and caregiver.

CPP is grounded in two primary principles. First, the counselor must never *out-parent the parent*, which means the counselor is always mindful of how his or her actions in the session are being interpreted. In every session, the counselor must carefully consider the impact the chosen CPP intervention will have on the *child's* perception of self, caregiver, and the relationship, as well as the impact the intervention will have on the *caregiver's* perception of self, child, and the relationship. The second CPP principle focuses on the caregiver's rightful place as the child's guide through his or her recovery from the traumatic experience(s). Because the trauma occurred in the context of a family relationship, the trauma must be healed in the context of that relationship. Drs. Lieberman and Van Horn explain that when caregivers and children experience interpersonal violence, they often become traumatic reminders for one another, which can harm the security of their attachment relationship. Thus, the counselor can serve as an interpretive *guide* in helping the dyad see where they are triggering each other's traumatic memories; however, the caregiver and child must ultimately repair the relationship themselves.

The first step in CPP, and most mental health treatments with children, is a thorough assessment of the child, caregiver, and dyad's relationship.

Counselors must assess the child's history of exposure to trauma as well as the impact those exposures are having on the child's symptom manifestation. There are a number of tools available for this purpose, including the Young Child PTSD Checklist (Scheeringa, 2010), which is free, measures multiple trauma domains, and is available in English and Spanish. Other measures may be used to assess trauma exposures and trauma symptoms separately. A very comprehensive assessment of exposures is the Traumatic Events Screening Inventory for Children (Ford et al., 2002), which is available for free through the National Center for PTSD (http://www.ptsd.va.gov). A measure that assesses only exposures, such as this one, would then be paired with a measure that assesses only symptoms, such as the Trauma Symptom Checklist for Children (Briere, 1996) or the Trauma Symptom Checklist for Young Children (Briere et al., 2001). The counselor must be careful to check the ages of the various measures to ensure that they are normed with similar ages to the client being assessed. There are a number of other excellent trauma measures available for review at the National Child Traumatic Stress Network (http://nctsnet.org).

A broad social and emotional measure is also required to assess general child symptoms. This could include the Child Behavior Checklist (Achenbach & Rescorla, 2001), the free Strengths and Difficulties Questionnaire (Goodman, 1997), or the Eyberg Child Behavior Inventory (ECBI; Eyberg & Pincus, 1999), to name a few. Counselors are then required to assess the child's developmental functioning. This may be done through observation of the child and discussion with the caregiver, or through the use of a formal assessment measure, such as the Ages and Stages Questionnaire (Squires & Bricker, 2009). Because CPP was designed for children who have been exposed to domestic violence, it is especially important for the counselor to continue to assess for traumatic events throughout the treatment, including any new exposures to domestic violence, in this population.

Because CPP is a dyadic model, the caregiver's trauma history, symptoms, and functioning must also be assessed. This may be done through clinical interview or in conjunction with standardized assessment tools. One excellent, free measure to assess caregiver trauma history is the Life Stressor Checklist–Revised (Wolfe, Kimerling, Brown, Chrestman, & Levin, 1996). This can be used in conjunction with the free PTSD Checklist for the *Diagnostic and Statistical Manual of Mental Disorders* (5th ed.; *DSM-5*; American Psychiatric Association, 2013; Weathers et al., 2013). Both are available at the National Center for PTSD website (www.ptsd.va.gov). It is also useful to include a measure of caregiver depression, such as the free Center for Epidemiological Studies Depression Scale–Revised (Eaton, Smith, Ybarra, Muntaner, & Tien, 2004). Some counselors also include a general measure of functioning, such as the Brief Symptom Inventory (Derogatis, 1993), which screens not only for depression but also for anxiety and somatization.

In addition to assessing the caregiver's trauma history and symptoms, CPP focuses on the benign influences in a caregiver's history on which he or she may draw for support. The developers of CPP have created a wonderful semi-structured interview titled, "Angels in the Nursery," which is based on an article with the same name (Lieberman, Padrón, Van Horn, & Harris, 2005), to help caregivers think as they move through treatment about relationship strengths from their past. This interview is currently only available through CPP-endorsed trainers.

The strengths and difficulties in the child–caregiver relationship can also be assessed through observation of their attachment interactions. The counselor may note how a child explores the environment and seeks out the caregiver to regulate his or her affect and behavior, and how the caregiver supports the child's exploration and provides comfort when needed. These are typical attachment interactions seen in child–caregiver dyads. Other caregiver assessments that may be helpful include the Working Model of the Child Interview (Zeanah, Benoit, Barton, & Hirshberg, 1996) and the Parenting Stress Index (Abidin, 1983).

After the assessment, the counselor can begin weekly CPP treatment. In the beginning of the CPP intervention, the counselor's goal is to simply create an emotionally safe environment in which the dyad can engage one another. Based on the trauma described in the assessment, the CPP counselor brings developmentally appropriate toys such as animal and dollhouse families, blocks, play dishes and doctor kits, toy phones, and any other toys that reflect some of the dyad's traumatic experiences. Unlike the other filial models reviewed in this chapter, CPP is very flexible in its approach to the session-to-session techniques. There is no agenda brought into the weekly sessions; instead, the counselor focuses the weekly sessions on the traumatic material the dyad may be trying to avoid. The counselor provides reflective, unstructured, developmental guidance; models protective behavior; provides concrete assistance with problems of daily living; promotes development through language, play, and physical contact; interprets the child's and caregiver's intentions, feelings, and behaviors to one another; and helps both link their current behaviors to their trauma histories when appropriate (Lieberman & Van Horn, 2011).

Each week, the CPP counselor determines what is needed in a session, based on the caregiver's and child's state of mind and the immediate and long-term goals for the dyad, and intervenes based on his or her *core competencies*. These core competencies include knowledge of human development as well as psychopathology, knowledge of the core concepts of trauma, cultural competence, ability to observe behavior, ability to collaborate with service systems, and, most important, the capacity to act as a bridge between the child and caregiver and be self-reflective. These core competencies allow the counselor to flexibly intervene in a number of ways in order to meet the goals of (a) strengthening physiological and affective regulation in both child and caregiver; (b) increasing reciprocity in the child–caregiver relationship; (c) increasing emotional and physical safety and stability; (d) enhancing understanding of the impact the trauma has had on the child, the caregiver, and their relationship; (e) enhancing the caregiver's ability to understand the meaning of the child's behavior in the context of the trauma, as well as enhancing the child's view of the caregiver's behavior as having protective intentions; and (f) helping the child and caregiver differentiate the time of the trauma from their current circumstances and put the trauma in a helpful perspective so the dyad can return to a healthy developmental trajectory (Lieberman & Van Horn, 2005).

CPP is based on the concept of parallel processes, whereby the reflective function of the counselor is used to facilitate enhanced reflective function in the caregiver. Reflective function, a process akin to empathy, is the degree to which an individual is both aware of his or her own internal states (affective, physiological, and cognitive) in relation to others, as well as the influence of those internal states on the other, and is able to consider the internal states of the other. A caregiver who has well-developed reflective function is better able to facilitate a secure attachment relationship with his or her child because he or she is better able to accurately read and respond to the child's needs. This is a core concept of CPP because the dyad's perceptions of themselves, one another, and their relationship are considered to be the focus of the treatment (i.e., the *client*). The counselor uses his or her own capacity for reflective function, which is strengthened in the context of reflective supervision, to strengthen the reflective functioning in the caregiver. Because this is such a core concept in CPP, a counselor must receive consistent reflective supervision in order to claim fidelity to the model.

PCIT Techniques

PCIT is a structured intervention designed to strengthen the caregiver–child relationship and improve the child's disruptive behaviors. To determine whether a child's symptoms are appropriate for PCIT, the child's caregiver completes the ECBI (Eyberg & Pincus, 1999). The ECBI is a norm-referenced measure of disruptive behavior; thus, a clinically significant score on the ECBI indicates the child's behaviors are appropriate for the PCIT intervention.

During the first phase of PCIT, CDI, the caregiver is taught some basic play therapy skills designed to provide interactions that minimize conflict between the parent and child and promote the caregiver's use of differential attention to increase the child's prosocial behavior. The caregiver is coached to use *P-R-I-D-E* skills while playing with the child using PCIT-appropriate toys (unstructured toys promoting imagination, such as stacking blocks, play food, and crayons with blank paper). In the P-R-I-D-E acronym, the *P* stands for *praise*, specifically, a labeled praise for any prosocial child behavior. The *R* stands for *reflect*, which means for any prosocial speech the child gives, the caregiver repeats the content of the child's prosocial speech back to the child. The *I* stands for *imitate*, which means the caregiver physically imitates any of the child's prosocial play with the toys. The *D* stands for *describe*, specifically behavior description, which means the caregiver describes any prosocial child behavior. Finally, the *E* stands for *enjoy*, which means the caregiver shows enjoyment when playing with the child when the child is being prosocial. Caregivers are coached to avoid giving their child commands, asking questions, and using any negative talk, including criticism. Caregivers are also taught to ignore whining and any other ignorable behavior. Aggressive or harmful behaviors during the session are not ignored; depending on the function of the behavior, the play session is stopped as a consequence. During these sessions, the PCIT coach rates the caregiver on his or her CDI behaviors on a CDI coding sheet provided to those trained in the model. Mastery of the CDI phase of treatment occurs when the caregiver provides the child 10 labeled praises, 10 reflections, and 10 behavior descriptions and no more than three total commands, questions, and criticisms during the 5-minute coding period. Imitation and enjoyment are rated qualitatively.

On caregiver mastery of the CDI skills, the second phase of PCIT begins: PDI. With the caregiver's skill base of differential attention learned in the first phase, the caregiver is taught how to give effective commands and to follow a specific discipline procedure when the child does not follow the commands. Caregivers are taught eight criteria that make a command effective (e.g., only one command given at a time, commands should be positively stated). The discipline procedure is a version of time-out with no loopholes, including having a backup plan for the potential that the child will leave the time-out chair. Mastery of the second phase of treatment occurs when 75% of the parent commands are effective and that the parent follows through correctly with the discipline procedure for 75% of the commands during the 5-minute coding period.

At the beginning of both the CDI and PDI treatment phases, caregivers participate in a session without their child present where the counselor thoroughly teaches each set of skills. The majority of sessions are coaching sessions, in which the caregiver plays with the child while a counselor watches and listens to the interactions from another room and provides immediate feedback to the caregiver frequently through a wireless ear bud. Because coaching is an essential element of PCIT, technology is needed that allows the counselor to hear and see the interaction and that permits the counselor to speak to the caregiver without the child hearing. Furthermore, to ensure that only appropriate toys are used and to reduce the child's access to potentially dangerous objects, the PCIT room should be stripped of everything except for what is needed for therapy. Due to the technology and environmental requirements needed to implement the treatment, most of the research on the effectiveness of PCIT has been done in clinics. Coaching lasts approximately 30 minutes per session, which occur weekly. Coding of the caregiver skills for 5 minutes precedes coaching to provide the counselor with the caregiver's baseline skill level for the week and to determine whether the caregiver and child are able to move to the second phase of treatment or graduate.

Five minutes of daily at-home practice between caregiver and child is assigned to give the caregiver an opportunity to practice the skills and for the child to receive a frequent therapeutic benefit. Caregivers also complete the ECBI at the beginning of each session. The counselor shares a graphic display of the scores weekly with the caregiver to gauge progress. Successful completion of PCIT occurs when the caregiver has met mastery of both the CDI and PDI skills and the child's behavior is subclinical on the ECBI.

CASE EXAMPLE: SOPHIA'S STORY

Sophia's fictional story follows her through several events in her young life. After each life event, Sophia is referred to one of the three filial models described in this chapter. This format provides a window into each of the three filial models and how they work best with Sophia's developmental age and social–emotional issues.

(*continued*)

(*continued*)

Attachment and Biobehavioral Catch-Up

Sophia is a 10-month-old baby girl who was recently placed in foster care by the local child welfare agency when the police received a report of domestic violence between Sophia's mother and her boyfriend. When the police arrived on the scene, Sophia's mother and boyfriend were both clearly intoxicated. Sophia's mother was holding the crying Sophia while screaming at her boyfriend. Both adults appeared bloodied and distraught. Sophia was placed in a foster home with an older foster mother, Mrs. Nash, who has been fostering for 20 years.

After a month in care, Mrs. Nash reports to the child welfare social worker that Sophia continues to be very fussy during the day and wakes up crying several times in the night. Mrs. Nash tells the social worker she typically has little trouble getting her foster children down to bed, but Sophia had not seemed to adjust. She continues to cry no matter how much Mrs. Nash ignores the behavior. The social worker calls the local mental health agency that supports children ages birth to 5 years. Tara, one of the agency's counselors, determines that Sophia and Mrs. Nash would benefit from the ABC intervention due to the adversities Sophia experienced living with, and being separated from, her mother.

In the first few ABC sessions, Tara video records Mrs. Nash and Sophia playing together. Commenting in-the-moment as Mrs. Nash and Sophia play, Tara praises Mrs. Nash when she shows nurturing behaviors toward Sophia. Over the next sessions, Tara shows Mrs. Nash video excerpts from previous weekly sessions where Mrs. Nash nurtured Sophia when she was distressed. Tara also helps Mrs. Nash learn what it means to follow Sophia's lead in the play activities with delight.

In the fifth ABC session, Tara engages Mrs. Nash in a discussion about how babies can sometimes feel overwhelmed in an interaction with their caregiver, and it can be challenging for a caregiver to recognize the shift in the baby from engagement to disengagement. Tara explains that she brought puppets to help Mrs. Nash

(*continued*)

practice following Sophia's need for disengagement during play with puppets, which can sometimes be scary for young children who do not understand why the puppets sometimes move and sometimes do not. Mrs. Nash and Sophia sit on the floor with Tara and the puppets. Sophia looks at the puppets but does not reach for them. Mrs. Nash notices that she looked at them and holds one out to Sophia. Sophia looks away from the puppets, and Mrs. Nash puts the puppet down. Tara comments, "You put the puppet down when she turned away! That was a wonderful job following her lead. You are letting her know that she has a say in her environment."

When Sophia looks back at the puppets, Mrs. Nash puts one of the puppets on her hand. "Oh!" Tara exclaims. "You did it again! Well done! You noticed she showed an interest in the puppets and you followed her lead by putting it on your hand. . . ." As Tara speaks, Sophia begins to cry. Mrs. Nash frowns and shakes her head slightly as she says to Sophia, "You're fine. It's just a puppet. Why do you get so upset?" Tara pauses and says to Mrs. Nash, "I think you're right that Sophia is upset right now. What do you think she needs you to do?" Mrs. Nash sighs and picks up Sophia. Sophia continues to cry.

Mrs. Nash says to Tara, "You see? I do what you say, but she keeps crying." Tara nods and reminds Mrs. Nash that sometimes Sophia is difficult to read and that Mrs. Nash's goal is to let Sophia know she is there for her, not to make her stop crying. As Mrs. Nash continues to hold Sophia, Sophia begins to snuggle into her. Tara notes this change, remarking, "You are doing a beautiful job nurturing her right now. You are letting her know you are here when she needs you and she can count on that." Sophia nuzzles into Mrs. Nash, and Mrs. Nash gives Sophia a squeeze.

The sessions continue for several more weeks. Tara shares, through video recordings or in-the moment praise, all the great ways Mrs. Nash is nurturing Sophia, following her lead, and helping her feel supported when she is distressed. By the end of 10 weeks, Mrs. Nash reports that Sophia is sleeping through the night and is much less irritable.

(*continued*)

(*continued*)

Child–Parent Psychotherapy

By the time Sophia is 30 months old, her biological mother, Ms. Smith, has successfully completed a residential substance abuse treatment program and is no longer in a relationship with her abusive boyfriend. The child welfare agency returns Sophia to Ms. Smith's care, but Sophia and Ms. Smith struggle in their relationship. The social worker from the child welfare agency observes that Ms. Smith appears impatient with Sophia and frequently yells at her. The social worker notices that Sophia appears alternately clingy with and withdrawn from her mother. Out of fear Sophia would again be removed from her custody, Ms. Smith tells the social worker that Sophia is whiny, but she can handle it. The social worker suggests a referral to a local mental health agency for CPP, and Ms. Smith reluctantly agrees.

The CPP counselor assigned to the dyad is a young counselor named Joe. He completes a thorough assessment of Sophia, Ms. Smith, and their relationship. He learns that Ms. Smith had an abusive family environment when she was growing up, and no adult intervened. She started using drugs after she ran away from home at the age of 17 to get away from her abusive stepfather. Joe begins meeting weekly with the dyad in their apartment.

After working with the family in the intervention phase of CPP for several months, Joe expresses in a reflective supervision session that he feels stuck. He informs his supervisor that the play had been going well and that Ms. Smith was able to tolerate increasingly difficult content in Sophia's play, but that Ms. Smith would still lose her temper with Sophia and threaten to spank her. Joe's supervisor asked him to explain what had happened in the latest session. Joe explains, "I arrived for the session and Sophia ran outside to meet me even though her mother was screaming at her to get back inside. When we got in the house, I explained to Sophia that it was not safe for her to run out to meet me and that mommy was trying to be sure you did not get hurt." Joe tells his supervisor that Sophia did not appear to hear him, but started grabbing his bag of toys and taking all of them out. Then, Ms. Smith yelled at Sophia to take out one thing at a time.

(*continued*)

Joe's CPP supervisor asks how he felt when Sophia's mother yelled at her. Joe considers the question and explains that he knew Sophia's mess making was an issue for Ms. Smith, and he had previously reassured her that this was what young children did and it was OK for Sophia to make a mess. He says he no longer says it, because he thinks it might make Ms. Smith and Sophia feel like Joe is taking Sophia's "side" and not supporting Ms. Smith's parenting. He tells his supervisor that it still bothers him, because he feels like Ms. Smith is unnecessarily controlling of Sophia. He shares with his supervisor that he began to feel a familiar tension in his chest when Ms. Smith reprimanded Sophia. His supervisor asks Joe what Sophia did when Ms. Smith yelled. Joe notes Sophia ignored her. When asked how Ms. Smith responded to this, Joe acknowledges he could not really remember. He notes he was watching what Sophia was taking out of the bag. Sophia took out dinosaur and policeman figures and began having the dinosaur eat the policeman; Sophia became very aggressive in the play. Joe's supervisor again asks how Ms. Smith had responded. Joe states she had again reprimanded Sophia for playing roughly with the toys. Joe notes, "It was so clear that Sophia was playing out a theme of violence and that the authority figures can't control the violence and keep everyone safe. All Ms. Smith cared about was the toys. She just didn't get it!"

Joe's supervisor asks him how he was feeling watching Sophia play and how he thought Sophia felt. Joe notes that Sophia appeared "lost" in the play. He described her face as serious and rigid. He notes she got louder as she played. Joe expresses that he was feeling excited because "she was actually doing the trauma processing! She was putting it out there!" Joe's supervisor asks him what he thought Ms. Smith was feeling watching her daughter play in this manner. Joe states he believed she was angry that Sophia was playing so roughly and that she had not been compliant when Joe first arrived. When asked if Joe might have any other hypotheses about Ms. Smith's feelings, Joe states he can not think of any. His supervisor notes it seemed that Joe wanted very much to help Sophia heal from all the violence and turmoil she had experienced.

(*continued*)

(*continued*)

Joe agrees this was true. His supervisor asks if he thought Ms. Smith also needed healing from all of the violence and turmoil she had experienced. Joe nods silently. He then notes, "I forgot to hold Ms. Smith's perspective in mind. I got so wrapped up in what Sophia was doing, I was just irritated that Ms. Smith wasn't responding the way I wanted her to." Joe's supervisor asks him to again consider what might have been happening for Ms. Smith when Sophia was playing out this theme. Joe suggests, "I wonder if she was maybe remembering the violence herself? Or maybe her violent experiences as a child? Maybe she was feeling out of control and she yelled at Sophia to play differently because she was trying to figure out a way to get back in control." Joe's supervisor asks him how this hypothesis could be useful to him in his next session. Joe says, "Next time, I'm going to attend more carefully to Ms. Smith's state of mind. Ask her what she's feeling and thinking. And help them both to remember that when they remember their scary history, it doesn't mean it is happening again." Joe states he will let Ms. Smith know that he had been thinking about this interaction and that he would need to make a relationship repair with Ms. Smith, because he had not attended to her emotional needs in that moment. The sessions continue over the next 6 months; eventually, Ms. Smith is able to see how her childhood history and the traumas she experienced are impacting her and Sophia's relationship.

Parent–Child Interaction Therapy

Sophia is now 4.5 years old. Ms. Smith hears from the child-care provider that Sophia is at risk of being expelled from her child-care center and, admittedly, that she has tolerated Sophia's difficult behaviors at home too long. She calls the local mental health agency and asks for help. The dyad is assigned to a counselor named Angela, who begins an assessment. On the Child Behavior Checklist (CBCL; Achenbach & Rescorla, 2001), Sophia had a clinically significant score on Rule-Breaking Behavior; Sophia also had a significant score on the ECBI (Eyberg & Pincus, 1999). During the

(*continued*)

Observation Session (split into three parts: child-led play, parent-led play, and clean-up), Sophia played well during the child-led play, but she was more resistant to playing with her mother when it was her mother's turn to take the lead. When told to clean up, Sophia cleaned extremely slowly, protesting throughout. Her mother yelled at her and resorted to helping her clean up despite the instructions for Sophia to clean up independently. Ms. Smith indicated that she usually does more things for Sophia than she thinks she should because "it's just easier."

Ms. Smith comes in for the next session without Sophia so that Angela can explain and demonstrate the types of skills Ms. Smith will use with Sophia during the upcoming PCIT sessions and during a daily 5-minute therapeutic play session ("special play time") completed at home. Angela and Ms. Smith select appropriate toys from those the family already owns. Angela clarifies how Ms. Smith will get the sets of toys out and declare that special time is starting. Ms. Smith is instructed to record her special time homework on the provided sheet to be turned in at the next session.

When Ms. Smith and Sophia return for the next session, Angela has Ms. Smith complete the ECBI and hand in her homework sheet. Discussion with Ms. Smith reveals that she was implementing special time incorrectly, making it too onerous. Sophia had "thrown a fit" when Ms. Smith tried to end the special time after 5 minutes, so Ms. Smith had substantially lengthened special time, which made her less likely to fit it into the day. Angela clarifies that Ms. Smith should declare that special time is over after 5 minutes but allow Sophia to continue to play with the toys independently. Angela instructs Ms. Smith to ignore any nonaggressive protesting and specifically praise Sophia when she plays independently.

During the coaching portion, Angela coaches Ms. Smith, through a listening device in her ear and a one-way mirror, to ignore Sophia's protests when her mom describes her play and when Sophia plays with the light switch. Ms. Smith initially demonstrates her frustration with Sophia's behavior in her body language and tells Sophia to stop playing with the light switch and to play with the toys,

(*continued*)

(*continued*)

which makes Sophia's behavior worse. Ms. Smith learns that the play interactions are very positive when she completely ignores Sophia's inappropriate behaviors and takes every opportunity to follow Sophia's lead when Sophia appropriately plays with the toys. After eight coaching sessions, in which Angela prompts Ms. Smith to increase her labeled praises, behavior descriptions, and reflections, Ms. Smith completes these skills independently! She also decreases her questions, commands, and negative talk to meet mastery on the CDI skills.

After participating in the PDI teaching session, Ms. Smith is coached on giving effective commands to Sophia. Sophia complies well with multiple play commands during the first session, but she did go to time-out during the second session for refusing to clean up (e.g., "Put the crayons in the bin"). Angela provides encouragement and support to Ms. Smith over the listening device in her ear while Ms. Smith ignores Sophia's yelling and crying during the time-out. Ms. Smith learns that Sophia can understand that no amount of crying will get her out of complying with her mother's command, and it was just easier to comply. Over the next few weeks, Ms. Smith begins to focus on everyday commands at home (e.g., "Put your shoes by the door" and "Put the blocks in the bucket") and following through with the discipline sequence when Sophia does not comply. Angela helps Ms. Smith overcome the challenges she experienced when she used the strategies in the home and in the community. Angela also has a meeting with Ms. Smith and Sophia's child-care teacher. Angela listens supportively to the teacher's frustrations with Sophia and talks with the teacher about how to incorporate more specific praise for Sophia and, when giving commands, to provide only one warning before implementing a consequence. Angela gives Sophia's teacher the teacher handouts from the PCIT manual to reinforce the strategies.

Over time, Sophia's behavior with adults begins to reflect her new understanding that adults are in charge. Ms. Smith and the counselor complete a session on developing "house rules," in which Sophia learns that she would go straight to time-out for hitting her younger sister. Because Sophia's behavior has been too difficult for

(*continued*)

Ms. Smith to take her to the grocery store anymore, another session is completed at the grocery store. Angela coaches Ms. Smith on how to prevent and address Sophia's difficult behaviors in the grocery store.

After nine sessions of PDI, the ECBI indicates that Sophia's behaviors are now in the normal range. Ms. Smith is consistently able to use effective commands with Sophia and can follow through with the discipline sequence. Ms. Smith can praise Sophia regularly, following through with her commands and using special time on a regular basis. Ms. Smith says to Angela, "I feel more connected with her, we laugh and play more. I'm not angry with her all the time. We are a happier family."

REFERENCES

Abidin, R. R. (1983). *Parenting Stress Index: Manual, administration booklet, [and] research update*. Charlottesville, VA: Pediatric Psychology Press.

Achenbach, T. M., & Rescorla, L. A. (2001). *Manual for the ASEBA school-age forms & profiles*. Burlington: University of Vermont, Research Center for Children, Youth, & Families.

American Psychiatric Association. (2013). *Diagnostic and statistical manual of mental disorders* (5th ed.). Arlington, VA: American Psychiatric Publishing.

Anda, R. (2007). *The health and social impact of growing up with adverse childhood experiences: The human and economic costs of the status quo*. Retrieved from http://www.nacoa.org/pdfs/Anda%20NACoA%20Review_web.pdf

Anda, R. F., Whitfield, C. L., Felitti, V. J., Chapman, D., Edwards, V. J., Dube, S. R., & Williamson, D. F. (2002). Adverse childhood experiences, alcoholic parents, and later risk of alcoholism and depression. *Psychiatric Services, 53*(8), 1001–1009. http://dx.doi.org/10.1176/appi.ps.53.8.1001

Bagner, D. M., & Eyberg, S. M. (2007). Parent-child interaction therapy for disruptive behavior in children with mental retardation: A randomized controlled trial. *Journal of Clinical Child and Adolescent Psychology, 36*(3), 418–429. http://dx.doi.org/10.1080/15374410701448448

Bernard, K., Dozier, M., Bick, J., Lewis-Morrarty, E., Lindhiem, O., & Carlson, E. (2012). Enhancing attachment organization among maltreated children: Results of a randomized clinical trial. *Child Development, 83*(2), 623–636. http://dx.doi.org/10.1111/j.1467-8624.2011.01712.x

Bernard, K., Hostinar, C. E., & Dozier, M. (2015). Intervention effects on diurnal cortisol rhythms of child protective services—Referred infants in early childhood. *JAMA Pediatrics, 169*(2), 112. http://dx.doi.org/10.1001/jamapediatrics.2014.2369

Bick, J., & Dozier, M. (2013). The effectiveness of an attachment-based intervention in promoting foster mothers' sensitivity toward foster infants. *Infant Mental Health Journal, 34*(2), 95–103. http://dx.doi.org/10.1002/imhj.21373.THE

Booth, P. B., & Jernberg, A. M. (2009). *Theraplay: Helping parents and children build better relationships through attachment-based play* (3rd ed., Vol. 6). Hoboken, NJ: John Wiley & Sons.

Bratton, S., Ray, D., Rhine, T., & Jones, L. (2005). The efficacy of play therapy with children: A meta-analytic review of treatment outcomes. *Professional Psychology: Research and Practice, 35*(4), 376–390. http://dx.doi.org/10.1037/0735-7028.36.4.376

Briere, J. (1996). *Trauma symptom checklist for children*. Lutz, FL: Psychological Assessment Resources.

Briere, J., Johnson, K., Bissada, A., Damon, L., Crouch, J., Gil, E.,...Ernst, V. (2001). The Trauma Symptom Checklist for Young Children (TSCYC): Reliability and association with abuse exposure in a multi-site study. *Child Abuse & Neglect, 25*(8), 1001–1014. http://dx.doi.org/10.1016/S0145-2134(01)00253–8

California Evidence-Based Clearinghouse for Child Welfare. (2015a). Attachment and biobehavioral catch-up (ABC). Retrieved from http://www.cebc4cw.org/program/attachment-and-biobehavioral-catch-up/detailed

California Evidence-Based Clearinghouse for Child Welfare. (2015b). Child parent psychotherapy (CPP). Retrieved from http://www.cebc4cw.org/program/child-parent-psychotherapy/detailed

California Evidence-Based Clearinghouse for Child Welfare. (2015c). Parent child interaction therapy (PCIT). Retrieved from http://www.cebc4cw.org/program/parent-child-interaction-therapy

Carrion, V. G., & Wong, S. S. (2012). Can traumatic stress alter the brain? Understanding the implications of early trauma on brain development and learning. *The Journal of Adolescent Health: Official Publication of the Society for Adolescent Medicine, 51*(2 Suppl.), S23–S28. http://dx.doi.org/10.1016/j.jadohealth.2012.04.010

Chaffin, M., Silovsky, J. F., Funderburk, B., Valle, L. A., Brestan, E. V., Balachova, T.,...Bonner, B. L. (2004). Parent-child interaction therapy with physically abusive parents: Efficacy for reducing future abuse reports. *Journal of Consulting and Clinical Psychology, 72*(3), 500–510. http://dx.doi.org/10.1037/0022-006X.72.3.500

Cicchetti, D., Rogosch, F. A., & Toth, S. L. (2006). Fostering secure attachment in infants in maltreating families through preventive interventions.

Development and Psychopathology, 18(3), 623–649. http://dx.doi.org/10.1017/S0954579406060329

Derogatis, L. R. (1993). *BSI, brief symptom inventory: Administration, scoring & procedures manual.* Piscataway, NJ: National Computer Systems.

Dozier, M., Higley, E., Albus, K. E., & Nutter, A. (2002). Intervening with foster infants' caregivers: Targeting three critical needs. *Infant Mental Health Journal, 23*(5), 541–554. http://dx.doi.org/10.1002/imhj.10032

Dozier, M., Lindhiem, O., Lewis, E., Bick, J., Bernard, K., & Peloso, E. (2009). Effects of a foster parent training program on young children's attachment behaviors: Preliminary evidence from a randomized clinical trial. *Child and Adolescent Social Work Journal, 26*(4), 321–332. http://dx.doi.org/10.1007/s10560-009-0165-1

Dozier, M., Manni, M., Gordon, M. K., Peloso, E., Gunnar, M. R., Stovall-McClough, K. C.,...Levine, S. (2006). Foster children's diurnal production of cortisol: An exploratory study. *Child Maltreatment, 11*(2), 189–197. http://dx.doi.org/10.1177/1077559505285779

Dozier, M., Peloso, E., Lewis, E., Laurenceau, J.-P., & Levine, S. (2008). Effects of an attachment-based intervention on the cortisol production of infants and toddlers in foster care. *Development and Psychopathology, 20*(3), 845–859. http://dx.doi.org/10.1017/S0954579408000400

Dozier, M., Peloso, E., Lindhiem, O., Gordon, M. K., Manni, M., Sepulveda, S., ...Levine, S. (2006). Developing evidence-based interventions for foster children: An example of a randomized clinical trial with infants and toddlers. *Journal of Social Issues, 62*(4), 767–785. http://dx.doi.org/10.1111/j.1540-4560.2006.00486.x

Eaton, W. W., Smith, C., Ybarra, M., Muntaner, C., & Tien, A. (2004). Center for Epidemiologic Studies Depression Scale: Review and Revision (CESD and CESD-R). In M. E. Marush (Ed.), *The use of psychological testing for treatment planning and outcomes assessment: Instruments for adults* (Vol. 3, pp. 363–377). Mahwah, US: Lawrence Erlbaum Associates.

Eyberg, S. M., & Pincus, D. (1999). *Eyberg child behavior inventory and Sutter-Eyberg student behavior inventory-revised: Professional manual.* Odessa, FL: Psychological Assessment Resources.

filial. (2015). In *Oxford English Dictionary (OED)* online. Oxford, UK: Oxford University Press. Retrieved from http://www.oed.com

Ford, J. D., Racusin, R., Rogers, K., Ellis, C., Schiffman, J., Ribbe, D.,...Edwards, J. (2002). *Traumatic Events Screening Inventory for Children (TESI-C) version 8.4.* Dartmouth, VT: National Center for PTSD and Dartmouth Child Psychiatry Research Group.

Goodman, R. (1997). The Strengths and Difficulties Questionnaire: A research note. *Journal of Child Psychology and Psychiatry, 38*(5), 581–586. http://dx.doi.org/10.1111/j.1469-7610.1997.tb01545.x

Guerney, B. (1964). Filial therapy: Description and rationale. *Journal of Consulting Psychology, 28*(4), 304–310. http://dx.doi.org/10.1037/h0041340

Hood, K. K., & Eyberg, S. M. (2003). Outcomes of parent-child interaction therapy: mothers' reports of maintenance three to six years after treatment. *Journal of Clinical Child and Adolescent Psychology : The Official Journal for the Society of Clinical Child and Adolescent Psychology, American Psychological Association, Division 53, 32*(3), 419–429. http://dx.doi.org/10.1207/S15374424JCCP3203_10

Landreth, G. L. (2006). *Child parent relationship therapy (CPRT): a 10-session filial therapy model*. New York, NY: Routledge.

Lewis-Morrarty, E., Dozier, M., Bernard, K., Terracciano, S. M., & Moore, S. V. (2012). Cognitive flexibility and theory of mind outcomes among foster children: Preschool follow-up results of a randomized clinical trial. *Journal of Adolescent Health, 51*(2 Suppl.), S17–S22. http://dx.doi.org/10.1016/j.jadohealth.2012.05.005

Lieberman, A. F., Padrón, E., Van Horn, P., & Harris, W. W. (2005). Angels in the nursery: The intergenerational transmission of benevolent parental influences. *Infant Mental Health Journal, 26*(6), 504–520. http://dx.doi.org/10.1002/imhj.20071

Lieberman, A. F., & Van Horn, P. (2005). *Don't Hit My Mommy!: A manual for child-parent psychotherapy with young witnesses of family violence*. Washington, DC: Zero to Three Press.

Lieberman, A. F., & Van Horn, P. (2011). *Psychotherapy with infants and young children: Repairing the effects of stress and trauma on early attachment*. New York, NY: Guilford Press.

Lieberman, A. F., Van Horn, P., & Ippen, C. G. (2005). Toward evidence-based treatment: Child-parent psychotherapy with preschoolers exposed to marital violence. *Journal of the American Academy of Child and Adolescent Psychiatry, 44*(12), 1241–1248. http://dx.doi.org/10.1097/01.chi.0000181047.59702.58

Lind, T., Bernard, K., Ross, E., & Dozier, M. (2014). Intervention effects on negative affect of CPS-referred children: Results of a randomized clinical trial. *Child Abuse & Neglect, 38*(9), 1459–1467. http://dx.doi.org/10.1016/j.chiabu.2014.04.004

Markiewicz, J., Ebert, L., Ling, D., Amaya-Jackson, L., & Kisiel, C. (2006). *The learning collaborative toolkit*. Los Angeles, CA, and Durham, NC: National Center for Child Traumatic Stress.

Nixon, R. D. V., Sweeney, L., Erickson, D. B., & Touyz, S. W. (2003). Parent-child interaction therapy: A comparison of standard and abbreviated treatments for oppositional defiant preschoolers. *Journal of Consulting and Clinical Psychology, 71*(2), 251–260. http://dx.doi.org/10.1037/0022-006X.71.2.251

Scheeringa, M. S. (2010). *Young Child PTSD Checklist*. New Orleans, LA: Tulane University Institute of Infant & Early Childhood Mental Health.

Schuhmann, E. M., Foote, R. C., Eyberg, S. M., Boggs, S. R., & Algina, J. (1998). Efficacy of parent-child interaction therapy: Interim report of a randomized trial with short-term maintenance. *Journal of Clinical Child Psychology, 27*(1), 34–45. http://dx.doi.org/10.1207/s15374424jccp2701_4

Shonkoff, J. P. (2010). *The foundations of lifelong health are built in early childhood.* Cambridge, MA: Harvard University Center on the Developing Child. Retrieved from http://developingchild.harvard.edu/wp-content/uploads/2010/05/Foundations-of-Lifelong-Health.pdf

Sprang, G. (2009). The efficacy of a relational treatment for maltreated children and their families. *Child and Adolescent Mental Health, 14*(2), 81–88. http://dx.doi.org/10.1111/j.1475-3588.2008.00499.x

Squires, J., & Bricker, D. (2009). *Ages & stages questionnaires, third edition (ASQ-3).* Baltimore, MD: Brookes.

Thompson, R. A. (2008). Early attachment and later development: Familiar questions, new answers. In J. Cassidy & P. R. Shaver (Eds.), *Handbook of attachment: Theory, research, and clinical applications* (2nd ed., pp. 348–365). New York, NY: Guilford Press.

Weathers, F. W., Litz, B. T., Keane, T. M., Palmieri, P. A., Marx, B. P., & Schnurr, P. P. (2013). *The PTSD Checklist for* DSM-5 *(PCL-5).* Scale available from the National Center for PTSD at www. ptsd.va.gov

Weisz, J. R., Jensen-Doss, A., & Hawley, K. M. (2006). Evidence-based youth psychotherapies versus usual clinical care: A meta-analysis of direct comparisons. *The American Psychologist, 61*(7), 671–689.

Wolfe, J., Kimerling, R., Brown, P. J., Chrestman, K. R., & Levin, K. (1996). Psychometric review of the life stressor checklist-revised. In B. H. Stamm (Ed.), *Measurement of stress, trauma, and adaptation* (pp. 198–201). Brooklandville, MD: Sidran Press.

Zeanah, C. H., Benoit, D., Barton, M. L., & Hirshberg, L. (1996). *Working model of the child interview coding manual.* Unpublished manuscript. New Orleans: Division of Infant, Child and Adolescent Psychiatry, Louisiana State University School of Medicine.

Zeanah, C., & Zeanah, P. (2009). The scope of infant mental health. In C. H. Zeanah, Jr. (Ed.), *Handbook of infant mental health* (3rd ed., pp. 3–21). New York, NY: Guilford Press.

(p. 810). Thus, humanistic therapists focus more on *what* clients are experiencing and *how* they experience it than why. Humanistic therapists facilitate a process with clients in which the focus is describing their subjective inner experiencing without explaining it (Hansen, 2005). What is directly perceived and felt is considered more reliable than explanations and interpretations (Yontef & Simkin, 1989).

How People Develop Problems

In humanistic therapy, maladjustment is seen as something deeper than symptoms or self-defeating behavioral patterns. The focus is on internal processes that hinder the individual's ability to reach his or her potential. Kirschenbaum and Henderson (1989) noted:

> As humans grow from infancy to adulthood, an internal rift gradually develops, a rift that separates our immediate awareness from our own deeper "experiencing." In order to receive approval and love, we learn to suppress those feelings and expressions of ourselves that are deemed unacceptable to the important caretakers in our lives. Our need to be loved and accepted can impair our ability to be "congruent," to be whole and genuine. (p. 155)

In addition to this internal rift between awareness and experiencing, children begin to develop conditions of worth as they interact with the primary caregivers in their environment (Wilkins, 2010). Children are born trusting their perceptions and evaluations of the world as they experience it but they also have a need for positive regard from their significant others. This need for positive regard from others is so strong that their internal evaluation of experiencing can be overwhelmed if love and acceptance are withheld (i.e., conditional). So, in order to gain and maintain the positive regard of others, children *disregard* or *inhibit* "the expression of aspects of inner experiencing that conflicts with the needs and opinions of others because to do otherwise would risk the withdrawal of love and acceptance" (Wilkins, 2010, p. 39).

How People Change

Numerous theories exist that explain how clients change and grow. In cognitive therapy, clients learn to challenge their distorted thinking patterns and information processing and examine their beliefs about themselves, other people, and the world. In behavioral therapy, clients learn to "act as if" or "fake it till you make it." By intervening in a person's behavioral patterns, change can occur when clients learn how to experiment with new behaviors. Humanistic sandtray therapists do not deny that intervening through clients' cognitive systems or behavioral patterns can be helpful and therapeutic, but the kind of change these approaches pursue is quite different from humanistic therapy. Symptom relief and improved coping are important goals in therapy, especially if clients are experiencing some self-defeating symptoms, such as mood regulation or struggling to cope with dysphoria. If clients are not coping to an extent, they are not ready for humanistic sandtray therapy because it brings emotion and images to the surface. Thus, if clients are struggling to regulate their own emotions, they do not need more unsettling emotions to surface.

In humanistic sandtray therapy, the primary goal is not to improve coping or relieve symptoms, though these outcomes may happen as clients grow and change. By contrast, humanistic therapists believe that change occurs within the individual. The goal of humanistic sandtray therapists is to create a growth-enhancing climate of exploration, awareness, and acceptance. Behavioral therapists initiate change from the outside in and humanistic therapists from the inside out. In other words, humanistic therapists are initiating change indirectly through a qualitatively different relationship that is characterized by empathy and acceptance. Humanistic sandtray therapists have tremendous faith in the inner resources of the client. Without attempting to change clients, the process of change in humanistic therapy is paradoxical. As therapists accept clients without conditions, clients begin to be more self-accepting. Rogers (1961) noted that "we cannot change, we cannot move away from what we are until we fully *accept* what we are. Then change seems to come about almost unnoticed" (p. 17).

Therapeutic Relationship

In several meta-analyses, the therapeutic relationship, regardless of theoretical approach, has been the factor in counseling most highly associated with positive treatment outcomes (Asay & Lambert, 2008; Frank & Frank, 1991; Hansen, 2005; Norcross & Wampold, 2011; Wampold & Bhati, 2004). In humanistic therapy, the quality and depth of the relationship is viewed as the causal factor that facilitates growth and change. The therapist–client relationship is the heart of the humanistic approach. According to Warner (2001), people are uniquely individual and relational at the same time. She noted that "we cannot process experience without being in relationship and we cannot be in relationship without processing experience" (p. 181). Warner acknowledged that clients "may feel repelled by much of what they experience" (p. 181). If clients are going to be able to move toward self-acceptance, they need a relationship with a person who is nonjudgmental and genuine at the same time.

The primary goal of humanistic therapists is to create optimal therapeutic conditions for their clients. Humanistic therapists place an emphasis on therapists' attitudes and qualities necessary for therapy to be effective. Self-awareness and openness to inner experiencing are important attributes for humanistic sandtray therapists because they are facilitating a process that focuses on awareness and experiencing in the here and now. Rogers (1957) hypothesized six conditions (known now as the core conditions) for constructive personality change, including the third, fourth, and fifth conditions: congruence, unconditional positive regard, and empathy. In most counseling literature, the other three conditions are ignored, but they are important to humanistic therapists.

Rogers's (1957) first condition, contact, is essential in an effective therapeutic relationship. If a therapist cannot make initial contact or some connection, it will be difficult for therapy to proceed effectively. The second condition, client incongruence, implies that clients come into therapy in a vulnerable or anxious state. This condition can be a significant one when working with children or involuntary adolescent and adult clients. Children are almost never self-referred and may come into therapy with no awareness of their problems. Involuntary adolescent and adult clients may come to therapy wanting nothing from it and unwilling to assume responsibility for their inner experiencing or the choices they have made. These first two conditions are important even if they are generally disregarded in the literature. In addition, in the sixth condition Rogers indicates that it is necessary for clients to be receptive to therapists' facilitative attitudes for constructive personality change to occur. This condition may, for example, impact many traumatized and abused clients who may find it difficult to be open to another person who cares on a deep level. In other words, it is not enough for the therapist to be congruent, unconditionally accepting, and warm and empathic. Clients have to receive what therapists offer or the therapeutic outcomes will be limited. These three lesser known conditions—contact, client incongruence, and client receptivity—are an integral part of a whole. Because congruence, unconditional positive regard, and empathy are viewed as critical in the effectiveness of humanistic therapy, we describe these conditions in some detail.

Congruence

Rogers's (1957) third condition, congruence (or genuineness), means that in the therapeutic relationship the counselor is "freely and deeply himself, with his actual experience accurately represented by his awareness of himself" (p. 97). Without a high level of self-awareness, humanistic therapists may increase the risk of being incongruent with clients and unaware of discrepancies between their words and behaviors that are evident to clients. In addition to self-awareness, congruence in therapists will be challenging without high levels of self-acceptance. Self-acceptance allows therapists to be more congruent in the relationship because they do not censor or reject inner experiences that are uncomfortable or unpleasant (Bozarth, 2001). Bozarth believed that self-acceptance is such an integral part of congruence that it is included in his definition of congruence. According to Bozarth, congruence is "the manifestation of unconditional positive self-regard (UPSR) and can be identified as the therapist's presence" (p. 185).

Congruence is a "way of being in which outward behavior is an accurate reflection of inner state; that is, there is a matching of awareness and experience" (Wilkins, 2010, p. 57). Congruent therapists are not necessarily doing anything but they are being themselves and are fully present (Wilkins, 2010). According to Rogers (1977), "the more the therapist is herself in the relationship, putting up no professional front or personal façade, the greater is the likelihood that the client will change and grow" (p. 9). Wilkins (2010) noted that congruent therapists are "not necessarily *doing, saying, or expressing* anything: they are being totally themselves and are fully present and aware of the flow of their inner experiencing" (p. 57).

Unconditional Positive Regard

In 1954, Stanley Standal, one of Carl Rogers's doctoral students, introduced the term "unconditional positive regard" in his doctoral dissertation. Three years later, Rogers incorporated Standal's term in his seminal article on the core conditions (Moon, Rice, & Schneider, 2001). Rogers (1957) described unconditional positive regard as a "warm acceptance of each aspect of the client's experience as being a part of that client" (p. 98). Rogers acknowledged that one potential problem with the term *unconditional positive regard* was it sounded like an absolute, all or nothing concept. He also noted that complete unconditional regard would never exist except in theory. To clarify the concept further, Rogers stated, "The effective therapist experiences unconditional regard for the client during moments of his contact with him, yet from time to time he experiences

CHAPTER 9

Humanistic Sandtray Therapy With Children and Adults

STEPHEN A. ARMSTRONG, RYAN D. FOSTER, TIM BROWN, AND JOAN DAVIS

Therapists who practice play therapy often provide the intervention to children who are still in the preoperational stage of cognitive development. Fantasy play, a natural mode of expression for children aged 3 to 8 years, spontaneously flows in children who feel safe and free with therapists trained in this modality. In contrast, sandtray therapy is most often used by mental health professionals who are working with children in the concrete operational stage or older and are capable of more abstract thought and verbal expression. In this chapter, we focus on using humanistic sandtray as a structured play therapy intervention with clients aged 9 years and older.

Sandtray therapy is:

> An expressive and projective mode of psychotherapy involving the unfolding and processing of intra- and inter-personal issues through the use of specific sandtray materials as a nonverbal medium of communication, led by the client(s) and facilitated by a trained therapist. (Homeyer & Sweeney, 2011, p. 4)

In sandtray therapy, clients use miniature figures to create scenes in the sand that represent their inner experiences. Sandtray provides clients with a safe, indirect, nonverbal, and symbolic way to express emotions and issues that they may struggle to voice in traditional talk therapy.

HUMANISTIC THEORY

Humanistic therapy includes several major schools of psychotherapy: (a) person-centered, (b) existential, (c) gestalt, and (d) experiential therapies. Humanistic sandtray therapy is theoretically grounded in two of these major schools: person-centered and gestalt therapy. According to Even and Armstrong (2011), "humanistic sandtray therapy is a dynamic and expressive form of psychotherapy that allows clients to express their inner worlds through symbol and metaphor" (p. 395). In humanistic sandtray, therapists facilitate a process of exploration and expression in the context of a deep and personal relationship that focuses on here and now inner experiencing.

Inherent Nature

Humanistic therapists believe people are experiencing organisms that have the capacity to grow and develop into fully functioning beings (Cain, 2002; Rogers, 1961) if they receive consistent nurturing interaction from their caregivers (Greenspan & Shankar, 2004). All people are born with an actualizing tendency that propels them to grow involving "increasing complexity and the fulfillment of potential" (Wilkins, 2010, p. 29). According to Wilkins (2010), the actualizing tendency is a "biological force common to all living things. It directs all organisms towards survival, maintenance, and growth" (p. 29). Wilkins stated that the actualizing tendency is the motivating force for development and behavior in human beings. According to Rogers (1980), this actualizing force is part of a formative tendency that moves in the direction of greater order. "Trust in the client's capacity for growth and development" (Raskin & Rogers, 2005, p. 145) is an essential attitude in humanistic therapists.

Children and adults possess the capacity to be aware and to choose. If they feel safe, valued, and accepted, they will naturally experience and express fully a wide range of emotions and trust the accuracy and reliability of their perceptions and experiences. All children need positive regard from their caregivers in order to trust their perceptions and internal evaluations and are born with a vulnerability to negative appraisals from others (Wilkins, 2010).

Humanistic theory is phenomenological. Spiegelberg (1970) defined *phenomenology* as "the direct investigation of and description of phenomena as consciously experienced, without theories about their causal explanation and as free as possible from unexamined preconceptions" only a conditional positive regard" (p. 98). In other words, the extent to which even an accomplished therapist experiences unconditional positive regard will fluctuate from client to client and day to day. Some therapists view unconditional positive regard as the curative factor in humanistic therapy because it addresses conditions of worth acquired during childhood (Bozarth, 2001).

Empathy

Though empathic *responses* are valued in many theoretical orientations in counseling and discussed frequently in counseling literature, empathy is an attitude more than a behavior. Landreth (2012) referred to empathy as sensitive understanding. Rogers (1957) described empathy as sensing "the client's private world as if it were your own, but without ever losing the 'as if' quality. To sense the client's anger, fear, or confusion as if it were your own, yet without your own anger, fear, or confusion bound up in it" (p. 99). Rogers (1975) also described the limits of empathy.

> It means temporarily living in the other's life, moving about in it delicately without making judgments; it means sensing meanings of which he or she is scarcely aware, but not trying to uncover totally unconscious feelings since this would be too threatening. (p. 4)

Sanders (2006) noted, "I cannot feel anyone else's hurt, fears, and joys. I can, though, see their thoughts and feelings accurately and understand them" (p. 66). Wilkins (2010) stressed that understanding and seeing is not enough. Part of the empathic process in therapy is to communicate what you see and understand about the client's experiencing.

RESEARCH SUPPORT

Sandtray therapy is considered to be a type of play therapy. According to Flahive and Ray (2007), "play therapy is an empirically supported treatment option and facilitates the use of play as the natural language for children" (p. 363). Humanistic play therapy was originally developed by Axline (1947), a student of Rogers, and research on play therapy began in earnest in the 1960s. In a meta-analysis of play therapy from various theoretical approaches, Ray, Bratton, Rhine, and Jones (2001) found that treatment groups receiving play therapy performed better than control groups (Cohen's $d = .80$). The Ray et al. (2001) study was an extensive meta-analysis based on almost 100 quantitative play therapy studies. More humanistic play therapy studies were in the meta-analysis than any other theoretical approach.

By contrast, the number of quantitative studies on sandtray therapy in general, and humanistic sandtray therapy in particular, is few. Jungian sandplay has been researched using case studies and qualitative methods. Mitchell and Friedman (1994) stated that, "the effectiveness of sandplay has been demonstrated by analysis of individual case studies, along with a few studies that have examined the sandtrays of small populations" (p. 113). In a grounded theory study of sandplay, Lagutina, Sperlinger, and Esterhuyzen (2013) found that "the focus and themes unfolding in sandplay process may vary depending on whether the clients present with somatization, chronic illness, or terminal illness" (p. 105).

In recent case studies, researchers have also indicated anecdotally the effectiveness of humanistic sandtray therapy. Lyles and Homeyer (2015) found great benefit in the use of sandtray with adoptive families, noting that the sandtray therapist's embodiment of deep empathic attunement provided adoptive families an opportunity to heal attachment wounds. Eberts and Homeyer (2015) described two approaches to processing sandtray—Adlerian and gestalt—and concluded that each model of processing had the potential to bring about client change when the authors processed sandtrays with each other. Schadler and De Domenico (2012) discussed a case study in which an adult male psychiatric inpatient diagnosed with schizoaffective and bipolar disorders engaged in a model of sandtray called Sandtray-Worldplay (ST-WP). The authors reported that through processing his sandtrays, the client was able to communicate feelings of anger and fear as well as the challenging nature of relationships with hospital roommates and staff, eventually resulting in positive behavioral change and decreased aggressive behaviors. Additionally, Armstrong, Brown, and Foster (2015) reported two case studies of the use of humanistic sandtray therapy in a school counseling setting and noted the benefit to preadolescents struggling with emotional expression. According to Armstrong et al. (2015), teacher reports indicated that several months post-sandtray sessions, a 10-year-old boy and an 11-year-old boy had not disrupted class even once due to outward expressions of anger.

However, beyond anecdotal evidence based on case studies, there is a substantial lack of empirical evidence to support clinical outcomes of sandtray therapy from both a qualitative and quantitative approach. We found only two quantitative studies that supported humanistic sandtray therapy with children. Both studies used group sandtray therapy rather than individual. Flahive and Ray (2007) investigated the impact of group sandtray therapy on behavioral problems in preadolescents, and Shen and Armstrong (2008) examined the impact of group sandtray therapy on the self-esteem of young adolescent females.

Sandtray With Preadolescents Having Behavioral Difficulties

Flahive and Ray (2007) used humanistic sandtray therapy to address behavioral problems in preadolescents in a school setting. Their explanation for choosing group sandtray therapy was that

> [P]readolescents need to learn how to do things near and with others and need to become familiar with the various social roles they may play in society. They need a facilitative and therapeutic environment to enhance their social competence and need to learn more sufficient social skills in order to make friends and maintain positive peer relationships. (p. 364)

Flahive and Ray (2007), using an experimental design, examined the effectiveness of group sandtray therapy with 56 preadolescents (28 in the experimental group and 28 in the control group) who were experiencing behavioral difficulties, such as disruptive behaviors in class. Flahive and Ray found a statistically significant difference with a medium effect size between the experimental and control groups on the Behavior Symptom Index (BSI) of the Behavioral Assessment Scale for Children–Teacher Rating Scale (BASC-TRS), F (1, 53) = 4.98, p = .03, Cohen's d = .52. The researchers reported that the behavior of the experimental group mean improved slightly and the problem behavior of the control group mean worsened. Flahive and Ray also found a statistically significant difference with a medium effect size on the Internalizing Behavior Problem Scale of the BASC-TRS, F (1, 53) = 4.04, p = .04, d = .59. In addition, the researchers found a statistically significant difference with a medium effect size on the Externalizing Behavior Problem Scale of the BASC-TRS, F (1, 53) = 10.44, p < .01, d = .54. Flahive and Ray also found a statistically significant difference with a medium effect size on the Externalizing Behavior Problem Scale of the BASC-PRS, F (1, 43) = 4.90, p = .03, d = .63. In a summary of the impact of group sandtray therapy with preadolescents, Flahive and Ray stated, "Results of this study suggest that group sandtray therapy may have a positive therapeutic impact on preadolescents with behavioral difficulties, or at least may have prevented a worsening of symptoms" (p. 379).

Sandtray With Young Adolescents and the Effect on Self-Esteem

Shen and Armstrong (2008) examined the impact of humanistic group sandtray therapy on the self-esteem of seventh-grade girls. This study, like the Flahive and Ray (2007) study, was also conducted in a school setting. According to Shen and Armstrong (2008), research has demonstrated that self-esteem declines in girls moving from early to late adolescence. Research on the self-esteem of boys at the same age did not show a similar trend. Therefore, girls of this age appear to be particularly vulnerable to lower levels of self-esteem. Research indicates that early adolescent girls from diverse populations may be even more vulnerable to drops in self-esteem.

Shen and Armstrong (2008) used similar procedures as Flahive and Ray (2007). The sandtray therapy was delivered in small groups of four girls. However, random assignment was not used but girls were assigned to conditions (treatment and control group) based on the mean scores of the pretest to ensure that the groups were equal before the sandtray intervention. The girls received nine group sessions in this study.

The original participants in the Shen and Armstrong (2008) study were 40 seventh-grade girls, but three girls were not able to complete the intervention and the posttest. After the attrition, 19 girls were in the wait-list control group and 18 in the treatment group. Of the 37 participants, 20 were African American, 12 European American, and 5 Hispanic. The groups were led by two doctoral students and one licensed practitioner trained in play therapy and sandtray by the second author. All three of the therapists were female.

The *Self-Perception Profile for Children* (SPPC) was used in the study to assess self-esteem. Shen and Armstrong (2008) found statistically significant interactions with medium to large (.52–.83) Cohen's *d* effect sizes on five of the six subscales used in the study. The researchers noted that findings on the Physical Appearance subscale seemed to be the most important because the girls in the study expressed serious concerns about their appearance in the groups. Shen and Armstrong believed that the girls were able to help each other to become more self-accepting in this area of self-esteem. The girls encouraged each other to value inner beauty more and physical beauty less. Shen and Armstrong (2008) summarized their findings by stating that

> [T]he findings of the current study support the effectiveness of group sandtray therapy in improving self-esteem with young adolescent girls. The findings indicate that girls can improve how they feel about their physical appearance, peer relationships and academic achievement as a result of participating in this group intervention. (p. 134)

In summary, sandtray therapy has some burgeoning evidence to support its effectiveness with clients from a variety of populations in multiple settings who present with a number of concerns. Although two quantitative studies can be considered supportive of humanistic sandtray therapy as a potentially effective intervention, the majority of evidence is based on anecdotal case studies, which are important to set the stage for further research based in rigorous qualitative and quantitative methodology.

HUMANISTIC SANDTRAY THERAPY: RATIONALE AND CLINICAL APPLICATION

The most widely used theoretical approach to sandtray is Jungian and it is often referred to as sandplay (Kalff, 1980). Sandplay therapy has been practiced for several decades and sandplay articles have appeared in many journals and books. Though humanistic play therapy began to emerge in the 1940s (Axline, 1947), humanistic sandtray therapy did not appear in the literature until the late 20th century. In this section, we will provide a rationale for humanistic sandtray, an explanation of the phases in a sandtray session, an in-depth description of the processing phase of humanistic sandtray, and the facilitative responses used by humanistic sandtray therapists.

Rationale for Humanistic Sandtray Therapy

Humanistic sandtray therapy is situated in a broader category of expressive therapies (ET; Pearson & Wilson, 2009) and thus shares several points of rationale with ET. This approach to sandtray is kinesthetic, indirect, inclusive, cathartic, metaphoric, can be effectively used with clients who have suffered trauma, and stimulates neurointegration. We now briefly detail the rationale underlying humanistic sandtray therapy.

Humanistic Sandtray Is Kinesthetic

Humanistic therapy is holistic and organismic. We recognize that people connect to their senses and experience much of life through their senses. Sandtray is sensual and many clients of all ages touch the sand throughout the sandtray therapy session. Sand is soothing to many clients and provides a physical way to reconnect to earlier positive experiences and memories from childhood. Many clients have pleasant memories of going to a beach and enjoying the ocean. Homeyer and Sweeney (2011) noted that "[t]he very tactile experience of touching and manipulating the sand is a therapeutic experience in and of itself" (p. 8). However, sand can also evoke uncomfortable sensory experiences or reminders of hurt (Badenoch, 2008). In either case, the kinesthetic quality of sand can be powerful. The miniatures are three-dimensional, textured, and carefully shaped so that clients experience them through touch as well as sight. Many clients have tears in their eyes when they pick up certain miniatures and hold them.

Humanistic Sandtray Is Indirect

Verbal expression of painful memories and experiences is very challenging for many clients in therapy and most try to avoid it if possible. All clients are afraid to an extent of experiencing certain emotions in the moment and talking about here and now emotions is especially difficult (Rogers, 1961; Wilkins, 2010). Humanistic sandtray provides clients with an alternative mode of expression in which they can create a safe, psychological distance using metaphorical figures to represent emotions, problematic people, and situations and barriers that they face without saying a word. When clients choose miniatures to represent themselves, they often say they chose the figure because it is *like* them. Using a symbol to represent who they are provides a distance that helps clients feel safe. In humanistic sandtray therapy, we emphasize the exploration of deeper emotions in the here and now, which can be threatening for many clients; however, the miniatures act as a buffer between experiencing and expression.

Inclusivity of Humanistic Sandtray Therapy

Armstrong and Simpson (2002) noted that many family therapists exclude young children from sessions because they do not know how to provide interventions that are developmentally appropriate. Humanistic sandtray therapy can be used with children as young as 9 years old, which gives family therapists a developmentally appropriate intervention they can use with the whole family. Likewise, Homeyer and Sweeney (2011) noted that "[s]andtray therapy creates a level playing field for every family member, giving each person the opportunity to express him or herself" (p. 9). Sweeney and Rocha (2000) argued that it is essential to include all members of the family in therapy. Using humanistic sandtray with families is one way to include children as young as 9 years old in family therapy sessions.

Catharsis in Humanistic Sandtray Therapy

In humanistic sandtray therapy, we believe in the value of experiencing emotions fully. During childhood, significant caretakers often discourage and even punish full expression of emotion, and parents often withhold positive regard if children do not inhibit their emotional expression. Later in life, as adolescents and adults experience emotions, they have developed habitual ways of responding to them to cope, have control, and avoid feeling overwhelmed. Catharsis is "an intense expression of emotion previously unexpressed and sometimes outside of awareness" (Armstrong, 2008, p. 11). Letting go of emotional pain and fear can be very difficult for many clients because they do not want to lose control or they may fear if they experience an emotion intensely it will result in a state of disequilibrium that persists for days or longer. In fact, some clients have never experienced a sense of relief or release when painful emotions come to the surface. Sandtray can help clients connect to experiences and emotions in a new way, see their lives and relationships in a new light, and enable them to get some movement with emotions and areas that have become fixed and rigid.

Metaphor in Humanistic Sandtray Therapy

Play therapy and sandtray therapy provide clients a place in which metaphoric and symbolic expressions are available. In humanistic sandtray therapy, clients choose the figures to represent their inner worlds and project their meanings onto the symbols they have chosen. Many clients describe the metaphors in the tray, and the tray as a whole, as deeply meaningful. Some clients state that the symbols in the tray helped them connect to who they really are or that they felt a pull or calling from the images they felt compelled to follow (Hillman, 1996). Metaphoric expressions allow clients to find another way to describe an experience or emotion, and in sandtray they have the opportunity to choose their own symbols to represent their inner lives. Therapists do not have to try to make educated guesses about metaphors that describe the subjective inner experiencing of clients because they provide the metaphors in their trays. Then, in the tray, they cluster figures together to represent a part of their lives so that therapists can see how clients operate in various situations, such as interactions with their families of origin and intrapsychic relating.

Humanistic Sandtray With Traumatized Clients

Humanistic sandtray therapy is an effective approach with traumatized clients because it provides a safe and trusting relationship and a mode of expression that is less threatening. According to Homeyer and Sweeney (2011), "there are neurological effects of trauma that point to the need for nonverbal interventions. The sensory nature of trauma may be best addressed by a sensory intervention such as sandtray" (p. 9). Homeyer and Sweeney contended that traditional talk therapy may be less effective and even detrimental with traumatized clients if therapists insist on focusing on emotionally charged content. In humanistic sandtray therapy, if clients begin to experience fear as emotions come to the surface, client safety becomes far more important than the resolution of an issue. Clients who are afraid of inner experiencing in the here and now cannot go deeper into their experiencing or awareness at that moment.

Humanistic Sandtray Stimulates Neurointegration

Because sandtray involves clients' multidimensional awareness of body, feelings, and thoughts, sandtray stimulates both right brain and left brain processes. The client's awareness of body and emotion is typically a right hemisphere process and awareness of thought and narrative is a left hemisphere process (Cozolino, 2010). Badenoch (2008) noted that kinesthetic experiences in sandtray involve structures, such as the thalamus and parietal lobe. As a three-dimensional visually encompassing world, the tray and figures trigger the occipital lobe. Attachment and emotional safety experiences lodged both in the present and past activate structures, such as the limbic system and hippocampus, which become a feedback loop of memory and emotion. Finally, the insula and middle prefrontal cortex produce understanding of symbolism, metaphor, and relational experiences with the tray. Badenoch contended that "[t]his whole experience encourages vertical integration, linking body, limbic region, and cortex in the right hemisphere" (p. 221). In our experience, when clients are experiencing deep awareness, they are energized by these right hemisphere processes. Over time, as clients grow in awareness and eventually understanding of their sandtrays, the right hemisphere begins to flow to the left hemisphere, stimulating neurointegration.

Phases of the Structured Sandtray Session

Homeyer and Sweeney (2011) delineated several phases in a structured sandtray therapy session: room setup, introduction of sandtray and miniatures, scene creation, processing, cleanup, and documentation. Before setting up the room, however, therapists must acquire the materials used in the session. The standard tray used in humanistic sandtray is rectangular, 30 × 20 inches, and 3 inches deep. The best trays have a blue interior to represent sky and water. The type of sand used in sandtray varies widely among therapists. For children younger than 15 years we recommend using play sand. It is inexpensive, easy to find, and can be used wet or dry. For adolescents and adults, we use silica sand, which is white and dry. Putting together a collection of miniatures used in sandtray can be time consuming, expensive, and challenging. Homeyer and Sweeney (2011) recommend having a minimum of 300 miniatures, including people, animals, vegetation, buildings, vehicles, fences, and numerous other categories. They provided a comprehensive list of the types of miniatures therapists need as they begin to include sandtray into their practice.

One concern that often emerges when putting together a collection of sandtray miniatures is use of figures based on popular media or that are recognizable. Examples of these types of figures are superheroes, cartoon characters, movie characters, and the like. Although there are differing opinions as to the inclusion of these types of characters, we have found in our own practices that use of miniatures that clients might recognize can help them to frame their experience metaphorically.

The ideal display for miniatures in sandtray therapy is a cabinet with shelving that is dedicated to the arrangement of miniatures. The shelves should not be above eye level, which can be a challenge if therapists use the sandtray with adults and preadolescents. Some preadolescents who are less than 5 feet tall would be unable to see figures on a 5-foot shelf. In addition to height, the depth of the shelves is important because deeper shelves make it more difficult to see the miniatures. We recommend shelving that is no more than 10 inches deep. Once therapists have obtained the materials, they are ready to set up the therapy room for a sandtray session.

Room Setup and Introduction to Materials

Setting up the room for a sandtray session is much easier if shelving is available to display the miniatures. If therapists are using sandtray with children it is important for the miniatures to be displayed at eye level and below. If shelving is unavailable, the miniatures can be displayed on a table. Once the client arrives—if he or she has not seen the miniatures—he or she may walk over and begin to notice and touch them. This introductory phase may be unstructured because many clients naturally are drawn to the figures and need no direction or structure. Some clients may find one or two miniatures attractive almost immediately. Others may be more tentative in approaching the miniatures and need some explanation and guidance about how the figures will be used.

Scene Creation Phase

After this brief orientation in humanistic sandtray, we do a short centering activity with clients to shift their focus to the present, settle their energy, and help them feel grounded. In the centering activity, we have clients close their eyes for approximately 2 minutes and place their awareness on their breathing. During the 2-minute centering activity, we make occasional comments like, "If you notice your awareness is drifting to your thoughts, gently guide your awareness back to your breathing." To conclude the centering activity, we have clients shift their focus to their eyelids and suggest that they open them slowly. This activity can be a helpful way for clients to detach from the hectic pace of their days.

After completing the centering activity, we provide instructions about how they will create their scenes. This part of the scene creation phase varies widely depending on the age and comfort level of the clients. In general, we use two different kinds of prompts to help clients create their scenes. With adolescents and adults, we provide this abstract prompt: "What I would like you to do is create a scene of your life the way it is now. You may include symbols from the past or future but focus mainly on how your life is now. I want you to be brutally honest with yourself as you create your scene. What you choose to share with me is up to you." With preadolescents, we may provide a more structured prompt to create the scene: "I'd like you to make a scene in the tray about you and your family." The length of the scene creation phase of sandtray can vary widely. Many adult clients take 15 minutes or longer to create their scenes, but some take 5 minutes or less. In general, preadolescents take the least amount of time in this phase, although some put considerable thought into creating their scenes.

Many adult clients and some children begin to experience emotions during the scene creation phase. Some adult clients may cry throughout this phase if their tray is about a painful loss or if they have been distressed in the past few days. Creating the scene is therapeutic in the same way that playing out emotions is therapeutic for young children. If clients are experiencing sadness or pain during this phase, it influences how humanistic sandtray therapists begin the processing phase.

Processing Phase

The processing phase, in which the client talks about the scene, is one of the primary foci in this chapter. We discuss this phase at length in the next section, but we will focus on it briefly here. In humanistic sandtray therapy this phase is complex, challenging, and may elicit deep emotions. Like the scene creation phase, the length of the processing phase can vary widely, with preadolescents typically taking the least amount of time. Many adult clients need 30 to 45 minutes to process their scenes, but younger clients often take 15 minutes or less. Typically, preadolescents are more reluctant than adolescents and adults to experience and express emotion in the here and now, but even some preadolescent males have cried in humanistic sandtray therapy sessions that we have conducted and supervised.

In humanistic sandtray therapy, we usually begin the processing phase of sandtray in one of two ways. If clients are experiencing sadness or pain during the scene creation phase, we do not shift the focus to the tray. Humanistic sandtray therapists may begin this phase by reflecting the emotions expressed during the scene creation and say something like, "It looks like creating the scene has brought some pain to the surface for you." If the client acknowledges that she is experiencing pain, then the therapist postpones the description of miniatures in the tray until after the pain is processed.

If clients do not show any sign of emotions coming to the surface while creating their scenes, humanistic sandtray therapists typically begin the processing of the tray by saying, "Tell me about your scene." One question that comes up regarding the client's description of these scenes is, "How long should therapists allow clients to talk about their trays before intervening?" This question is difficult to answer; however, we would not allow clients to talk for 10 minutes before we responded to their emotions or the meaning of a figure in the tray. Some adults take a long time to tell about their trays. It takes clinical judgment to decide whether to interrupt the client at this point or not.

Cleanup Phase

After the processing phase is over, the cleanup phase begins. It is easy to minimize the importance of the cleanup phase and to think that it may be self-explanatory, but one issue in this phase is significant: the dismantling of the tray. We believe it is essential to dismantle the tray after the client has left the room. This procedure allows clients to leave the session with the visual image of the scene in their minds (Badenoch, 2008; Pearson & Wilson, 2009). As Homeyer and Sweeney (2011) noted, many clients "will continue to do their own processing and thinking about the imagery and metaphor of their sandtray" (p. 42) after they leave the session and throughout the next week. The final procedure that we use in humanistic sandtray is documenting the tray with a photograph. We ask the client if we can take a picture of his or her scene and save the picture for future reference. With older adolescents and adults, the picture can be used in subsequent sessions to do more work on significant images in the tray.

Documentation

Sandtray therapists document their session in similar ways as play therapists. Homeyer and Sweeney (2011) provided an example of sandtray case notes that we recommend clinicians to follow. Using Homeyer and Sweeney's sandtray case notes method, sandtray therapists document the general categories of miniatures used during the session, clinical themes or metaphors that emerged, and recommendations for future sessions. There is also a place to attach a printed photograph of the tray. Their example aligns with Ray's (2011) assertion that play therapy case notes should align with a structured system of documentation such as data, assessment, and plan (DAP).

Humanistic Sandtray Processing

What sets humanistic sandtray therapy apart from other approaches is the processing phase of sandtray. Other approaches, such as Jungian sand play, do not focus on verbal elucidation of the inner experiencing of the client in the here and now like humanistic sandtray therapists do. In addition, Rogers's six core conditions (1957) are very important in humanistic therapy and lay the foundation for everything in the processing phase of sandtray. Any techniques or interventions used in humanistic sandtray therapy are only effective if the six core conditions described by Rogers are experienced by the therapist and received by the client. Trust is especially significant at this phase of a humanistic sandtray session. Humanistic sandtray therapists do not recommend using sandtray with clients until they trust the therapist to a significant degree. Asking clients to focus on here and now experiencing is frightening to many clients and if they do not trust the therapist to a significant degree, they will probably be unwilling to allow themselves to experience painful emotions on a deeper level.

Working in the here and now during this phase of sandtray poses other challenges, such as length of time available and developmental level of clients. Adult clients tend to provide extensive content as they describe their scenes and therapists can become intrigued and curious about specific details of clients' stories. The details of clients' stories are important to clients and the therapist, but during this phase of therapy, time is usually limited; therefore, therapists have to make choices about what to respond to and how to respond. It is easy to make a mistake that may negatively impact the therapeutic impact of the session. If therapists rush clients or ignore parts of clients' stories that are especially important to them, they will feel misunderstood and invalidated.

On the other hand, if humanistic sandtray therapists are too laissez-faire in their therapeutic responses, the depth of the processing phase may be sacrificed. In humanistic sandtray therapy, details of clients' stories are significant and meaningful, but the primary focus of the processing phase in humanistic sandtray is on the inner experiencing of clients in the moment. Therefore, the choice for therapists as clients are describing the meaning of the symbols in the tray to pursue a line of inquiry about clients' stories or to focus on *how* the clients are experiencing the metaphors in the moment. For example, if clients say they were hurt by something from the past, humanistic sandtray therapists might ask, "What is it like to remember that experience now?" Another option would be to ask, "When you think about that hurtful experience now, what do you experience?" In a good sandtray session, there is usually a rhythmic dance between focusing on the tray and various aspects of the scene and focusing on the inner experiencing of the client and *how* they are experiencing the scene.

With children younger than 15 years, the challenges during the processing phase of sandtray are quite different. Many children either do not possess the verbal and cognitive capacity to process a tray on a deeper level or do not feel safe enough to experience the vulnerability necessary to feel their emotions in the moment. Also, many children (and some adults) use avoidance and denial as coping skills. If sandtray therapists are trying to process trays with child clients who use these defenses during the processing phase, the therapists may be asking the children to do something that will feel unsafe. All clients want to avoid pain and vulnerability to an extent, but many children work very hard to avoid it altogether. Humanistic sandtray therapists believe that children can benefit from going deeper into their inner experiencing and are capable of doing it, but during the processing phase, if children are afraid to stay with an experience, it is very important not to force the issue. The relationship always trumps the goal of facilitating a process of awareness and growth. As a general rule, if clients of any age begin to feel unsafe during this phase of therapy, our primary goal as therapists is to help them feel safe at that moment.

By contrast, many clients are able to stay with emotions and feel vulnerable to an extent if they trust the therapist to a significant degree and their own inner experiencing to an extent. One important goal of the processing phase of humanistic sandtray is to help clients reconnect to who they really are. Humanistic therapists believe that clients are by nature experiencing and expressive beings that have developed a tendency to distrust and even fear emotion in the here and now (Rogers, 1961; Wilkins, 2010). Therapists can facilitate healing by accepting and acknowledging what clients truly experience emotionally and conveying verbally and nonverbally that clients' inner experiencing is trustworthy and valuable. In this approach to therapy, symptom relief is not the primary goal: The goal is movement toward becoming a fully functioning person. Movement toward becoming a fully functioning person means moving in the direction of trusting inner experiencing and being open to feeling it. Humanistic therapists believe "fully functioning people rely on inner experiencing to direct their behavior" (Meador & Rogers, 1984, p. 146).

Earlier in this chapter, we stated that an internal rift between awareness and experiencing gradually develops in people during childhood. We also noted that children need positive regard from adults so strongly that they disregard and inhibit the expression of aspects of inner experiencing to gain love and approval. In this processing phase of sandtray, humanistic therapists are helping clients to restore what was there in the beginning: a connection between awareness and inner experiencing and a validation of the goodness of clients' innermost emotions.

Humanistic sandtray therapists help clients access their emotions on a deeper level by staying in a descriptive mode of processing. Instead of explaining or analyzing an experience, therapists explore and describe it without looking for the cause (Yontef & Simkin, 1989). Helping clients to stay in a descriptive mode is difficult and may be uncomfortable to clients. For many clients, it is natural and habitual to explain why they are having a particular experience, and they may shift into this mode so effortlessly the therapist may not even notice it.

Consider the following example to illustrate a descriptive processing exchange. An adult female client has used a three-headed dog figure (Cerberus in Greek mythology) to represent her male boss. In talking about her boss, she recounts a moment from the previous week in which he berated her in front of her coworkers. As she talks about the experience, a tear rolls down her cheek. A humanistic sandtray therapist would focus on her experience in the moment and possibly respond in this manner. First, the therapist might slow the pace, lean forward, and nonverbally convey empathy. Then the therapist might reflect the emotion expressed by saying, "It must be painful to remember that moment now." Next, instead of analyzing or explaining the experience, the therapist might ask, "What is your pain like?" This response keeps the client in a descriptive mode and helps her to stay with the experience.

Facilitative Responses and Interventions in Humanistic Sandtray Therapy

Though the therapeutic relationship is the most critical factor related to therapeutic outcomes in humanistic sandtray therapy, therapists using this approach to sandtray use numerous facilitative responses to communicate empathy and acceptance, enhance client awareness, go deeper into inner experiencing, and respond to resistance. Without a trusting relationship in which clients feel safe to explore and express all emotions, however, these responses have limited value. If a deep level of trust has been established, many clients are receptive to experiencing emotion in the moment and becoming aware of how they operate. However, one factor that hinders clients' responsiveness to experiencing their emotions is a distrust of their own inner experiencing in the moment. All clients to some degree distrust here and now inner experiencing because it is somewhat unpredictable and uncomfortable. Clients have developed habits of how they respond to their own emotions and usually these habits include ways to avoid here and now experiencing. However, if clients are willing to stay with the process of moving toward being fully functioning, their distrust of their own emotions can begin to heal and new possibilities of experiencing can unfold.

Although these responses are presented separately and in different categories, humanistic therapists may use all of the responses listed in the following sections in a 15-minute part of one session. These responses are all designed to go deeper into the client's inner experiencing and awareness. Knowing when to use them and how to use them most effectively takes time and experience.

Reflective and Descriptive Responses

Humanistic therapists place a greater emphasis on emotion than many other therapeutic approaches. Though cognition and behavior are discussed and explored, inner experiencing of emotions in the moment and awareness are the primary foci of humanistic sandtray therapy. The goal of this approach to sandtray is to go deep enough into experiencing and awareness to get to core issues and enhance movement with these issues on an underlying level.

Reflection of feeling responses are taught almost universally in counselor preparation programs and most graduates of quality master's programs in counseling are capable of responding to clients with reflections of feeling. However, what we have noticed in our supervision of advanced master's and doctoral students, licensed interns, and licensed counselors is less skill in reflecting emotions than we expected. In particular, we have noticed in our training of therapists that reflections of feeling responses to *nonverbal* expressions of emotion are sometimes less than adequate. In humanistic sandtray therapy, our emphasis is on the here and now and many expressions of emotion in the moment are nonverbal. Like children in play therapy, we have found that adults tend to often show how they feel in the moment more than say it. Therefore, a critical facilitative response in humanistic sandtray therapy is reflection of feeling to nonverbal expressions of emotion.

When clients are in an experiencing mode, humanistic sandtray therapists want to stay with the experience and avoid analyzing or interpreting it. One way that is accomplished in sandtray is to use a descriptive mode of responding. After reflecting emotions, therapists in a descriptive mode might ask questions like, "What is your pain like?" Questions like these help clients stay with their experience in the moment and out of their head. Using descriptive responses like this are helpful to clients who are willing to stay in an experiencing mode.

Body Awareness Responses

We have noticed that many adult men in sandtray therapy have difficulty processing descriptive questions. We have experienced several male clients who respond to the question, "What is your pain like?" with a bewildered expression. We have found that many men respond better to body awareness questions. Instead of asking a male client the aforementioned question, therapists might ask, "What do you notice in your body right now?" Emotions are physical. All people experience sensations in their bodies when they are feeling an emotion. Humanistic therapists believe experiencing—including physical sensations—is a more reliable source of therapeutic information than explanations and analyses, which tend to be repetitive and unhelpful (Yontef & Simkin, 1989). When therapists are trying to enhance body awareness, they may focus on areas of tension, pressure, numbness, or tingling. When clients acknowledge tension in their bodies, humanistic therapists help clients to explore and describe the tension. Therapists may ask, "How would you describe the tightness in your chest?" Like the previous facilitative response of describing an emotion, the goal of this technique is to stay with inner experiencing in the moment and continue to explore it. In addition, these body awareness responses enhance clients' awareness of how various parts of their bodies connect to their emotions.

Guiding Clients Into the Present Moment

One way that clients avoid their own emotions and maintain self-control in therapy sessions is to focus on the past and future instead of the present. Humanistic sandtray therapists emphasize and explore the here and now inner experiencing of the client. Because almost all clients are afraid of experiencing emotions in the moment and try to avoid it, this facilitative response can be especially challenging for therapists in training to learn. Imagine that a client is talking about her divorce being finalized 4 days ago. When she talks about the finality of her marriage, she focuses on the day the divorce was final. One way to gently guide her into the moment is to ask, "When you think about your marriage being over right now, what do you experience?"

At this point in our discussion of facilitative responses it might be helpful to show how the responses described so far can be used together. If the aforementioned client responds to this question with more emotion, therapists can use some of the other facilitative responses to explore it such as, "It still hurts to think about it being over and now it's more real." If the client is experiencing the pain, a descriptive question may be effective: "What is your pain like?" After the client attempts to describe her pain, it might be helpful to have her focus on her body: "What are you noticing in your body right now?" Of course one of the most powerful and helpful responses therapists can use with many different kinds of clients is supportive and attentive silence. Sometimes therapists try to do too much when it may be more helpful to silently be with the client where she is in the present moment. Silence and a slower pace are usually even more effective with introverted clients.

According to Rogers (1961), even clients who have considerable self-awareness and openness to their emotions fear and distrust experiencing emotions in the immediate present. One goal of this focus on here and now experiencing is to "intensify and expand the client's subjective activity and consequent awareness" (Bugental, 1999, p. 19). When a client becomes more aware of her own subjective inner experiencing in the moment, it "helps the client to discover ways in which she is self-defeating and thus releases the client's creative (or self-healing) potential" (p. 19).

Enhancing Awareness

When emotions surface in therapy, clients tend to stop their inner experiencing by increasing tension in their bodies; shifting into a thinking, rational, or analytical mode; changing the subject; or telling a story. All clients avoid the present to an extent. Humanistic sandtray therapists enhance clients' awareness in the moment by noticing *how* clients avoid their inner experiencing. For example, imagine that a client is beginning to experience pain over the loss of her partner. As the pain comes to the surface, her throat begins to tighten and her tone of voice reflects this increased tension. Humanistic sandtray therapists might work with this moment by saying, "It looks like you're beginning to experience the pain but I'm noticing that you seem to be stopping the pain as well. Are you aware that you're stopping it?" If the client says yes, the therapists might ask, "How are you stopping your pain?" Many clients will say, "I don't know," or something similar, but some who are less afraid and more self-aware might say, "I'm noticing that my throat is tight." Humanistic therapists do not believe that clients choose consciously to tighten their throats to control or stop the flow of emotion. When clients tighten their throats in this manner it is because they have developed a habit of doing so when they find an emotion unsettling or frightening. This example of how to respond to this habit illustrates how humanistic sandtray therapists enhance clients' awareness of *how* they are responding to their emotions in the here and now.

Responding to Polarities

Humanistic therapists recognize the complexity of emotion and accept the ambiguities of being human. Clients often present their struggles in the form of polarized emotions or desires. In humanistic sandtray therapy, polarities are viewed as an important aspect of inner experiencing, and responding to them effectively can help clients feel understood, validated, and accepted. In humanistic sandtray therapy, polarities—two opposing parts, wants, or desires—emerge during the processing phase of sandtray (Armstrong, 2008). In fact, when therapists look at clients' trays, polarities are apparent. For example, imagine that a client has a princess figure representing herself with a bridge in front of her. On the other side of the bridge is a treasure chest. However, on the short path between the princess and the bridge are snakes. This cluster of miniatures is typical of how clients portray a polarity in the sand.

The client might say, "I want to get my doctorate but I'm afraid of failing." Here are some common examples of polarities that many clients experience:

- "I want to lose weight but I can't get motivated."
- "I don't love my husband but I'm afraid if I leave I'll wind up alone."
- "I want to quit my job but I need the money."

With many clients we have seen, some polarities can persist for months or years.

Why are polarities important? Clients feel misunderstood if therapists only acknowledge part of their experience when they are conflicted. Years ago, I (S.A.A.) was doing sandtray with a domestic violence victim who wanted to end her relationship with her partner but was afraid to leave. Due to my inexperience, I neglected to recognize the importance of the fear and thought I should help my client put herself in a position where she could end a destructive relationship. In addition, when clients are stuck in the middle of a polarity, their energy stops flowing. They may even feel trapped and sometimes hopeless. Carson (2003) described the flow of energy this way: When people are in a natural, relaxed state of experiencing, their energy flows freely and is available to them to use as they wish, but when they are experiencing a polarity, their energy is tied up in an internal conflict. This inner struggle may drain the person's resources to the point of feeling physically tired or lethargic.

Another reason to respond to polarities is that it helps clients and therapists go deeper into clients' awareness and experiencing. Therapists who believe in here and now work will encounter polarities: they will emerge. If therapists do not know how to respond to polarities when they come to the surface, therapists will struggle to stay in the here and now and clients will feel misunderstood.

The first step in responding to polarities is seeing or recognizing them in clients' trays and their stories. Often when clients express a polarity, the word *but* may be a helpful indicator that a polarity may be present. The next step is naming the polarity. It may sound fairly simple but sometimes it is not. Typically, we ask clients if we are wording the polarity in a way that captures their experience. After identifying and naming the polarity, it is very important to separate it and work with one part at a time. Going back to the domestic violence example, the therapist might ask, "When you think about the two parts of you right now—the part that wants to leave and the part that is afraid—which part are you more aware of?" It has been our experience that usually the client will be experiencing the fear more than the desire to leave. After clarifying the part that is in the client's foreground, the therapist will explore the fear. The therapist might ask, "Are you experiencing the fear now?" If the client says yes, we might respond using some of the techniques we have described, such as asking a descriptive question or a body awareness question. Once the polarity is separated into two parts, therapists explore that part like they would any inner experiencing of the client.

Now that we have reviewed the process of using humanistic sandtray, we move to present a case example that demonstrates the attitudes and skills effective sandtray therapists use in clinical work. After we discuss the case, then we provide reflections and implications.

CONCLUSION

Humanistic sandtray therapy is a type of play therapy that can be used with clients of many ages from preadolescents to older adults. Humanistic play therapy began to emerge in the 1940s and has extensive empirical support, but research support for humanistic sandtray therapy is still limited. This approach to sandtray emphasizes the primacy of the therapeutic relationship and views the relationship as the curative factor in therapy. In sandtray, therapists and clients benefit from the symbolic nature of the experience because it increases safety and provides clients with a metaphorical and indirect mode of expression that is less threatening than using an intervention that is completely verbal. The safety of the tray and a relationship based on Rogers's (1957) core conditions enable clients to do deeper work and have the courage to express and become who they really are. If clients trust the therapist to a considerable degree and Rogers's core conditions are experienced by the therapist and received by the client, humanistic sandtray therapy can facilitate increased awareness and growth. The facilitative responses presented in this chapter and illustrated in the case example are designed to help clients go deeper into their inner experiencing and awareness so that they might move in the direction of becoming a more fully functioning person. Fully functioning people are moving in the direction of increasingly trusting their inner experiencing and becoming open to a wide range of emotions.

CASE EXAMPLE: ZOE'S STORY

The following case illustration represents the third author's (T.B.) sandtray therapy with a preadolescent female in a public school setting. The name of the client used is fictitious and I changed some details to protect the client's identity.

Zoe is an 11-year-old girl whom I had seen in my office previously for concerns related to relationships with her friends and self-injury. When Zoe revealed she was cutting and scratching herself, we met together with her mother to talk about the concern. During this visit, her mother committed to take Zoe to an outside counselor. However, follow-up visits with Zoe revealed her mother had not taken her. This is typical at my school. I work at a low socioeconomic status elementary school in the southwestern United States. The students primarily live in low-income subsidized apartments. Due to many factors, including lack of transportation, lack of legal documentation, inability to pay, lack of insurance, and inability to take time off from work, parents typically do not follow through on commitments to take their children to outside counseling. When working with Zoe, I was conscious she would likely not receive any counseling besides what occurred in my office.

During one of the follow-up visits, Zoe shared that she was continuing to self-injure and had begun to have suicidal thoughts. We met with her mom again to share and discuss the emergence of these thoughts. We discussed what Zoe was experiencing. Mom seemed eager to help her daughter. We discussed ways the mother and daughter might better communicate, especially when Zoe was experiencing suicidal thoughts or a desire to injure herself. I also provided resources for outside counseling, and received an additional commitment from her mom to take her daughter.

During the next visit, Zoe reported her mom had been too busy to make an appointment with an outside counselor. We discussed Zoe's desire to self-harm and her desire to die. Although Zoe was open to discussing these issues, the discussion stayed surface level. I decided to use sandtray to bring more of what she was experiencing to her awareness.

(*continued*)

(*continued*)

Tray 1

I showed Zoe the sandtray and the miniatures. I explained how the miniatures could be used to make scenes, and prompted Zoe to make a scene from her life. As she worked, I stayed present but quiet. It took her about 5 minutes to complete the scene. She began by describing her scene as a historic ghost town she had visited with her parents. Zoe represented herself with a miniature of a little girl. The girl was facing gemstones set in front of a tombstone. She placed houses to the left and to the right of the tombstone. She also placed a black cat in front of one of the houses. The cat was positioned with its gaze toward Zoe's figure. Next to the other house, Zoe placed a tree and a church. In front of the church, she placed a man and a woman. These represented her mom and former stepfather. Next to the church, she used fencing to create a pen. Inside the pen, she placed a lion.

As often happens, Zoe began explaining her scene by telling me which miniature represented her. She said she placed herself in front of the tombstone to represent her desire to challenge her fears. Next, she described the cat looking at her as a symbol of fear. With the theme of fear emerging, we began to process her fears. As we talked, it became clear that she was primarily afraid of people's judgments. I empathized with this overarching fear. We talked only a little more about fears before she changed the focus to her parents.

Zoe had chosen to represent this scene from her past because it was a happy time in her life. She had visited a ghost town with her mother and former stepfather. She did not know her biological father, and regarded her former stepfather as her dad. During the past few years, her parents had divorced, and her mom had begun a new relationship with another man. This new boyfriend had moved in, and took a great deal of mom's attention from Zoe. Zoe had previously been used to having a great deal of her mom's attention because she was an only child.

(*continued*)

This scene represented the last time she saw her dad. It was after her parents' breakup. Her mother wanted Zoe to still see her dad, but the new boyfriend would not allow it. This led her mother to take Zoe in secret to meet with her dad. Zoe enjoyed these times but did not like sneaking to see her dad. Zoe was also polarized about her mother's new relationship. She wanted her mom to be happy, but did not like all the attention this new boyfriend was given. Zoe felt marginalized. We processed this polarity. Zoe was far more aware of frustration about the lack of attention her mother gave her; however, her strong desire to see her mother happy kept conflicting with this feeling of frustration. As we talked, she presented feelings of anger, sadness, loneliness, and guilt. I empathized with these feelings as they presented. Part of her believed her mom had betrayed her. She said her mom was not initially honest about her relationship with her new boyfriend. The memory of this dishonesty seemed to strengthen Zoe's sense of betrayal. Zoe also missed her dad. She said she cried on the way home from this outing. I empathized with her and we talked about both her sense of betrayal and missing her dad.

Zoe did not say much about the other miniatures in the tray. They were essentially props from her memory about the town she visited. As we talked about this tray, Zoe revealed a great deal about her relationship with her parents. From previous visits, I knew she lived with her mom and the boyfriend. I also knew her dad was not in the picture. From her language and presenting affect, I got the impression she was not happy with her mom's current relationship, but she did not say much about it when asked. Processing the scene in this tray allowed us to address issues important to Zoe, but not necessarily present in her mind when she came into my office. Typically, Zoe would talk about things related to school and friends, or talk about her desire to self-harm or die. These strong surface level issues, while important, kept Zoe from coming into contact with some of the problems behind her desire to injure herself or die. By using the sandtray, we were able to address the pressing issues sitting just below the surface.

(*continued*)

(*continued*)

Tray 2

Although it is possible to process one tray over the course of many sessions by taking a picture of the tray and returning to it again and again, I will often have kids create a new tray each time. I find kids enjoy creating the tray, and it helps them come into contact with what is going on inside of them. The very act of making their scene in a sandtray seems to be therapeutic.

For this tray, I gave Zoe a slightly different prompt than I had the previous time. This time, I asked Zoe to create a scene from her life, but I added the words "as it is right now." In the previous tray, Zoe had created a scene from her past. Although the previous prompt proved to be very useful to her, I wanted Zoe to come into contact with what she was experiencing in the present moment. As before, Zoe took about 5 minutes to create the scene. I stayed present with her as she worked.

Her scene was divided into two halves. The left half consisted of a male and female miniature representing her mom and her mom's boyfriend. She represented herself with a miniature of a girl, and placed herself in between her mom and her mom's boyfriend. There was a notable closeness between Zoe's and the mom's figure. The figure of the boyfriend was slightly further away. In front of them were three dog miniatures, a bunny miniature, and some jewels. Dividing the tray were trees and a gravestone. To the right of the trees, there was a miniature man representing her dad. Next to her dad was a treasure chest. There was one house on each side of the tray. Like the previous tray, this tray did not have a great deal of miniatures in it. She left a lot of empty space.

Zoe began by talking about her current living situation. She said she used to live in a house with her mom and dad. Now she lived in an apartment with her mom and the new boyfriend. She said her dad lived alone. She did not get to see her dad often because he was both in the army and in college. The houses in the scene represented the change in her living situation.

After talking about the houses, Zoe went on to talk about the gravestones. She seemed eager to let me know what each thing in her tray represented. Zoe, referring to the gravestones, said they

(continued)

represented weird thoughts she had. She was often preoccupied with thoughts of death, fighting, and gore. Because of this, her mom had begun to limit the media Zoe could watch. Most of the media consisted of graphically violent cartoons and graphic novels.

The next part of the scene was the right half consisting of her dad and the treasure chest. She said she had visited her dad again. Her mom took her and her mother did not tell her boyfriend. She also said her mom would not leave her alone with her dad. This was confusing for Zoe. She said the treasure chest represented her dad's stuff. As she talked about his stuff, she began to talk about her dad having his own life. He was in college and the army now. He was busy. She did not like this separation.

The trees represented the sneaking around to see her dad. The sneaking around scared her. She did not feel guilty, but she was afraid the new boyfriend would find out. She was afraid, if he discovered the deception, Zoe would no longer be able to see her dad. She was also afraid something bad would happen to her mom's relationship with her boyfriend. This fear stemmed from Zoe's desire to see her mom happy. She wanted to visit her dad, but was afraid of the consequences. We identified and processed this polarity.

The miniature representing Zoe was standing in between her mom and her mom's boyfriend. Zoe had placed herself much closer to her mom than her mom's boyfriend. She said she does what she can to get close to her mom. She said her mom lets her talk when she feels down. When I reflected this idea, it seemed to be impactful for Zoe. She wanted to get close to her mom, and she was able to achieve this when she appeared depressed, suicidal, or had injured herself. I did not imply this was the sole or main reason for those feelings or actions, but she had not been aware of the possible connection between them previously.

We continued the session as she talked about the change in the time her mother spent with her. When her mom was married to her dad, she was able to spend a lot of time with her. After the divorce, her mother got a boyfriend, and the time she had with her mother dramatically decreased. We talked about the difference

(continued)

(*continued*)

between the two times in her life. She continued by saying there was a time between the divorce and the new boyfriend when she and her mom lived with her grandparents. She said this was also a happy time. Mom had time for her. She described herself as dressing differently. She did not dress in dark colors then. She also said that she was not ashamed of herself like she was now, she did not cut herself, and she was not suicidal. She said the major change in her life came when her mom got the new boyfriend. She talked a great deal about how her mom changed her focus from Zoe to mom's new boyfriend.

As Zoe talked, I empathized with her feelings and thoughts. I also noticed she would take a single deep breath in and out on occasion. I pointed out she did this when she seemed to be angry. Zoe talked again about how she cannot seem to get her mother's attention because her mother is busy. Zoe remarked she was glad her mother was at least concerned about her.

The conversation took a turn back to a previously identified polarity, the polarity between the desire to see her mom happy and the desire to have more attention from her mom. She had previously talked a great deal about her desire to have her mom's attention. She now focused on her desire to see her mom happy. Before her mom had met the new boyfriend, her mom would cry herself to sleep at night. I empathized to validate this side of the polarity. However, I also noted there was a lot of anger there. She wanted to see her mom happy, but the anger was on the surface. She commented that everything was about this new boyfriend. She joked maybe she would get more of her mom's attention if she wore a T-shirt with the boyfriend's face on it.

As she talked, I noticed she was picking at the fingerless gloves she was wearing. The floor had become littered with bits of black cotton. I remarked on this, and we talked about how she used this to soothe herself. We talked about ways she soothed herself. She said her mom was once her safety blanket, but now she turns to other things like games, friends, cutting, and thoughts of hurting herself to feel better.

We concluded this session shortly after. I did additional check-ins to ensure that she was safe, and met with her for another counseling

(*continued*)

session a week later. She reported that since our last session she had not been thinking about suicide. We briefly talked about some of the major points discussed in our previous sessions, such as her relationship with her mom, dad, and the new boyfriend. Things were largely the same. We also discussed additional options to self-soothe and cope, such as focusing her awareness on her five senses, using imagery, and progressive relaxation. Shortly after, the school year came to a close. The suicidal thoughts had moved to the background and she was not self-harming at the end of the year.

After the summer ended, I met again with Zoe. She was much more composed. Mom was pregnant, and she was polarized about whether she was happy for her mom or worried about what changes this might bring. We processed this polarity. She also said she no longer had suicidal thoughts or was self-injuring. Although there was a brief relapse during the summer, she was able to talk to her mom and work through things.

Zoe still had not seen an outside counselor. However, using sandtray as a counseling intervention had aided her recovery. Her awareness about what she was doing both to get her mom's attention and self-soothe had grown. She had become more empowered to choose how she did both of these things. In addition to these two marked areas of growth, she seemed more self-accepting.

Reflections on Zoe's Session

This case illustration is a good example of the value of humanistic sandtray therapy with preadolescent clients. Tim's relationship with Zoe allowed her to feel safe enough to be honest and willing to explore her emotions. As Tim indicated, before sandtray, Zoe tended to keep the session on a surface level, but in sandtray she was able to go deeper into her experiencing to an extent. The depth of these sessions shows how preadolescents can experience and discuss their issues and experience their emotions on a fairly deep level if they feel safe, accepted, and understood. Zoe's experience of

(*continued*)

(*continued*)

being torn between her mother's happiness and her own feelings of anger and betrayal are poignant examples of how children of this age are more complex and conflicted than they are often portrayed.

Many of the responses Tim made to Zoe are similar to those he would have made to an adult client even though Zoe is 11 years old. However, Zoe's reluctance to be vulnerable in the here and now is an age-appropriate response. With preadolescents, it is difficult for therapists to determine if the clients' reluctance to be vulnerable and open to painful emotions in the here and now is a developmental limitation or a defense similar to adult clients. Zoe expressed polarities and Tim explored them, but she did not experience her emotions on as deep a level as many adults would. Learning to trust inner experiencing in the here and now is difficult for most adults and preadolescents tend to avoid being vulnerable in front of adults. Alhough Tim did not confront Zoe about how she may be using depression and self-injurious behavior to get her mother's attention, he reflected that her mother let Zoe talk to her when she was down. If Tim's relationship with Zoe was not strong and based on mutual trust, she may have become defensive about the implications of getting her mother's attention in this manner.

REFERENCES

Armstrong, S. A. (2008). *Sandtray therapy: A humanistic approach.* Dallas, TX: Ludic Press.

Armstrong, S. A., Brown, T., & Foster, R. D. (2015). Humanistic sandtray therapy with preadolescents. *Journal of Child and Adolescent Counseling, 1*(1), 17–26.

Armstrong, S. A., & Simpson, C. S. (2002). Expressive arts in family therapy: Including young children in the process. *Texas Counseling Association Journal, 30*(2), 2–10.

Asay, T. P., & Lambert, M. J. (2008). The empirical case for the common factors in therapy: Quantitative findings. In M. A. Hubble, B. L. Duncan, & S. D. Miller (Eds.), *The heart and soul of change: What works in therapy* (pp. 23–55). Washington, DC: American Psychological Association.

Axline, V. M. (1947). *Play therapy*. New York, NY: Ballantine.

Badenoch, B. (2008). *Being a brain-wise therapist: A practical guide to interpersonal neurobiology.* New York, NY: W. W. Norton.

Bozarth, J. D. (2001). Congruence: A special way of being. In G. Wyatt (Ed.), *Congruence. Rogers' therapeutic conditions: Evolution, theory and practice* (pp. 184–199). Ross-On-Wye, UK: PCCS Books.

Bugental, J. F. T. (1999). *Psychotherapy isn't what you think.* Phoenix, AZ: Zeig, Tucker & Theisen.

Cain, D. J. (2002). Defining characteristics, history, and evolution of humanistic psychotherapies. In D. J. Cain & J. Seeman (Eds.), *Humanistic psychotherapies: Handbook of research and practice* (pp. 3–54). Washington, DC: American Psychological Association.

Carson, R. (2003). *Taming your gremlin: A surprisingly simple method for getting out of your own way.* New York, NY: Harper Collins.

Cozolino, L. (2010). *The neuroscience of psychotherapy: Building and rebuilding the human brain.* New York, NY: W. W. Norton.

Eberts, S., & Homeyer, L. (2015). Processing sandtrays from two theoretical perspectives: Gestalt and Adlerian. *International Journal of Play Therapy, 24*(3), 134–150. http://dx.doi.org/10.1037/a0039392

Even, T. A., & Armstrong, S. A. (2011). Sandtray for early recollections with children (SERCh) in Adlerian play therapy. *Journal of Individual Psychology, 67*, 391–407.

Flahive, M., & Ray, D. (2007). Effect of group sandtray therapy with preadolescents in a school setting. *Journal for Specialists in Group Work, 32*, 362–382.

Frank, J. D., & Frank, J. B. (1991). *Persuasion and healing* (3rd ed.). Baltimore, MD: Johns Hopkins University Press.

Greenspan, S. I., & Shankar, S. G. (2004). *The first idea: How symbols, language, and intelligence evolved from our primate ancestors to modern humans.* Cambridge, MA: Da Capo Press.

Hansen, J. T. (2005). The devaluation of inner subjective experiences by the counseling profession: A plea to reclaim the essence of the profession. *Journal of Counseling & Development, 83*, 406–415.

Hillman, J. (1996). *The soul's code.* New York, NY: Random House.

Homeyer, L., & Sweeney, D. (2011). *Sandtray therapy: A practical manual* (2nd ed.). New York, NY: Routledge.

Kalff, D. (1980). *Sandplay.* Santa Monica, CA: Sigo.

Kirschenbaum, H., & Henderson, V. L. (1989). *The Carl Rogers reader.* Boston, MA: Houghton Mifflin.

Lagutina, L., Sperlinger, D., & Esterhuyzen, A. (2013). Addressing psychological aspects of physical problems through sandplay: A grounded theory study of therapists' views. *Psychology and Psychotherapy, 86*(1), 105–124.

Landreth, G. (2012). *Play therapy: The art of the relationship* (3rd ed.). New York, NY: Routledge.

Lyles, M., & Homeyer, L. (2015). The use of sandtray therapy with adoptive families. *Adoption Quarterly, 18*(1), 67–80. http://dx.doi.org/10.1080/10926755.2014.945704

Meador, B. D., & Rogers, C. R. (1984). Person-centered therapy. In R. J. Corsini (Ed.), *Current psychotherapies* (3rd ed., pp. 142–195). Itasca, IL: F. E. Peacock.

Mitchell, R. R., & Friedman, H. S. (1994). *Sandplay: Past, present and future.* East Sussex, UK: Routledge.

Moon, K., Rice, B., & Schneider, C. (2005). Stanley W. Standal and the need for positive regard. In J. D. Bozarth & P. Wilkins (Vol. Eds.), *Rogers' therapeutic conditions: Evolution, theory and practice: Vol. 3, Unconditional positive regard* (pp. 19–34). Ross-on-Wye, Herfordshire, UK: PCCS Books.

Norcross, J. C., & Wampold, B. E. (2011). Evidence-based therapy relationships: Research conclusions and clinical practices. *Psychotherapy, 48*(1), 98–102.

Pearson, M., & Wilson, H. (2009). *Using expressive arts to work with mind, body and emotions.* Philadelphia, PA: Jessica Kingsley.

Raskin, N. J., & Rogers, C. R. (2005). Person-centered therapy. In R. J. Corsini & D. Wedding (Eds.), *Current psychotherapies* (7th ed.). Itasca, IL: F. E. Peacock.

Ray, D., Bratton, S., Rhine, T., & Jones, L. (2001). The effectiveness of play therapy: Responding to the critics. *International Journal of Play Therapy, 10*(1), 85–108.

Ray, D. C. (2011). *Advanced play therapy: Essential conditions, knowledge, and skills for child practice.* New York, NY: Routledge.

Rogers, C. R. (1957). The necessary and sufficient conditions of therapeutic personality change. *Journal of Consulting Psychology, 21*(2), 95–103.

Rogers, C. R. (1961). *On becoming a person*. New York, NY: Houghton Mifflin.

Rogers, C. R. (1975). Empathic: An unappreciated way of being. *The Counseling Psychologist, 5*(2), 2–11.

Rogers, C. R. (1977). *Carl Rogers on personal power: Inner strength and its revolutionary impact.* New York, NY: Delacorte Press.

Rogers, C. R. (1980). *A way of being*. Boston, MA: Houghton Mifflin.

Sanders, P. (2006). *The person-centred counseling primer*. Ross-On-Wye, UK: PCCS Books.

Schadler, G., & De Domenico, G. S. (2012). Sandtray-Worldplay for people who experience chronic mental illness. *International Journal of Play Therapy, 21*(2), 87–99. http://dx.doi.org/10.1037/a0027192

Shen, Y., & Armstrong, S. A. (2008). Impact of group sandtray therapy on the self-esteem of young adolescent girls. *Journal for Specialists in Group Work, 33*, 118–137.

Spiegelberg, H. (1970). Phenomenology. In *Encyclopedia Britannica* (14th ed., pp. 810–812). Chicago, IL: Encyclopedia Britannica.

Sweeney, D., & Rocha, S. (2000). Using play therapy to assess family dynamics. In R. Watts (Ed.), *Techniques in marriage and family counseling* (Vol. 1, pp. 33–47). Alexandria, VA: American Counseling Association.

Wampold, B. E., & Bhati, K. S. (2004). Attending to the omissions: A historical examination of evidence-based practice movements. *Professional Psychology: Research and Practice, 35*, 563–570.

Warner, M. S. (2001). Empathy, relational depth, and difficult client process. In S. Haugh & T. Merry (Eds.), *Empathy. Rogers' therapeutic conditions: Evolution, theory and practice* (pp. 181–191). Ross-On-Wye, UK: PCCS Books.

Wilkins, P. (2010). *Person-centered therapy: 100 key points*. London, UK: Routledge.

Yontef, G. M., & Simkin, J. S. (1989). Gestalt therapy. In R. J. Corsini & D. Wedding (Eds.), *Current psychotherapies* (4th ed., pp. 323–362). Itasca, IL: F. E. Peacock.

CHAPTER 10

Directive Approaches When Working With Parents

JENNIFER N. BOSWELL

Many child therapy researchers recommend parents to be included in their child's counseling process (Athanasiou, 2001; Kottman, 2009; Landreth & Bratton, 2006; McGuire & McGuire, 2001; Sommers-Flannagan, 2007), but many times parents are left out of the process. These researchers have demonstrated that inclusion of parents in the counseling process leads to greater parent satisfaction of the counselor and treatment for the child. Oftentimes, parents are left wondering what the counselor is working on with their child, what progress is being made, and how the parent plays a role in the overall process. Typically, parents desire to be included and to be up-to-date with their child's progress but are unsure of ways in which to be included in the dialogue with the counselor. At the same time, counselors are often unsure of how to include parents and what can be said to parents about the child. Counselors working with children are often conflicted about this because they would like to inform parents of the progress and the goings on of the counseling relationship but have an ethical responsibility to protect the child's privacy within the counseling relationship. How does a counselor ethically include a parent in the child's counseling process while also maintaining the child's privacy, knowing that parents play a vital role in the success of the child's counseling?

Parent consultations can be used by play therapists and child and adolescent counselors as a means of including parents in the therapeutic process. Parent consultations have been widely used and researched in various fields. Consultations are commonly used in school and counseling settings (Dettmer, Dyck, & Thurston, 2004; Holcomb-McCoy & Bryan, 2010; Ritchie & Partin, 1994). Consultations with parents encourage collateral work with the parent and the counselor to solve a problem versus the treatment being counselor directed. Consultations allow for specific interventions and family strategies unique to the child and parent. By working in collaboration, parents feel more encouraged and empowered to work toward a solution to the problem; this increases the possibility of a long-lasting change. Specifically related to the counseling field and in working with children and families, parent involvement in a child's therapeutic process has been linked to a greater overall satisfaction in the counseling process and a noted decrease in the behavioral problems at home and school (Israel, Thomsen, Langeveld, & Stormark, 2007; Kottman, 2001a, 2003; Landreth & Bratton, 2006; McGuire & McGuire, 2001), but when parents are left out of the counseling relationship and therapeutic work, there is evidence that this results in a reduced amount of cooperation by the parents in the counseling process and then may result in premature termination of counseling for the child (O'Conner, 1991). Moreover, when parents are involved in the process, McMahon (2009) observed that children and parents continue to report gains and improvement after the counseling relationship has ended.

A RATIONALE FOR USING PARENT CONSULTATIONS

McGuire posited that parent involvement in a child's life is one of the strongest factors in the child's overall well-being and growth (McGuire & McGuire, 2001). McGuire and McGuire, therefore, advocated for the increased and frequent use of parent consultations in any work with children and adolescents. Specifically, they focused on two overarching goals of parent consultation: (a) educate parents on improving communication between the parent and child and (b) explain the process and goals of play therapy. Educating and engaging with parents begins at the first contact (phone call or meeting) and should include multiple and ongoing points of contact throughout the duration of the counseling relationship until termination. Sharing the same viewpoint, Garry Landreth (2002), a prominent researcher in the play therapy field, suggested that counselors using parent consultations should focus on obtaining the parent's cooperation, explaining and helping the parent understand the process of play therapy, and exploring ways to engage the parent in the ongoing process of counseling. Meeting with a parent on a regular schedule to discuss the child's progress, both in counseling and in other significant areas, can help the parent feel included and involved in the counseling process.

Based on McGuire and McGuire and Landreth's interest in parent consultations, Cates, Paone, Packman, and Margolis (2006) developed helpful outlines structuring the steps of an effective parent consultation. Cates et al. (2006) recognized parents who are informed about the process of play therapy, are in agreement with the child's therapeutic goals, and recognize the benefits of play therapy are more likely to continue bringing their child to play therapy and complete tasks at home to build on the gains that the child is making in the play sessions. This lends itself to a greater likelihood that the child will create movement toward the counseling goals. Parents may understand their role as parent, but they may be unfamiliar with their role in the overall play therapy process. It is the counselor's job to teach parents about the process during the first session (Association for Play Therapy Ethics and Practices Committee, 2001; Haworth, 1982; Landreth, 2002). This includes an explanation of the rationale of play therapy, the benefits, time commitment by both the child and parent, and the limits of confidentiality. A discussion about the limits of confidentiality is especially important when working with parents and older children and/or adolescents. Contributing to successful outcomes in treatment, counselors are encouraged to discuss and recognize all positive parenting skills, even those that seem minor, so that the parent is encouraged by his or her effort (McGuire & McGuire, 2001; Sori, Dermer, & Wesolowski, 2006). This recognition of positive parenting skills exhibited can then begin to build up the parents' level of self-confidence in their skill set which, in turn, leads to an improvement in the parent–child interaction.

During parent consultations, counselors and other mental health professionals should continually work on educating parents regarding normal child development and behaviors so that parents can better understand their child by improving parent–child relationship patterns and family communication (McGuire & McGuire, 2001). Each element discussed between counselor and parent (e.g., development, skills, techniques) help facilitate positive change in the child and the parent–child relationship. The parent consultation is a significant part of the counseling process when working with children and families and should not be discounted. As much time and energy that is placed into work with the child should also be expended in the relationship and work with the parent(s).

METHODS AND TECHNIQUES FOR PARENT INVOLVEMENT

Generally, parent consultation models consist of parent education, developing solutions to problems faced by the parent and child, and intensive parent training (Sommers-Flannagan, 2007). All parent consultations should include the following four stages: (a) engagement, (b) cooperation, (c) incorporation, and (d) termination (Steen, 2010). During the engagement stage, counselors work to dispel any apprehension or worry that the parent might have about the counseling process. Counselors should actively use encouragement, empathy, and genuineness to help a parent feel respected, validated, and included in the process. During the cooperation stage, the counselor works to include the parent in a more active and direct way. During this time, the parent and counselor work on limit-setting skills, ongoing communication and behavioral problems, and any other concerns that the parent may have about the child and family. In the third stage, incorporation, parents are encouraged to use the new skills they are learning at home and in other settings with the child. Counselors assist the parents in using empathy and communication skills to better understand the perspective of the child. The parent should become more active and responsible for using the new parenting skills with the child. In the last stage, termination, the counselor should be listening for parent and child cues that change is happening at home and newly developed parenting skills are being used consistently. It should be noted that parent consultation does not mean that the counselor becomes the parent's therapist. Care should be taken to avoid dual relationships with the parents. If a counselor notices that a parent may be in need of his or her own mental health services, then the child's counselor should suggest referrals.

Parent consultations can be used as a single-session model to a more intensive and long-term model of work with parents. Two directive models common to play therapy practice are (a) the solution-focused behavioral approach and (b) the Adlerian parent consultation approach. In addition to these two theoretical models, two therapeutic approaches include parents in an active way throughout the therapy process. These are (a) systematic training for effective parenting (STEP) and (b) filial therapy.

Solution-Focused Behavioral Approach to Parent Involvement

Many of the current approaches and models to parent consultations and greater involvement in counseling are intensive and ongoing. Due to many responsibilities and obligations that parents have today, this level of involvement, while desired, is not often feasible. Shaw and Magnuson (2006) developed a short-term behavioral and solution-focused approach to conducting parent consultations. This approach was created from behavioral, solution-focused brief therapy, as well as Adlerian principles.

Shaw and Magnuson suggested this model as a way to enhance the play therapy process through the use of parent consultation. As such, parents are encouraged to find time to meet with the counselor without the child present. This may mean that another professional or family member watches the child before or after the play therapy session. If this does not work, the counselor can suggest that the parent find time to meet on a different day. Using this model, a counselor meets with parents for the first or last 10 minutes of each counseling session and then spends the remaining 45 minutes with the child in the play therapy session. During the parent consultation, Shaw and Magnuson focus on five key tasks: (a) following a consultation model to create a working alliance that allows parents to feel heard, respected, and included; (b) defining the presenting problem in behavioral terms that allow the parents to understand the behavior antecedents and consequences and allow the parent to develop measures to track and observe the behaviors; (c) using solution-focused language to help the parents focus on the behavioral goal and solutions rather than focusing on what is not working; (d) using behavioral reinforcements within the family to encourage members to catch the child engaging in positive behaviors; and (e) educating parents on common childhood issues, developmental levels and milestones, and reasons children typically act out. Common prompts that counselors using this model might encourage parents to discuss during the meeting include (Shaw & Magnuson, 2006):

- Describe what your child is doing that is creating concern or disruption within the family.
- Provide an example of the problem behavior this past week.
- How did you, or other family members, respond to this behavior?
- What was the child's next course of action? What happened next?
- Looking back, what might you have done differently on that occasion?

In 2007, Sommers-Flannagan assessed the use of a short-term, single-session, solution-focused approach to parent consultations. This approach was created in response to the move toward more brief, short-term, strengths-based services for clients. Sommers-Flannagan's (2007) Parenting Consultant and Consultation Model comprises six core areas of focus: (a) explaining the consultation; (b) supporting and allowing the parents' concerns to feel heard; (c) identifying and noting the presenting problem as explained by the parent; (d) modeling counseling skills, such as empathy, compassion, reflection, and genuineness; (e) offering advice and education to parents for management of the presenting problem; and

(f) summarizing the learning and behavioral plan for the parents. In an analysis of this consultation model, Sommers-Flannagan conducted a single-session parent consultation with 33 parents and then administered a Parenting Questionnaire and Satisfaction Inventory to assess each parent's views on the parent consultation process. Using a paired-sample *t*-test, Sommers-Flannagan found that parents perceived the consultations as beneficial in managing the child's behaviors and decreasing parental stress.

Adlerian Approach to Parent Involvement

In Adlerian play therapy, Terry Kottman encourages continued work and inclusion of parents on a regular basis. Adlerian counselors and play therapists use the tenets of Individual Psychology as developed by Alfred Adler in order to understand the child's style of life and way to connect and belong in the world, along with the family dynamics to understand the presenting problem and methods to help the child and family. At the core of Adlerian counseling, Alfred Adler believed that all people (a) have a need to belong in the community; (b) are teleological in that all human behavior has a goal; (c) are creative and unique in how they view and approach their personal goals; and (d) view the world from their own subjective perspective (Kottman, 2009). Adlerian play therapists actively involve the parents, teachers, and other significant adults in the therapeutic process. Other significant adults who might be included in the therapeutic process may include other family members that have close connections with the child, religious leaders, and/or daily caregivers.

In Adlerian play therapy, the counselor meets with parents on a regular basis, beginning with the initial session, to learn about the child and family and assess behavioral goals. During the initial meeting with the parents, the play therapists will begin constructing a conceptualization of the family and child including the relationships and communication styles between parents and between each parent and the child. Throughout the initial phases of therapy, the Adlerian play therapists will continue to work with the parents to assess the child and begin to develop hypotheses of behavior related to the child's style of life, private logic, and faulty assumptions. These hypotheses come from work with the child in therapy and ongoing discussions with the parents about the child and about the parents' families of origin and how they have impacted their relationships, interactions, and discipline styles while raising the child. In the later phases of therapy, after the relationships have been built and assessment of the child and family has been completed, the counselor continues to work with the parents in a more directive, teaching role. The Adlerian counselor teaches the parents about the child's identified goals of misbehavior (i.e., attention, power, revenge, and displays of inadequacy). These goals of misbehavior are used as the foundation to develop parenting strategies to help the child improve (Driekurs, Grunwald, & Pepper, 1971). During these ongoing meetings, the counselor reeducates the parents on helpful parenting strategies that meet the child's specific needs and help the child learn positive and socially acceptable ways of meeting his or her needs rather than through misbehavior. The counselor continues to encourage positive parenting skills and evaluates how the parents are using their newly adopted parenting skills on a day-to-day basis.

Systematic Training for Effective Parenting

Dinkmeyer and McKay (1989) developed the STEP curriculum as a way to assist parents and other significant caregivers. This training program was created in 1976 after the creators, Dinkmeyer and McKay (1973), coauthored a book, *Raising a Responsible Child,* and subsequently turned the book into a discussion group and then a parenting program. Adlerian counselors and play therapists actively include parents, teachers, and other caregivers in the treatment process as they recognize the value and influence that each has on the child's daily world. These adults provide valuable insights and information into the development, daily concerns, and previously attempted solutions (Kottman, 2011). Depending on where the presenting problem is manifesting itself, the play therapist will include that caregiver. For example, if a behavior is consistently causing difficulty at school, the play therapist might include the parent, school counselor, and teacher in the consultations and treatment planning. The STEP program is grounded within Adlerian theoretical constructs and tenets.

The STEP parent education training can be completed by parents independently, with a play therapist, or in a parent training group. Most professionals encourage parents to complete the training with a professional counselor or play therapist either in an individual session or in a group format so that the play therapist can discuss areas of concern for the parent and ensure that the activities and components are understood. Each chapter or module of the training can be completed each week and the training program consists of component areas (Dinkmeyer, McKay, & Dinkmeyer, 1997). Play therapists using the STEP program with parents include the parent's handbook, discussion prompts, videos, and parent needs and expectations of the child to reach the desired behavioral goals (Dinkmeyer & McKay, 1989). Like other parent training programs, STEP encourages parents to attend each consultation session with the play therapist in order to reap the greatest benefit for both the child and the parent. The STEP program begins with the parent gaining a greater awareness into the needs and perceptions of both the parent and child and having the parent reflect on his or her own parenting beliefs. The parent learns how the family parenting style affects the child and the parent–child relationship. In addition, common developmental issues and milestones are discussed as a way to help the parent normalize some of the child's behavior. Next, the parent begins to understand the child's goals of misbehavior (Driekurs et al., 1971) and how these goals serve a purpose for the child. Common parental reactions to each goal of misbehavior and positive and encouraging parent responses to the identified goals are also covered. Encouragement as a form of communication and means of loving and supporting the child are reviewed. After these components are addressed, the STEP program moves into teaching the parent positive parenting strategies to increase the parent's positive regard and self-esteem of the child, thereby developing a stronger and healthier parent–child relationship within the family. Parenting strategies include the use of I-messages versus You-messages; the use of active, reflective listening to the child; teaching the parent and child to collaboratively problem solve; developing routine family meetings; using choices when disciplining the child; and allowing the child to learn from logical consequences (Dinkmeyer et al., 1997). As a result of the STEP program, parents have reported a greater connection and a positive view of their child; an increase in positive, healthy parenting skills; and a greater self-esteem in the child (Gibson, 1999; Jackson & Brown, 1986; Noller & Taylor, 1989).

Much of the research demonstrating the STEP program to be an effective parent training program was conducted from the 1970s to the 1990s. In 1993, Gibson completed a meta-analysis of the 40 research studies where mental health professionals studied the effectiveness of the program on a wide range of participants and child concerns. Gibson found that the STEP program was effective in most of the parent populations and, overall, parents reported positive changes in parenting styles and strategies, greater understanding and parental empathy toward the child, greater positive interactions and relationships between the parent and the child, and a decrease in the child's problematic behaviors. In 1999, Gibson did a follow-up to the previous meta-analysis and included an additional 21 studies for a total of 61 studies evaluating the STEP program. Gibson again found strong support and research efficacy for the STEP program.

Finally, in 2010, the STEP program was added to the Substance Abuse and Mental Health Services Administration's (SAMHSA) National Registry of Evidence-Based Programs.

Filial Therapy

Filial therapy is both a therapeutic intervention and a preventative intervention in which a parent is trained to become the therapeutic change agent in his or her child's life (Guerney, 1964; Landreth & Bratton, 2006). Filial therapy originated from Rogerian tenets and uses a group format to teach parents how to interact with their children using play therapy methods (Guerney, 1964). One of the first models of filial therapy was used in the 1960s by Bernard and Louise Guerney. It was designed to be a long-term parenting program for parents of children with emotional and behavioral issues (Bratton, Ray, Rhine, & Jones, 2005; Landreth & Bratton, 2006). VanFleet (2005) also described a filial therapy model, which can be used with smaller groups or individual parents. She adapted the original filial therapy model as described by the Guerneys for individual families rather than groups of parents. The VanFleet model is the same as the Guerneys' original one except that each meeting time is 1 hour in duration and the entire training process typically lasts between 15 and 25 sessions.

In the filial therapy model, parents are involved in the counseling process and incorporate relationship skills that strengthen the parent–child relationship (Kottman, 2001b; Landreth, 2002; VanFleet, 1994, 2000). Through filial therapy, the counselor teaches parents how to (a) use play therapy techniques in daily interactions and communication with their child; (b) reflect the child's feelings so that he or she feels heard and accepted; and (c) set appropriate limits on inappropriate behavior (Landreth & Bratton, 2006). In Landreth's intensive 10-week filial therapy model, child–parent relationship training (CPRT), parents meet for biweekly training groups, 2 hours per session, to learn basic play therapy skills using a specialized kit of toys (Landreth & Bratton, 2006). The basic skills include reflecting, limit setting, and encouragement (Landreth & Bratton, 2006). Via didactic and skills-based practice, parents are taught how to recognize the child's feelings; demonstrate acceptance, empathy, and encouragement of the child; and to master limit-setting skills to facilitate both child and parent growth. During the parent training process, the counselor models attending and reflecting skills and teaches the parents principles of the CPRT model. Parents are able to practice the skills learned in the group parent sessions as they conduct weekly, child-centered play sessions at home.

Unique to this approach to working with parents is the support group aspect and the continuous supervision by the counselor to ensure that parents are learning the skills being taught. Those counselors interested in the use of the 10-week model can use the CPRT treatment manual that accompanies the textbook with specific instructions and guides for following the model along with printable parent materials and worksheets (Bratton, Landreth, Kellam, & Blackard, 2006). It is important to explain that parents are not in group counseling, but are in a supportive group designed to help them learn skills and ways of communicating with their child that will improve the parent–child relationship.

COMMON ISSUES: PERCEPTIONS AND TIME INVESTMENT OF PARENT CONSULTATIONS

Parent perceptions and the time investment of parent consultations are rarely mentioned in the parent consultation and play therapy literature. Landreth (2002) encouraged the use of "periodic parental sessions" (p. 154). In his child-centered model of counseling, counselors typically meet with parents every four to five sessions for ongoing parent consultations. Child-centered counselors endorse the use of parent consultations to inform parents about the progress being made, whereas counselors using the other three models incorporate parents more into the ongoing counseling sessions or through skills-based learning during the consultation meeting. Regardless of the time investment, counselors using child-centered counseling tenets focus on building a strong parent–counselor working alliance, assessing ongoing changes with both the parent and the child, and educating the parent on developmental issues and resources that are available to the parent (Post, Ceballos, & Penn, 2012). Furthermore, Post et al. (2012) stated that ongoing parent consultations assist counselors in meeting the requirements of managed care as well as attending to agency needs for continuing evaluation of progress toward counseling goals. McGuire and McGuire (2001) encouraged counselors to meet with parents for 15 minutes each week, whereas Landreth suggested that counselors should meet with the parents during the first 15 minutes of the therapeutic session so the child does not perceive the counselor is "telling on them" (Landreth, 2002, p. 154). Regardless of when counselors choose to hold the meeting, these consultations are to review any changes in the child, report changes in play themes, and make new homework assignments for the parent for the next week. McGuire and McGuire noted that weekly sessions might not be possible for all parents due to work and family schedules. Counselors should be flexible in scheduling parent consultations. In child-centered play therapy, when it is clear that more intensive services are needed for the parent, then filial therapy and parent education sessions are suggested. McGuire and McGuire did not provide a rationale as to why 15-minute weekly sessions are encouraged over other models.

Similar to McGuire and McGuire, Kottman (2003) recommended that Adlerian counselors meet with parents on an ongoing, weekly basis so that parents are actively engaged in the counseling process. These weekly meetings are specifically designed for each family. Some parents have equal time in consultation as the child has in counseling, whereas other parents may just need 15 to 20 minutes before or after the child's counseling session to consult with the counselor. She also recognized that some parents are not able to meet weekly or counselors do not have the resources available for regular consultations with parents. In these cases, Kottman suggested that counselors attempt to meet with parents every other week or have regularly scheduled phone conversations about the child's behaviors and any changes being noted. In Adlerian counseling and play therapy, counselors believe that, by having the parents actively involved, the child is more likely to "alter their attitudes and behaviors" (Kottman, 2003, p. 66).

In another parent-consultation approach, Athanasiou (2001) discussed an ecobehavioral model of consultation in which she met with both the parent and the child on a weekly basis for counseling and consultation. Using this model, Athanasiou met with the grandmother for 25 minutes and with the child for the remaining 25 minutes of the session. The family system and both the child and grandparent's needs were being addressed and discussed each week. She suggested that significant improvement in the different sublevels of the family system occurred in 5 weeks due to the use of this consultation model.

CASE EXAMPLE: THE STORY OF ANDREW AND MS. V

Ms. V brought her son Andrew, aged 8 years, to counseling for behavioral problems at school and home. She reported that Andrew had significant behavioral, acting out problems. Andrew would become angry and aggressive toward teachers at school, which would lead

(continued)

(*continued*)

to him throwing the contents of his desk out across the classroom, running away from teachers and administrators, and yelling and screaming in the lunchroom. At home, Ms. V reported that when reprimanded, Andrew would lash out at her and her older daughter. This resulted in physical fights with Andrew and the older daughter. Ms. V also mentioned that, after one argument, she found that Andrew had opened the window of his bedroom and climbed out onto the roof of the house. Ms. V was a single parent and had adopted Andrew at birth. She explained to the counselor that she knew that Andrew's biological parents abused drugs before and during pregnancy. Ms. V had no other medical or mental health information on the parents or Andrew. The biological parents terminated their parental rights and Ms. V adopted Andrew at that point. Ms. V attributed Andrew's behavior to the drug use. Ms. V has been active in working with the school administrators, teachers, and school counselor in finding solutions to manage Andrew's behaviors at school. She reported that she is beginning the process of having him tested for services by the school. Ms. V stated that she is overwhelmed and frustrated with a lack of improvement in Andrew's behaviors and worries that it will only get worse as he gets older.

When Ms. V called the counselor to make the initial counseling appointment for Andrew, the counselor encouraged Ms. V to attend the first session without Andrew so as to complete all of the necessary intake paperwork and discuss the plan for treatment. During the initial session, the counselor spoke to Ms. V about the developmental, medical, and family background of Andrew and the behaviors and issues she was seeing both at home and in school. As Ms. V spoke about her concerns for Andrew, the counselor began to conceptualize the problems Andrew was experiencing and how those might be addressed in play therapy. She began to gather ideas about the ways in which Andrew was using his anger and aggression to express himself and get what he needed from others (his goal of misbehavior). In addition, the counselor also began to gain a better understanding of Andrew's way of viewing and understanding the world (his style of life). As the counselor spoke with Ms. V, she made sure to empathize with her frustration and concern for Andrew and affirmed all of the work Ms. V had done to help

(*continued*)

Andrew and find solutions to improve his behavior. As Ms. V began to talk through her frustration and worry for her son, the counselor could see her begin to relax as she felt heard and understood by the counselor. Behavioral goals were also developed for Andrew with Ms. V's input.

During the initial meeting, the counselor spent the first half of the session educating Ms. V on play therapy and the structure of the counseling relationship and sessions. She also discussed the ways in which Ms. V would actively participate in the process. This included explaining what play therapy was, the benefits of play versus talk therapy for children, and what Ms. V might expect at each session and what she might begin to see at home and school. In addition, the counselor discussed confidentiality and how she would be updated on his progress in counseling. Next, the counselor discussed how Ms. V was going to be included in the treatment. The counselor explained that she would meet with Ms. V on an ongoing basis, usually for 20 minutes before Andrew's session. During these consultation meetings, the counselor would review any changes Ms. V had noticed or heard about from school administrators or teachers. Time would also be spent delving into Ms. V's family of origin and how her childhood and relationships with her parents impacted her current relationships with her children, especially Andrew, and her parenting style. This would also include discussions about Ms. V's view on discipline in the home. As sessions moved forward with Andrew, the counselor explained that the parent consultations would also begin to include different parenting skills, strategies, and interventions that Ms. V could use at home, and explain to teachers for consistency across settings to help Andrew learn more socially appropriate ways of expressing his needs and having those needs met. Ms. V reported that she was very interested in learning different ways she could work with Andrew at home.

During the initial play session with Andrew, the counselor observed Andrew's need to test relationship boundaries. This entailed Andrew continually wanting to leave the playroom for a variety of reasons, opening and closing the playroom door, and playing with a variety of toys in the playroom and then tossing them on the floor when he was ready to move on to something else. As the counselor set limits on Andrew's desire to leave the

(*continued*)

(*continued*)

playroom, Andrew would give a sly grin but would change his behavior and continue to explore the playroom. At the end of the session, Andrew refused to leave the room. A limit needed to be placed two times before Andrew left the playroom independently. At the beginning of the following session, the counselor met with Ms. V to review any changes that were happening at home and school. Ms. V reported little change but did mention that Andrew was excited to return to the playroom. During this consultation time, the counselor discussed the use of basic empathy and reflection skills with Ms. V to help her begin to recognize and respond to Andrew's feelings of anger and frustration at home. The counselor provided Ms. V with a feelings list to help her respond to the different levels of anger that Andrew was displaying in addition to providing examples of response statements. After the consultation meeting, the counselor again met with Andrew for his play session. The session continued as the first with Andrew testing limits and boundaries throughout the session and the counselor consistently responding to his need to test the relationship with the counselor and with appropriate limits to maintain the child–counselor relationship, safety of Andrew during the session, and Andrew damaging the playroom.

During the following month, Andrew was brought to counseling once a week and the counselor continued to meet with Ms. V before each session. During each parent meeting, Ms. V would provide a short update on any behavioral changes at school and home. Next, the counselor would work with Ms. V in reviewing her use of positive communication skills and appropriate limit setting at home. Each week, the counselor would focus on a new skill for Ms. V to incorporate at home. Along with the skills being practiced, the counselor also encouraged Ms. V to spend one-on-one time with Andrew each week for at least 30 minutes. Andrew would be encouraged to help decide on the activity each week, such as taking a walk in the park, going to eat ice cream, playing a board game, or playing a game of basketball with mom. These one-on-one activities allowed Andrew and Ms. V to connect during a special mom and son time and to remove the focus on the problem behavior and instead focus on positive relationship time.

In the second month of treatment, the counselor began to notice an increase in aggressive behaviors in the playroom. Andrew would

(*continued*)

test the playroom limits and, instead of redirecting his behavior, would follow through with the action. In the conceptualization of Andrew and his anger and aggression, the counselor recognized Andrew's acting out as a way, although negative, to get his need of attention and control over a situation met. To feel significant in his world, Andrew learned that acting out led to significant adults giving him the desired attention he wanted. In addition, when Andrew felt scared and unsure of his relationship with significant adults in his world he would lash out. By doing so, Andrew would test the response of the adult to determine if he was desired or unwanted. Throughout the duration of the counseling relationship, the counselor would remain consistent in her use of limits in the playroom in order to reinforce socially appropriate ways of behaving. The counselor also used reflection and tracking skills to note when Andrew became frustrated with a game he devised in the playroom or with toys he was playing with to help him recognize his frustration. The counselor also used esteem-building statements and encouragement when she recognized Andrew becoming frustrated but continuing to attempt to solve the problem. This helped Andrew learn that it was okay when he was not successful with his attempt; he could try again, and the counselor would continue to remain supportive.

From this conceptualization of Andrew and the presenting problem, the counselor also tailored the parent consultations to address Andrew's need of feeling wanted and cared for by the adults in his world. The counselor spent several consultation sessions explaining the idea of children's goals of misbehavior. It was explained to Ms. V that when a child does not feel his or her needs have been met, the child may turn to misbehavior as a way to get the need met. Time was spent explaining each of the goals of misbehavior (attention, power and control, revenge, and inadequacy). The way each of these goals of misbehavior present themselves, how the parent feels when these behaviors are used, what the child is actually needing from the parent, and how the parent can respond to the actual need were discussed. Ms. V clearly and quickly identified Andrew's goals of misbehavior as being attention, power, and control. During this consultation, the counselor observed Ms. V visibly relax and take a sign of relief as she began to understand the purpose

(*continued*)

(*continued*)

behind Andrew's behavior and that she had a solution. Ms. V was eager to go home and continue using the communication skills she had learned to help correct Andrew's behavior, and also address his underlying need to feel safe and connected to Ms. V along with needing some sense of control in his world.

In the following consultations, Ms. V began to report a decrease in the number of acting out incidents at school and a stronger parent–child relationship at home. Ms. V continued to place limits on Andrew's behavior when he began acting out, but also started allowing him to make age-appropriate choices to give him a sense of control over some of his decisions. This even transferred over to the one-on-one time Ms. V spent with Andrew each week. She reported that she now allowed him to make the decision on their weekly activity / time and that he always looked forward to the time they spent together. The counselor worked with Ms. V to also find ways to incorporate more physical activity in Andrew's daily routine and alternatives for expression of anger and frustration at home instead of lashing out and destroying property or attacking Ms. V. Special emphasis was placed on developing a routine for Andrew to provide consistency. This routine allowed for homework time, downtime, and weekly mom and son activities. The routine of play therapy and weekly parent consultations with Ms. V continued throughout Andrew's treatment. Although Andrew remained consistent in his acting out behaviors in therapy, Ms. V continued to report significant improvement at school and home. By the fourth month of treatment, Ms. V reported that she was feeling comfortable and empowered in her new skill set and improved relationship at home with Andrew. She was also pleased with the behavior change at school as she was contacted less and less frequently by the principal and teachers.

REFERENCES

Association for Play Therapy Ethics and Practices Committee. (2001). Consultations with parents of minors. *Association for Play Therapy Newsletter, 20*(3), 1–29.

Athanasiou, M. S. (2001). Using consultation with a grandmother as an adjunct to play therapy. *The Family Journal, 9*, 445–449. http://dx.doi.org/10.1177/1066480701094014

Bratton, S. C., Landreth, G. L., Kellam, T., & Blackard, S. R. (2006). *Child Parent Relationship Therapy (CPRT) treatment manual: A 10-session filial therapy model for training parents*. New York, NY: Routledge.

Bratton, S. C., Ray, D., Rhine, T., & Jones, L. (2005). The efficacy of play therapy with children: A meta-analytic review of treatment outcomes. *Professional Psychology: Research and Practice, 36*, 367–390. http://dx.doi.org/10.1037/0735-7028.36.4.376

Cates, J., Paone, T. R., Packman, J., & Margolis, D. (2006). Effective parent consultation in play therapy. *International Journal of Play Therapy, 15*, 87–100.

Dettmer, M. A., Dyck, N., & Thurston, L. P. (2004). *Consultation, collaboration, and teamwork for students with special needs*. Boston, MA: Allyn & Bacon.

Dinkmeyer, D., & McKay, G. D. (1973). *Raising a responsible child: Practical steps to successful family relationships*. New York, NY: Simon & Schuster.

Dinkmeyer, D., Sr., McKay, G. D., & Dinkmeyer, D., Jr. (1997). *The parent's handbook: Systematic training for effective parenting*. Circle Pines, MN: American Guidance Service.

Driekurs, R., Grunwald, B. B., & Pepper, F. C. (1971). *Maintaining sanity in the classroom: Illustrated teaching techniques*. New York, NY: Harper & Row.

Gibson, D. G. (1993). *A meta analytical review of the literature on the efficacy of the systematic training for effective parenting (STEP) program*. Logan, UT: Utah State University, Department of Psychology.

Gibson, D. G. (1999). *A monograph: Summary of the research related to the use and efficacy of the systematic training for effective parenting (STEP) program*. Retrieved from www.steppublishers.com/sites/default/files/Monograph.pdf

Guerney, B. G., Jr. (1964). Filial therapy: Description and rationale. *Journal of Consulting Psychology, 28*, 303–310.

Haworth, M. R. (1982). Explaining play therapy to parents. In G. L. Landreth (Ed.), *Play therapy: Dynamics of the process of counseling with children* (pp. 233–234). Springfield, IL: Charles Thomas.

Holcomb-McCoy, C., & Bryan, J. (2010). Advocacy and empowerment in parent consultation: Implications for theory and practice. *Journal of Counseling and Development, 88*, 259–268.

Israel, P., Thomsen, P. H., Langeveld, J. H., & Stormark, K. M. (2007). Parent-youth discrepancy in the assessment and treatment of youth in usual clinical care setting: Consequences to parent involvement. *European Child & Adolescent Psychiatry, 16*(2), 138–148.

Jackson, M. D., & Brown, D. (1986). Use of systematic training for effective parenting (STEP) with elementary school parents. *School Counselor, 34*, 100–104.

Kottman, T. (2001a). Adlerian play therapy. *International Journal of Play Therapy, 10*, 1–12.

Kottman, T. (2001b). *Play therapy: Basics and beyond*. Alexandria, VA: American Counseling Association.

Kottman, T. (2003). *Partners in play: An Adlerian approach to play therapy* (2nd ed.). Alexandria, VA: American Counseling Association.

Kottman, T. (2009). Adlerian play therapy. In K. J. O'Connor & L. M. Braveman (Eds.), *Play therapy theory and practice: A comparative presentation* (pp. 237–282). New York, NY: John Wiley & Sons.

Kottman, T. (2011). *Play therapy: Basics and beyond* (2nd ed.). Alexandria, VA: American Counseling Association.

Landreth, G. L. (2002). *Play therapy: The art of the relationship* (2nd ed.). New York, NY: Brunner-Routledge.

Landreth, G. L., & Bratton, S. (2006). *Child parent relationship therapy: A 10-session filial therapy model*. New York, NY: Routledge.

McGuire, D. K., & McGuire, D. E. (2001). *Linking parents to play therapy: A practical guide with applications, interventions, and case studies*. Philadelphia, PA: Brunner-Routledge.

McMahon, L. (2009). *The handbook of play therapy and therapeutic play* (2nd ed.). New York, NY: Routledge.

Noller, P., & Taylor, R. (1989). Parent education and family relations. *Family Relations, 38*, 196–200.

O'Conner, K. (1991). *The play therapy primer: An integration of theories and techniques*. New York, NY: John Wiley & Sons.

Post, P. B., Ceballos, P. L., & Penn, S. L. (2012). Collaborating with parents to establish behavioral goals in child-centered play therapy. *The Family Journal, 20*, 51–57. http://dx.doi.org/10.1177/1066480711425472

Ritchie, M. H., & Partin, R. L. (1994). Parent education and consultation activities of school counselors. *School Counselor, 41*, 165–170.

Shaw, H. E., & Magnuson, S. (2006). Enhancing play therapy with parent consultation: A behavioral/solution-focused approach. In H. G. Kaduson & C. E. Schaefer (Eds.), *Short-term play therapy for children* (pp. 216–241). New York, NY: Guilford Press.

Sommers-Flannagan, J. (2007). Single-session consultations for parents: A preliminary investigation. *The Family Journal: Counseling and Therapy for Couples and Families, 15*, 24–29. http://dx.doi.org/10.1177/1066480706294045

Sori, C. F., Dermer, S., & Wesolowski, G. (2006). Involving children in family counseling and involving parents in children's counseling: Theoretical and practical guidelines. In C. F. Sori (Ed.), *Engaging children in family therapy: Creative approaches to integrating theory and research in clinical practice* (pp. 139–158). New York, NY: Routledge.

Steen, L. (2010). Parent consults: Beyond engagement. In P. Goodyear-Brown (Ed.), *Association for Play Therapy Mining Report, October 2010*. Clovis, CA: Association for Play Therapy.

VanFleet, R. (1994). *Filial therapy: Strengthening parent-child relationships through play. Practitioner's resource series.* Sarasota, FL: Professional Resource Press.

VanFleet, R. (2000). Understanding and overcoming parent resistance to play therapy. *International Journal of Play Therapy, 9,* 35–46.

VanFleet, R. (2005). *Filial therapy: Strengthening parent-child relationships through play*. Sarasota, FL: Professional Resource Press.

APPENDIX A

Directive Play Therapy

CASE NOTES

Client Name: ______________________ Age: ____________
Date of Session: ____________________ Session # __________

I. Subjective: (Feelings and/or Concerns Expressed)

Underline all that apply (including capitalized words). Indicate predominate feeling(s) by circling.

HAPPY: relieved, satisfied, pleased, delighted, excited, surprised, silly

CONFIDENT: proud, strong, powerful, determined, free

SAD: disappointed, hopeless, pessimistic, discouraged, lonely

HESITANT: timid, confused, nervous, embarrassed, ashamed

ANGRY: impatient, annoyed, frustrated, mad, mean, jealous

CURIOUS: interested, focused

AFRAID: vulnerable, helpless, distrustful, anxious, fearful, scared, terrified

FLAT: restricted, contained, ambiguous

OTHER:

II. Objective (Facts and Issues)

A. Play Themes/Toys

____ hammer/log/woodworking
____ sandbox/water/sink
____ puppets/theater
____ kitchen/cooking/food

___ easel/paint/chalkboard
___ riding car
___ bop bag/bean bag
___ dress up/jewelry/hats/masks/wand
___ crafts table/clay/markers/paint/etc.
___ doll house/doll family/bottle/pacifier/baby
___ cash register/money/telephone/camera/flashlight
___ medical kit/bandages
___ musical instruments
___ games/bowling/ring toss/balls/etc.
___ constructive toys (tinkertoys, etc.)
___ vehicles/planes
___ animals: domestic/zoo/alligator/dinosaurs/shark/snake
___ soldiers/guns/knife/sword/handcuffs/rope
___ blocks/barricade
___ sandtray/miniatures

___ other: ___________________________________

Processing Notes

____

____

____

____

B. Verbal Themes

1. Therapist's directive prompt or question: ___________________

____

____

2. Client's significant verbalizations: ___________________

____

____

C. Changes in Play Behavior (First Time Happenings or Discontinued Behavior)

____

____

D. Limits Set (Type of Limit, Frequency, Outcome):

____

____

III. Assessment/Observations (General Impression and Clinical Understanding of Session)

____

____

____

____

Interventions/techniques used:

___ Cognitive therapy	___ Solution-focused therapy	___ Systemic therapy
___ Trauma counseling	___ Crisis management	___ Psychoeducation
___ Assessment	___ Social skills	___ Anger management
___ Behavioral therapy	___ Symptom/compliance	___ Treatment planning
___ Communication	___ Supportive psychotherapy	___ Play therapy
___ Assignment/evaluation	___ Homework/exercises	___ Building self-esteem
___ Narrative therapy	___ Parenting monitoring	___ Sandtray therapy
___ Client empowerment		Other:___________
___ Relaxation of homework		

IV. Plan

____

____

____

____

Therapist: _______________________ Date: ___________

Signature

III. Assessment Observations (General Impression and Clinical Understanding of Session)

APPENDIX B

Directive Play Skills Feedback

Category Content of Session	Present and Evident	Present and More Needed	Not Evident	Comments, Strengths, and Areas for Growth
NONVERBAL COMMUNICATIONS				
Lean forward/open				
Appear interested				
Relaxed/comfortable				
Expression/tone congruent with client				
VERBAL RESPONSES				
Greeting and use of client's name				
Introduction to session/play				
Goal Formulation				
Clarification of problem or need				
Directive Prompt				
Theoretically framed				
Relative to goal				

Play or Expressive Process				
Appropriate use of silence				
Tracking behavior				
Facilitating decision making and responsibility				
Succinct responses and replies				
Processing Play or Expression				
Theoretically framed				
Opened questions				
Reflection feeling				
Reflecting content/meaning				
Building esteem and encouragement				

(continued)

Category Content of Session	Present and Evident	Present and More Needed	Not Evident	Comments, Strengths, and Areas for Growth
Limit Setting as Applicable				
Tasks/Homework				
Applicable and relevant				
Concrete				
Simple and doable				
Closure				

APPENDIX C

Resources and Information

EYE MOVEMENT DESENSITIZATION AND REPROCESSING

Supplemental EMDR Resources for Children

Adler-Tapia, R., & Tapia, M. (2008). *My EMDR workbook.* Retrieved from www.emdrhap.org

Brochures on EMDR. Retrieved from EMDRIA.org

Courtney, D. (2010). *The EMDR journey game.* Retrieved from www.emdrhap.org

Gomez, A. (2007). *Dark, bad day...go away: A book for children about trauma and EMDR.* Retrieved from AnaGomezTherapy.com

Meignant, L., & Neignant, C. (2007). *Buddy, the dog's E.M.D.R.* France: Author. Retrieved from EMDR.buddy@mail.com

Waldon, A. (2004). *Goodbye yucky thoughts and feelings: An EMDR workbook for children.* Carrboro, NC: Author. Retrieved from www.annwaldon.com

Waldon, A. (2007). *Hello strength and bravery: A resource workbook for children.* Carrboro, NC: Author. Retrieved from www.annwaldon.com

Additional EMDR Resources

Child Dissociative Checklist. Retrieved from http://www.energyhealing.net/pdf_files/cdc.pdf

Children's Impact of Events Scale. Retrieved from http://www.swin.edu.au/victims/resources/assessment/ptsd/cites-r.pdf

EMDR International Association. Retrieved from www.emdria.org

EMDR HAP website. Retrieved from http://emdrhap.org/content/what-is-emdr/research-findings

ISSD position paper on the guidelines for the treatment of DID in children. Retrieved from http://www.isst-d.org/default.asp?contentID=50

Website for training information on EMDR. Retrieved from www.emdr.org

Adlerian Counseling and Step Program

The Encouragement Zone. *Adlerian Play Therapy Training and Workshops by Terry Kottman*. Retrieved from http://encouragementzone.com

The North American Society of Adlerian Psychology (NASAP). Retrieved from http://www.alfredadler.org

Step Publishers. *Systematic Training for Effective Parenting (STEP) Program*. Retrieved from http://www.steppublishers.com

Index

www.ingramcontent.com/pod-product-compliance
Ingram Content Group UK Ltd.
Pitfield, Milton Keynes, MK11 3LW, UK
UKHW021845100926
8556IPUK00019B/1062

9 780826 130655